Praise for *The Only Life I Could Save*

"From a mother's harrowing journey into the dark abyss of fear and to the bright light of hope, help, and healing, this story unfolds the vivid gamut of emotions any parent knows when a child becomes entangled in alcohol or other drug use. A must-read for anyone who wants to know what to do (and not to do) to help a loved one recover from addiction."

WILLIAM COPE MOYERS
New York Times bestselling author of *Broken*

"Kathy Ketcham is a gifted storyteller and uses her considerable resources from a life devoted to the telling of others' stories to provide an unfiltered, visceral immersion into her own family's experience with addiction. This book is both an essential, informed resource for any family facing addiction and a sacred tale of a mother's personal transformation. Kathy exposes the impotent powerlessness of a parent attempting to cure a child's addiction, as well as a powerful, personal portrayal of her healing journey. I recommend this book to any family struggling with addiction."

MARVIN D. SEPPALA, MD
chief medical officer, Hazelden Betty Ford Foundation

"Profound, raw, and visceral! Once again, Ketcham grips the reader with passion and clarity, disclosing the hidden nature of drug and alcohol addiction, its ravages, and the pathway to recovery. Unlike her resume of collaborative scholarly and objective works on the disease model of addiction, she now opens the curtain to her own story: A mother and her addicted son. A family in distress. What to do, how to cope, where to turn. In her usual poignant fashion, she uniquely exposes her own journey—'walking the walk,' unveiling the mystery of addiction—this time through the eyes and agony of life experience."

L. ANN MUELLER, MD
coauthor of *Eating Right to Live Sober*

"There are many books written on addiction, but this one will grab you and hold you tight. It will show you that beauty and love are always there for the finding."

DEBRA JAY
author of *It Takes a Family*

"What is it like for a mother (and an addictions expert) to experience her teenage son's drift into addiction and struggle through treatments before finding his own road to recovery? That question is answered in Katherine Ketcham's riveting story, *The Only Life I Could Save*. This heartbreaking and uplifting story will offer readers an insider's view of the family experience of addiction, treatment, and recovery. Highly recommended."

WILLIAM WHITE
author of *Recovery Rising*

"I've been treating addictions as a clinical psychologist for over forty years, and I've never met anyone who understands the emotional, spiritual, and psychological experience of an addicted human being as well as Kathy Ketcham."

ARTHUR P. CIARAMICOLI, EDD, PHD
author of *The Stress Solution*

"At a time when we lose 144 people a day to accidental drug overdose in our country, Kathy Ketcham captures the raw emotion of watching a child taken hold by addiction and a parent's desperate fight to save them. Her beautifully recounted journey will help countless families struggling in solitude to realize that they are not alone and give them hope that, like Ben, their child can find long-term recovery."

MARCIA LEE TAYLOR
chief policy officer, Partnership for Drug-Free Kids

"Ketcham has given us a treasured *must-read*. It belongs in every pediatrician's office and in the offices of every school counselor, assistant principal, youth minister, and adolescent therapist. It teaches countless lessons not only for other parents and families struggling to make sense of what is unthinkable to them, but it also carries a profound message to all the adults in the lives of young people about their missed opportunities to help. It can teach neighbors, pediatricians, youth ministers, coaches, school administrators, and counselors that treating any use of drugs other than as a major concern is a disservice to parents and an injustice to the child. To intervene, to speak up, to express concern to parents who cannot see their reality is the greatest kindness. I recommend this book broadly. There are critical messages for all of us between its covers."

SIS WENGER
president and CEO, National Association for Children of Addiction

"Katherine Ketcham captures the essence of a family deep in the throes of the insidious disease of addiction. Despite her expertise in the field, Kathy finds herself as helpless as any parent watching the deterioration of a loved one before her eyes, caught in the same fear and denial she has warned against in a trove of published works on the topic. As a person in long-term recovery, I found *The Only Life I Could Save* to be chillingly accurate in its description of a mother trapped in despair, actually rereading her own books in an effort to find comfort and perhaps some answers within. As a parent of a teenage son and daughter, I was gripped by the stories within the story, knowing there was a 'happy' ending to come but realizing my family's journey is still underway. Kathy has brought a needed light into this darkness called addiction, sharing a timeless story that addresses a very contemporary issue."

DON FERTMAN
chief development officer, Subway

"Eloquent and moving . . . Ketcham's engaging writing style will capture and sustain the interest of the many families battling addiction in their children as they fear the worst but hope for a good outcome modeled after [her son's] recovery."

DAVID SMITH, MD
founder of Haight Ashbury Free Clinics

"[A] wise and wonderful masterpiece . . . *The Only Life I Could Save* is a powerful and insightful work . . . The current national addiction crisis has created a plethora of books, podcasts, and documentaries on how to best respond to this epidemic, but this book is different. Katherine Ketcham knows addiction. Not only is she a bestselling author and expert on the disease, she has also experienced it firsthand through her son Ben's journey through addiction and recovery."

SUSAN BRODERICK
associate research professor, Georgetown University

"With addiction, no matter how deep the despair of the family, there is hope. No matter how sick the addict, the miracle of recovery is possible. These truths are beautifully brought home in Kathy Ketcham's latest wonderful book, *The Only Life I Could Save*."

CHARLIE KESTER
owner, Lakeside-Milam Recovery Centers

"Ketcham's powerful story and the vulnerability with which she shares it hit hard—both in your head and in your heart. Her storytelling elicits a visceral and emotional reaction that awakens and heals . . . I had to stop to wipe away tears. Her story is my story, my mother's story, and all of our stories. It's a must-read for anyone seeking to understand the inevitable rollercoaster ride of life, how awareness and acceptance are the landing pads to peace, and a reminder of the humanity and spirit that exists in all of us."

RICK SHAMBERG
CEO of Gray Wolf Ranch

"Remarkable book . . . I was so deeply touched with the rawness of Kathy's journey and her courage to hold nothing back . . . This is a MUST-read for all persons struggling with how to save their addicted loved ones from addiction."

JOYCE SUNDIN
intervention specialist

"An intimate, poignant description of one family's valiant efforts to cope as their son spirals into the cunning grip of addiction, told through the heart and lens of a loving mother. Katherine Ketcham, a deeply informed author and expert in addiction, painfully deconstructs her son's progression into the inferno, illustrating how addiction is nondiscriminatory even in loving, functional families. Her fear and anguish force her to seek understanding from her spiritual life, revealing that addiction is but another part of the family tapestry."

CHERLYNE SHORT MAJORS, PHD
behavioral health consultant

"There is a critical need for this courageous, inspiring book. Finally, those of us who work in the addiction treatment field have a book that we can recommend to suffering families, written by an addiction expert and loving mother who offers her firsthand perspective on the destructive nature of drug addiction and the difficulties so often encountered on the pathway to long-term recovery. The recovery process takes time, but with the family's loving support, exposure to good treatment, continuing care, mentoring, and mutual support, the 'miracle' of recovery is a reality for millions. A must-read for any parent concerned about the epidemic of drug addiction in this country."

NICHOLAS PACE, MD
clinical associate professor of medicine, NYU

"The statistics on the opioid epidemic currently devastating our country fail to reveal the true impact of substance abuse and addiction. Despite being an expert on teen substance abusers, Ketcham initially was blind to the extent of her son's problems. But, as the addiction exploded into the family, her expertise was shattered as her feelings as a mother overwhelmed her. This account, evolving as smoothly as a novel, reveals the soul-searching journey to recovery that Ketcham, her son, and each of her family members was compelled to undergo. The beauty of the book is that in telling her story, Ketcham's expertise comes back into play, helping make sense of what happened and serving as an inspiration and resource to the many families across the country that are dealing with this crisis."

ANGELA DIAZ, MD, PHD, MPH
director, Mt. Sinai Adolescent Health Center

"This is a story of real life: The life of a mother whose journey takes her full circle as she tries to help her child. Fearlessly honest, *The Only Life I Could Save* provides a clear vision into the reality families face when a loved one is struggling with the disease of addiction. Kathy and her family's willingness to share their story will help other families discover they are not alone and learn that regardless of how things look from the outside, there are other families with the same challenges, the same hopes, the same fears."

SCOTT MUNSON
executive director, Sundown M Ranch

"Through openly recounting her own desperate attempts to cope with her son's addiction, Katherine Ketcham vividly shows us that, despite vast personal knowledge and professional expertise, life's deepest and most gratifying existential realizations are borne of the humility that comes from the very real struggle between holding on and letting go."

JOHN F. KELLY, PHD, ABPP
Elizabeth R. Spallin professor of psychiatry in addiction medicine, Harvard Medical School; director, Recovery Research Institute, Mass. General Hospital

"Kathy Ketcham has written a mother's spiritual geography of witnessing her youngest child's descent into addiction. As she watches her teenage son begin to use drugs addictively, she engages in the inevitable self-blame and desperate search for solutions common among parents of addicted children. An author of many previous books about addiction and recovery, she ironically finds little comfort in those works—and thus, like so many authors, she has written the book she needed to read, with the desire to help just one other parent who at any given moment may be staring into a dark vortex of fear for their addicted child's life. The book offers many practical strategies for negotiating this fear, including the poignant practice of writing love letters to our children. Above all it is a lyrical, intelligent reflection about the nature of surrender and the myriad qualities of the providence that lives within all of us."

JENNIFER MATESA
author of *Sex in Recovery* and *The Recovering Body*

"*The Only Life I Could Save* is the very best of all the books written on the desperate challenges of addiction in a family. So many books on addiction are written with sad endings, but this is the beautifully written one that has many poignant new beginnings, hope, and yes, gratitude. An emotional and meaningful description of the pain and frustration family members experience when loving a chemically impaired child."

GINNY LYFORD ASP
coauthor of *Living on the Edge*

"This book gave me goosebumps—repeatedly. It is gripping, wise, and soulful. An instant classic."

JEFF JAY
author of *Navigating Grace*

"Katherine eloquently captures a rarely told story that hits close to home for me and for one in three households in America. When addiction enters your home, it leaves parents lost and searching for answers for one of the most challenging health issues any person can face—especially a child. This story articulates the struggle, but most importantly inspires optimism throughout a powerful journey to recovery that will lead families to continue to work through the challenges of addiction and remain hopeful."

GREG WILLIAMS
filmmaker, *The Anonymous People* and *Generation Found*, and cofounder of Facing Addiction

the only life
I could save

Also by Katherine Ketcham

Under the Influence: A Guide to the Myths and Realities of Alcoholism,
coauthored with James R. Milam, PhD

*Eating Right to Live Sober: A Comprehensive Guide to Alcoholism
and Nutrition*, coauthored with L. Ann Mueller, MD

Recovering: How to Get and Stay Sober,
coauthored with L. Ann Mueller, MD

*Living on the Edge: A Guide to Intervention for Families
with Drug and Alcohol Problems*, coauthored with Ginny Lyford Asp

*Witness for the Defense: The Accused, the Eyewitness, and the Expert
Who Puts Memory on Trial*, coauthored with Elizabeth Loftus, PhD

The Spirituality of Imperfection: Storytelling and the Search for Meaning,
coauthored with Ernest Kurtz

*The Myth of Repressed Memory: False Memories and Allegations
of Sexual Abuse*, coauthored with Dr. Elizabeth Loftus

In the House of the Moon: Reclaiming the Feminine Spirit of Healing,
coauthored with Jason Elias

*The Five Elements of Self-Healing: Using Chinese Medicine
for Maximum Immunity, Wellness, and Health*,
coauthored with Jason Elias

Beyond the Influence: Understanding and Defeating Alcoholism,
coauthored with William F. Asbury

*The Power of Empathy: A Practical Guide to Creating Intimacy,
Self-Understanding, and Lasting Love in Your Life*,
coauthored with Arthur P. Ciaramicoli, EdD, PhD

*Teens Under the Influence: The Truth About Kids, Alcohol,
and Other Drugs—How to Recognize the Problem and What to Do
About It*, coauthored with Nicholas A. Pace, MD

Broken: My Story of Addiction and Redemption,
coauthored with William Cope Moyers

*Miss O'Dell: My Hard Days and Long Nights with The Beatles,
The Stones, Bob Dylan, Eric Clapton, and the Women They Loved*,
coauthored with Chris O'Dell

Experiencing Spirituality: Finding Meaning Through Storytelling,
coauthored with Ernest Kurtz

*The Pain Antidote: The Proven Program to Help You Stop Suffering
from Chronic Pain, Avoid Addiction to Painkillers—
and Reclaim Your Life*, coauthored with Mel Pohl, MD

the only life I could save

a memoir

Katherine Ketcham

sounds true
BOULDER, COLORADO

Sounds True
Boulder, CO 80306

Published 2018

Cover design by Karen Polaski
Book design by Beth Skelley

Printed in Canada

Library of Congress Cataloging-in-Publication Data
Names: Ketcham, Katherine, 1949- author.
Title: The only life I could save : a memoir / Katherine Ketcham.
Description: Boulder, Colorado : Sounds True, 2018.
Identifiers: LCCN 2017033129 (print) | LCCN 2017043629 (ebook) |
    ISBN 9781622039784 (ebook) | ISBN 9781622039777 (hardcover)
Subjects: LCSH: Ketcham, Katherine, 1949- | Parents of drug addicts—United States—
    Biography. | Drug addicts—Family relationships—United States. | Drug addicts—
    Rehabilitation—United States. | Mothers and sons—United States.
Classification: LCC HV5805.K48 (ebook) | LCC HV5805.K48 A3 2018 (print) |
    DDC 362.29/13092 [B]—dc23
LC record available at https://lccn.loc.gov/2017033129

10 9 8 7 6 5 4 3 2 1

To Ben
the bravest soul I know

~

contents

THE JOURNEY

By Mary Oliver

One day you finally knew
what you had to do, and began,
though the voices around you
kept shouting
their bad advice—
though the whole house
began to tremble
and you felt the old tug
at your ankles.
"Mend my life!"
each voice cried.
But you didn't stop.
You knew what you had to do,
though the wind pried
with its stiff fingers
at the very foundations—
though their melancholy
was terrible.
It was already late
enough, and a wild night,
and the road full of fallen
branches and stones.
But little by little,
as you left their voices behind,
the stars began to burn
through the sheets of clouds,
and there was a new voice,
which you slowly
recognized as your own,
that kept you company
as you strode deeper and deeper
into the world,
determined to do
the only thing you could do—
determined to save
the only life you could save.

introduction

December 4, 2005

The place is deserted when we arrive. Log cabins set in a frozen landscape, not a human being in sight. I begin to panic. Where is everyone?

Ben stands with his long arms hanging loose at his sides, shoulders slumped forward. He shifts his weight, and the frozen ground crunches under his size thirteen Adidas sneakers. The look on his face speaks of fear. Dread. Despair.

I don't like this place. Where is everyone? I look around at the log cabins and imagine we're on a movie set. The actors and directors, cameras and production crew haven't arrived yet, maybe because it's a Sunday. Their day off.

Somewhere, out there, are the barns, outbuildings, and miles upon miles of split-rail fences. I remember these facts from the Internet description and photographs. A four-thousand-acre working cattle ranch with a stream running through it, surrounded by rolling hills; farther out, beyond sight, are the waterfalls, sheer rock walls, glaciers, forests, and tens of thousands of acres stretching up to the Canadian border.

Months later, Ben tells me that Saturday and Sunday are work days at the treatment center. The boys are probably in the barns, spearing frozen cow droppings with rebar poles ("that sucked") or riding on open-back trucks and tossing hay out to the chasing cattle ("that was fun"). But as we stand at the end of the driveway, shaking with the cold, I wonder if other parents decided to keep their boys home for Christmas. Why didn't we do that? What kind of people drive their child to the middle of nowhere and drop him off in a desolate place with the wind howling and the temperature dropping and not a soul in sight?

A door slams. A short, stocky man improbably dressed in a T-shirt walks toward us. He barely manages a smile. I wonder what we look like to him—this mother, father, and son standing in a ragged semicircle, waiting. Perhaps we are a familiar tableau: the boy standing apart, hands in his jean pockets, eyes on the ground; the mom fighting back tears; dad stepping forward with hand outstretched. I think about the faces we show to the world, the hiding we do behind those masks. The outside is holding together, just barely, but the inside is crumbling.

The stocky man says the boys will be back soon. He says they were expecting us earlier. I don't think he means to make me feel guilty, but I do. I mumble something about the long drive and the ice and the broken windshield wipers, but he doesn't care; he shrugs his shoulders. He's a mountain man standing there in a T-shirt, strongly muscled, tough, ruddy, preoccupied. He says his wife just fell off a horse and broke her pelvis. I look at Ben, and his face registers my thoughts. *Who cares about your wife? We're standing here in the cold in a barren empty godforsaken place, and it's taking everything we have not to bolt, jump in the car, and drive away, all of us. Why would we give a damn about your wife?*

He shakes Ben's hand. It feels as if the wind is blowing right through me. I am an empty shell. I plant my feet wide apart and dig in, willing myself to stand straight and tall, to be strong. I don't like this man. I don't like this place. I want the whole thing to blow away. There's no softness here, no friendly faces. It's hard. Bitter. I think about camping and waking up to the acidic taste of percolated coffee on a Coleman stove, chilled inside and out, the coffee grounds thick and chewy on my tongue.

I want hot chocolate with marshmallows. I want soft, cozy blankets. I want smiles, sunshine, warmth. I want my son to come home to me. I want to reach out to Ben, hold him close, turn back time, and carry him away in my arms, to start all over again. I want, I want, I want.

"Okay," the man says, ready to move on. "Don't worry. We'll take good care of him."

We give Ben a hug—me first, then Pat, then me again. We walk to the car. As we drive away, I turn around in my seat to look back at Ben.

He lifts his head and attempts a half-hearted wave. My heart feels as brittle and broken as the ice cracking beneath the tires of the car as we turn onto the highway for the long ride home.

I start to cry. I can't stop. I'm sobbing. Pat reaches over, takes my hand and squeezes it, but the roads are too slick, and he needs both hands on the wheel. Tears are running down his cheeks, and he wipes them off with the arm of his jacket. I look at his fingers gripping the steering wheel and think, *Hold on, honey, hold on.* I'm talking to myself. *Hold on, honey, hold on.* I feel the pieces of myself breaking apart.

It's three weeks before Christmas, and Ben will be in treatment for two months.

August 2016

On a family vacation at one of our favorite places in the world, Black Butte Ranch near Sisters, Oregon, Ben and I talk about this book. He just turned thirty and, in two months, will celebrate his ninth year of recovery.

The early morning sunshine filters through the Ponderosa pines, creating patterns of light and shadow on the patio table. We listen for a moment to the laughter inside the rental house where Pat is starting a new jigsaw puzzle with Ben's older sisters, Robyn and Alison. Ben and I are not fans of jigsaw puzzles; they're too abstract and time consuming, and they make our heads hurt. Sometimes Pat saves the last piece for me—if Ben hasn't hidden it somewhere, which he's been known to do—and I have to turn the thing right, left, and upside down before I can figure out where it fits. Sort of the way I look at life, it seems.

"I wouldn't change my life," Ben says, in a quiet, reflective tone. "I have a really good recovery and an amazing perspective on the past. It was just a crazy kind of vortex based on the combination of you being an expert in addiction and me struggling for all those years."

He smiles in a thoughtful way, and as he tilts his head, the sun lights up his auburn hair to a golden copper. I was always so afraid his red hair would fade away, a fluke of his childhood. But his Scottish genes held fast.

"Do you remember 'the Promises' in the Big Book of AA, Mom? 'We will not regret the past nor wish to shut the door on it.' I don't regret the past, and I don't wish it had been something different. I am who I am because of what happened. In the end, it's a positive thing."

Ben and I have talked before, often, about destiny and fate and coming to terms with the fact that there is no one goal, no one future, no one pathway. I look at him, and for the thousandth time, I am so grateful he is here with me. Alive, strong (all those CrossFit muscles), scarred—the forehead scar from running into a play structure at pre-school, the scar on his left hand when he broke several bones in a rugby game, the knee scar from a lacrosse injury. A deep thinker, a soul searcher, a good human being.

He takes a deep breath. "I have just one request for the book," he says. Sensing the hesitation in his voice, I feel a little hitch inside my heart. It feels like a cramp, like someone is squeezing my heart lightly, willing me to pay attention. I'm afraid of what he will say next. We've talked about the book dozens of times, and he tells me he is one hundred percent behind it; he believes it will help people. But maybe he has changed his mind. Maybe now that I am so close to finishing it, he doesn't want the exposure. Now that his life is so together, he doesn't want to go backward and experience all the bad stuff again. I gear myself up with the thought that I can handle it; if he does not want the book to be published, I will let it go. I'm surprised how easily that thought comes to me, after all the work of the past few years. I realize it might be because revisiting the past has been difficult for me, too. Writing this book may be the most god-awful, painful thing I have ever done.

"Over the years you've talked a lot about addiction as a demon that walked into your house and threatened to destroy your family." Ben pauses for a moment to collect his thoughts. "I need to ask you this one thing—don't demonize addiction. Addiction is not a demon. For me, at least, it's a spiritual malady, and understanding it at its depth requires asking questions and coming into a conversation. *What was I missing? What was I seeking?*

"Drugs were a means to an end for me. I was extremely unhappy in my own skin. I was coping with the death of my best friend. I was dealing with my spiritual deficiencies and my grief, my guilt and my shame, trying to heal myself. It was only when I came to the realization that I was using drugs as a means to fill up this hole inside, to find some meaning in life, that I was able to figure things out. Philosophy, bigger ideals, the truth, and the good—that's what allowed me to get and stay sober."

"The truth and the good," I repeat. "Can you tell me more about that?"

"Doing something right, however small it is," he explains. "Forgiving myself for the mistakes I've made and continue to make. Realizing that imperfection is okay. Struggling to create a new self, to believe in myself again, to trust that I'm worth the effort."

The long, hard work of recovery. But the other side of recovery is addiction. Ben has his perspective on "the demon," and I have mine. I can't let go of that image of a monstrous force that changed him from the inside out and took him away from us for seven long, tortuous years. By personifying addiction as a hideous, loathsome entity that captured and imprisoned my son, I was able to figure out how to fight it. Seeing addiction as a demon helped me understand that it wasn't Ben I was battling; it was his disease. Hating, loathing, detesting, hoping to destroy the addiction kept me sane, allowing me to love my child even when he seemed to hate everything in the world, including his family, including himself.

Silence joins the slanting of sunlight on the table, and I stretch out my hand to the warmth. *Arthritis*, I think. *I must be getting arthritis.* And at that moment, a sudden insight hits me hard: Maybe the demon was never inside Ben. Maybe it is inside me, and all those years, I was fighting myself. For seven long years, I struggled to take control, to reach in and pull Ben out of the addiction's clutches, believing that it was within my power to save him and alter the trajectory of his life. If I just do this or that. If I say the right words. If I say nothing at all. If I hold on. If I let go. If I could go back in time and relive some of the events of our lives . . . maybe things would be different. For how long did I live in those "what if" scenarios? For how long did I torture myself with wishing I could go back to revise the past?

The demon, I realize, is not something outside me. It is the illusion of control; the belief that I can change the world for someone else;

the fantasy that hope and faith, even love, are strong enough to battle fate. All those books I wrote about addiction led me to think I knew what to do—the words created a pathway before me, and all I had to do was follow them. But the words were just words, after all, and real life doesn't follow a straight line; instead, it leads to detours, dead ends, and sheer drop-offs.

So now, as Ben begins his fourth decade on this earth and as I approach seventy (how did *that* happen, I wonder), it is long past time to admit that I don't have the ability to alter the direction of my son's life. Only he has that power. And from there, it is not too big a leap to the understanding that this book I am writing is not about Ben and his addiction journey, nor is it about "the demon" that I lived with in my mind for all those years. This book is about the Big Know-It-All Who Realizes She Doesn't Know a Damn Thing.

Except this one daunting truth—the only life I can save is my own.

1

something happened

1976–1999

*A*ddiction *was handed to me, like a gift.*

Not so very long ago, those words came to me unbidden in the dark of night, startling me out of a deep sleep. It has taken decades to open my eyes to the nature of that gift, but here is the story of where it all began.

~

It's 1976, and I'm twenty-seven years old, a freelance writer with ambition that outstrips experience, and even perhaps, talent. I still can't believe my luck at finding a part-time job at the *Seattle Post-Intelligencer* newspaper, which pays enough to cover my food and rent, thus supporting my writing ambitions. I'm the secretary to the executive editor of the *P-I*, and from the moment I meet Bill Asbury, I fall in love with him. It's not a heart-thumping crush. He's cute but not all that attractive from the perspective of someone half his age; it is more along the lines of a heart-and-soul connection to his unbridled passion for life. He reminds me of my father, especially the way he cracks up at his own silly jokes.

The *P-I* is one of the largest morning dailies (number thirty-three) in the country. Bill is the quintessential old-time journalist—fiercely protective of his writers, fearless in the face of controversy, and stubbornly committed to reporting the truth no matter what the cost. What I love most about him is his irreverent wit and his goofy smile, all wrinkles, loose joints, and twinkling eyes. When Bill laughs, his whole body laughs with him.

On slow news days, Bill walks into my office, arms swinging, a big grin on his deeply lined face. If he's in a particularly exuberant mood, he'll do a little tap dance ("my five kids call it my soft-shoe shuffle," he says with a wink), his body tilting to one side and then the other, arms splayed out to the side for balance, heels clicking on the floor, hands spread at the end with a "ta-da." Although he has his moments of grace, Bill also has a sailor's mouth on him and a turn-your-head-around way with stories that paints words with colors, smells, and the snap of the wind in the sails.

He pulls up a chair, puts his feet on my desk, and tells me stories about his drinking days. I don't know why he trusts me with these dark tales. Maybe he senses that I have no real knowledge or experience of alcoholism and therefore no scores to settle and few judgments to make. Maybe he's simply spreading the word, hoping to enlighten me about a common but unmentionable disease that came close to destroying his marriage, his reputation, and his life.

Bill's stories take place in a small farming town in eastern Washington, a community so far removed from Seattle (over the mountains and through the woods, deep into the farms and irrigated deserts) that just saying the name makes sophisticated urbanites laugh out loud—Walla Walla. I'd never heard of Walla Walla, and Bill and I shared some good laughs at the expense of what would one day, ironically, become my home.

From January 1972 to August 1975, Bill was the editor of the *Walla Walla Union-Bulletin*. He was also, during those years, a high-functioning alcoholic who never had a drink before quitting time and never missed a day of work due to boozing. But alcohol was causing considerable havoc in his life, including a painful case of gout and an enlarged liver ("You might consider cutting down on your drinking," his doctor advised), chronic depression, anxiety, suicidal thoughts, and heated arguments with his wife, Janet. Despite these alcohol-related problems, only Janet and a few close friends knew that Bill had a serious alcohol problem.

One of Bill's stories says a lot about his character, even when he was under the influence. It was an early summer evening, and Bill was driving home from a dinner meeting in Pendleton, Oregon. A state trooper stopped him on the Milton-Freewater Highway and gave him a Breathalyzer test. He blew a 0.17, plenty high enough to earn him a ride to the county jail, where he drunkenly put his arms around his police buddies and asked them to pose with him for a picture, which he offered to publish in the next day's paper. ("They were not amused," Bill recalls.) The next morning, he showed up early for work, hungover and filled with shame. He summoned Jo Moreland, the *U-B*'s police reporter; after relating the details of his arrest, Bill told her to pursue the story, holding nothing back from the truth. In the evening paper, his name appeared in the arrest column along with other drunk drivers and lawbreakers.

"I had to put my own name in my own newspaper as a drunk driver," Bill remembers with a self-deprecating smile and a sad shake of his head. "That brought some interesting letters to the editor."

In one of the worst episodes "in those dark days," Bill drove up to Spokane, Washington, for a job interview. "I interviewed for a lot of jobs back then," he said with a sad, sideways smile. "I figured if I could only find the right job, I wouldn't drink so much." After his interview, he decided to celebrate at a fancy restaurant.

"Guess what?" he says, eyebrows raised, his smile somewhat subdued. "I lucked out and arrived at the beginning of the happy hour. The house specialty was martinis served in one of those wine goblets they call tulip glasses." He chuckles but without his usual mirth. "More like a goldfish bowl than anything else. I had three 'bowls' of martinis (because the price was so good, I told myself), and then I had a full bottle of wine and an unremembered amount of after-dinner brandy."

I think my eyes must be huge because Bill laughs. "Alcoholics can really put it away," he says. "But what may seem like a blessing is actually a curse."

After the brandy, he remembered only two things—looking at the speedometer, which read one hundred miles per hour, and stopping for gas in George, Washington. From George to Walla Walla, a distance of one hundred miles, Bill drove in a blackout.

Two months later, Bill was offered the job at the *P-I*. He asked for a month off and voluntarily entered Alcenas, a twenty-eight-day alcoholism treatment program in Kirkland, Washington. Three days after completing treatment, Bill started his new job and his new life.

I will never know why Bill told me his stories, except that maybe it was one of those "God things." I'm not a religious person. I don't believe there is a mythical figure sitting up in the clouds dispensing favors and hobnobbing with angels. But I do believe there is a force in this world that throws color, light, and goodness all around, a hidden power that is greater, stronger, more enduring than the dark energies of ignorance and prejudice. I am willing to call it "God" for want of a better word. Whatever this force is, however it happens to work its large and small miracles in the world, I do not doubt it is there, fighting the good fight, pushing us along when we hesitate, lending us grit and gumption when we are most in need, and helping us put up with our imperfections and the flaws and limitations of others.

God thing or not, some bizarre quirk of happenstance places me in that office with Bill Asbury, who gives me his stories, trusting (I believe) that they might spark something inside me. Somewhere along the way, my life switches tracks, and whatever I had planned or hoped for in terms of a career or a future was suddenly not mine to design or control. Bill's stories grab hold of me and don't let go. *Something had happened.* Some "thing" had come into Bill's life—it shook him empty of reason, right thinking, and good living and came perilously close to destroying him and all that he loved. Then some "God thing" did battle with this "some thing" and brought him back to the life he was meant to live, the person he was meant to be.

What happened? The question haunts me. Once planted, Bill's stories take root and grow to the point at which alcoholism is just about all I can think of. If my goal is to be a writer, then wow, here is a subject worth writing about. Now I'm the one walking into Bill's office (not quite comfortable enough to put my feet up on his desk), asking him questions; trying to figure out what he means when he says alcoholism is a disease, what causes it, why some people get it and others are spared, and how it can so totally change your personality, dreams, goals, and desires that everything you love becomes less important than the drug.

One day (and looking back, I wonder if this was Bill's plan all along), Bill suggests that I read a monograph by James R. Milam, PhD, the person who founded the treatment center where Bill got sober. He hands me a bright, yellow-covered booklet titled *The Emergent Comprehensive Concept of Alcoholism*. I devour every word, although I understand about half of them. It's the most incomprehensible document I have ever read.

"Milam is brilliant," Bill laughs, "but he can't write for beans. His head is up in the clouds. He needs someone to bring his ideas down to earth so normal people like you and me can understand them. Why don't you write an article about him?"

What a gift—a writing project! I jump headfirst into the research, attending Milam's lectures and interviewing him at Alcenas, filling entire notebooks with scribbled thoughts and verbatim quotes that I type up on my ten-year-old Smith-Corona (my high school graduation present from my parents). Milam slightly terrifies me. I'm five feet, three inches tall, and he's well over six feet, with a craggy face that looks as if it were carved out of granite (thus his great difficulty forming a smile) and a deep, resonant voice. After we spend several dozen hours together, he seems to warm up to me, but he never hesitates to tell me when I ask a stupid question ("You just don't get it," he thunders, more times than I can count) and constantly reminds me that I have a lot of work to do if I'm going to accurately communicate his concepts to the world. I don't have any set ideas and nothing really to prove, so I don't argue with him, but I can't pretend his comments don't sting. He's a tough one, but I console myself with the knowledge that he's got a point—I do have a lot to learn.

I write an article titled "Alcoholism: A Disease Not a Disgrace," followed by another article and then another, all three published in a Seattle magazine. Milam likes them enough to pull them together into a pamphlet that he hands out to patients and their families at his treatment center.

"Why don't you write a book with Milam?" Bill asks me one day.

"A book?" I'm not at all sure he's serious.

"Sure, why not? You're young; you've got the energy; Milam knows you and maybe even likes you, which is saying something," Bill chuckles heartily. "And people need this information in digestible form. Go for it!"

The idea excites and petrifies me. Who am I to think I could write a book? But, I argue with myself, this isn't about me—it's about the importance of communicating Jim Milam's brilliant concept of alcoholism to a larger audience. If I can break through the scholarly verbiage and impenetrable layers of his monograph to reveal the simple theory behind it all—that alcoholics become addicted to alcohol because their bodies are physiologically incapable of processing alcohol normally—then maybe, who knows, maybe such a book will offer help and hope to alcoholics like Bill, my sister's husband who is definitely showing signs of out-of-control drinking; my friend Elizabeth's elegant, binge-drinking mother; my favorite uncle; and all those other millions of struggling people.

I talk to Pat, my fiancé, about the book idea, expressing my doubts that I can "go the distance," as one writer friend describes the process of writing a book. "I have no doubt at all you can do it," Pat says. "You've got the passion and the drive."

I raise my eyebrows at him. "Oh, yeah," he laughs, putting his arms around me, "and the talent."

I write two letters: one to Little, Brown and Company in Boston and the second to tiny Madrona Press in Seattle. My letter is heartfelt, promising to change the world for alcoholics and their families. Little, Brown sends a nice letter back, letting me know that they have another similar book in the pipeline, but Dan Levant, Madrona's publisher, calls and asks me to lunch. We dine on Chinese food that he orders for both of us at a little hole-in-the-wall restaurant in Seattle's Chinatown. I offer to help pay the bill, but Dan just laughs.

"I don't know why I always make deals over kung pao chicken," he chuckles, "but I'd like to offer you and Dr. Milam a contract and a $3,000 advance." A contract! An advance! I can't control myself—I throw my arms around his neck and give him a big kiss on the cheek. Then I invite him to my wedding.

Pat is working on his master's degree in Bellingham, two hours from Seattle, spending his days searching in rock specimens for 300-million-year-old microscopic fossils called foraminifera, and I'm hunkered down in the University of Washington library with thick texts explaining the biochemical and neurophysiological mechanisms of alcohol addiction. I've never been particularly interested in biochemistry or neurophysiology, but I'm enthralled by descriptions of the microsomal ethanol oxidizing system, alcohol dehydrogenase, acetaldehyde, tetrahydroisoquinolines, and mitochondrial disfigurations. I'm hooked; I can't get enough of this stuff. I take all my notes by hand and later transcribe them on my electric, noncorrecting typewriter. Wite-Out correction fluid is my best friend.

Under the Influence: A Guide to the Myths and Realities of Alcoholism sells 50,000 copies in hardcover before Bantam Books buys the paperback edition for $17,000. I'm floating on air. Madrona buys my second book, which focuses on the benefits of nutritional therapy for alcoholics, titled *Eating Right to Live Sober* and coauthored by Ann Mueller, MD, medical director at Alcenas. Pat earns his PhD while I'm writing that book, and we have our first child, Robyn. Two years later, we have a second child, Alison, and Dr. Mueller and I write a book titled *Recovering: How to Get and Stay Sober*.

When Pat is offered a tenure-track job teaching geology at Whitman College, we move to Walla Walla and buy a small Cape Cod home for $55,000 (my father loans us the down payment). Two years later, Ben is born, and I start work on a book with intervention specialist Ginny Gustafson titled *Living on the Edge: A Guide to Intervention for Families with Drug and Alcohol Problems*.

Books and kids. Life is good. I'm head over heels in love with my husband, our children are healthy and tons of fun, we have a close group of friends, and Walla Walla is a peaceful, friendly place to live. I couldn't be happier. Over the years, I write books and more books—a book on the fallibility of eyewitness testimony with world-famous memory researcher Elizabeth Loftus; followed by a book with Ernest Kurtz titled *The Spirituality of Imperfection: Storytelling and the Search for Meaning*; another book, *The Myth of Repressed Memory* with Beth

Loftus; and two books on traditional Chinese medicine with acupuncturist and herbalist Jason Elias.

I'm moving away from addiction, and it feels good. After writing hundreds of thousands of words on the subject, it seems as if nothing has changed. I was so hopeful way back when, and now, when I hear people arguing about whether addiction is a physiological disease or merely a symptom of psychological or emotional problems, I want to scream, "Read the damn research!" Decades of scientific study by distinguished experts—biochemists, neurophysiologists, geneticists, pharmacologists, psychologists, and on and on it goes—provide the basic facts we need to understand addiction. We know what the disease is, and we know how to treat it.

The knowledge is in our hands, but it seems we keep shoving it into the background as new theories come rolling in. Anyone with a website or a PhD can promote a theory about drug addiction without paying much attention to the long-established facts. Medical students receive little or no training in addiction, and yet most of the people sitting in doctors' offices are, in one way or another, affected by the disease. Alcoholics are referred to psychologists and psychiatrists, who all too often have no training in addiction and who therefore mistakenly assume the causes of excessive drinking or drug use are emotional or psychological, which they treat with talk therapy or drugs. Would we send someone with a newly diagnosed cancer (also a chronic, progressive disease) to a psychologist to uncover the reasons behind the spreading malignancy? Treatment for addiction is haphazard, often substandard, and insurance often doesn't cover it. If they're lucky, addicted individuals are offered three or four weeks of inpatient care, after which they are released to fend for themselves with little or no follow-up. Would a heart attack patient be released from the hospital with no follow-up appointments or plans for ongoing continuing care?

It drives me crazy. I had high hopes once upon a time that the world would be a kinder, more generous and forgiving place for addicted people, but now I just feel frustrated and sad. I'm tired and worn out. I want to write books on happier subjects. Maybe I should stop writing altogether. I don't know. With the kids in high school and middle school, I wonder if it's time to cut back on work or even switch careers. Secretarial work sounds appealing—I'm a really fast typist and have years of experience. Why not? So, I get a part-time office job at Whitman College and have fun being out in the world again, talking to someone other than myself.

One weekend morning, I pick up the phone to hear Bill's cheerful booming voice. "Well, hello, Kathy!" We share news of our families, and then he drops the bomb.

"It's time for another book on alcoholism," he says. "The field has gone to hell. Managed-care companies are refusing to pay for inpatient treatment or are cutting way back on the days they will cover, outpatient treatment is all over the map in terms of quality, and recovery support services are virtually nonexistent. The stigma of addiction as a psychological 'illness' that happens to weak-willed people persists and is becoming more pervasive. People are dying because they can't get into treatment or because they don't want to admit they have this disease. The world has gotten much, much worse for alcoholics. You need to write another book."

I don't want to. I don't say it, but I sure think it. I figure I'll stall for a little while, listen to Bill, tell him I'll think about it. Then I'll come up with an excuse—wanting to be with my children during their last years at home, another book in the works—something, I'll think of something. I'm tired of alcoholism and addiction, exhausted by the heartbreaking stories and the darkness and doom surrounding it. Bill is right—people just do not get it. How the heck are we going to convince them that this is a real disease and it's all around us? *Maybe it is even in your family, so watch out!* Who wants to read that sort of book? Why shout into a wind tunnel? Really, no, thank you.

But Bill won't let go. He calls again. And again. I suggest that he write the book; he could even coauthor it with Jim Milam. He says he'll think about it, but a few weeks later, he writes me a letter full of writer's angst. "I am discovering that writing books—or even contemplating same—is an act of will and great courage," he writes in his surprisingly legible longhand script. In the end, I can't say no to William F. Asbury, my great friend and former boss, the person who so willingly and candidly offered his stories, who opened the door to a world I never knew existed, and who gave me all the advice and encouragement I needed to start my career.

The book, which we title *Beyond the Influence*, takes almost two years to write, and it's long, more than four hundred pages in manuscript form. Seven or eight months later, the publisher's page proofs arrive. I read through the pages, looking for any egregious errors that might need correcting, and experience a sense of relief, even triumph, when I finally get to the last chapter titled "Walking the Walk." It's a really short chapter, just five pages of the 297-page book. Phew! Almost done.

I read those five pages. Then I read them again. And that's when another "God thing" comes crashing into my life. I swear, if there is a God in the heavens, He or She or It took one look at this just-turned-fifty-year-old woman and said, "She needs to know whereof she speaks!" BAM! The lightning bolt crashes down, opening up the earth beneath me.

> We have an obligation, as human beings, to do what
> we can to ease the suffering of others. This is not
> superficial charity or the work of do-gooders—this
> is our responsibility as individuals who are part of a
> larger community. When a fellow human being is in
> pain, we are called upon to do what we can to alleviate
> the suffering. When people are powerless to help
> themselves, we are asked to do what we can to assist.
> When we are presented with an opportunity to change
> what does not work and in the process save even one
> life, it is our duty to seize the moment with all the
> passion that we can muster. . . .
>
> Looking with compassion at the panhandlers on our
> streets, the drunks passed out in our city parks, and
> the broken, bloodied bodies in our emergency rooms,
> we will renew our commitment to helping those who
> cannot help themselves. We will ask what we can do to

make the world a less hospitable environment for the drug alcohol and a more humane place for people who are addicted to alcohol. We will begin to walk the walk and not just talk the talk.

Now is the time.

Now is our chance.

Having written those words, believing in them with all my heart, what choice did I have? Once again, a door opens, and I walk through it.

2

walking the walk

1998–1999

I press the silver button on the wall and wait for the buzzer, signaling that the metal door is now unlocked. Pushing my hip and shoulder against the massive door (I bet it weighs a thousand pounds off its hinges), I walk a few steps, and it closes hard behind me. I press another button and, when the buzzer sounds, open the second heavy door.

Beige concrete walls frame a narrow hallway, at the end of which is a small table, two plastic chairs, and a pair of handcuffs soldered into the wall. A girl, no older than fifteen, sits cross-legged on the floor, one hand cuffed to the wall. When youth in detention are handcuffed to the wall, they're considered a danger to self and others; the handcuffs are not for punishment but protection.

"Who the fuck are you?" she says, looking up at me, her eyes narrowed in suspicion. My guess is she's coming down off meth, a nasty withdrawal process that often causes irritability, paranoia, violent outbursts, and intense drug craving, along with severe anxiety and depression.

"My name is Kathy. I lead a group here every week."

"What kind of fucking group?"

"We talk about alcohol and other drugs."

"Fuck drugs," she says, looking up and down the hallway and pulling against the chain. "Fuck this place. Fucking people lock me up to this fucking wall. Fuck them. Fuck you."

She's so tiny, no more than 80 or 90 pounds, with huge dark circles under her eyes—almost mirrors of the shape of her eyes, but upside down and solid black. Meth mascara, painted on her face by exhaustion and malnutrition.

"What's your name?" I ask.

She looks up at me, surprised. "Colleen," she mumbles. For just a moment, it's as if a door opens.

Then it slams shut.

"Why the fuck do you care?"

~

"What chance do some of these kids have?" I blurt out that night at the dinner table. Robyn and Alison are just back from high school soccer practice, their long hair tied up in messy ponytails, and Ben is still wearing his uniform from the game this afternoon. Pat coaches Ben's soccer team, the Hornets. I helped pick out the outfits—black-and-yellow striped socks, black nylon shorts, and bright yellow shirts. A buzzing hive of sixth-graders tearing up the soccer field.

I am never happier than when I watch our children play soccer. Of all the sports they play, it's my favorite because of the nonstop action, the green grass, the sun shining (most of the time), and the kids looking so healthy and energetic running up and down the field. If I had three soccer games to watch every day, one after another, every day of the year, I'd be in heaven. I wish I'd been able to play soccer as a kid (I think I would have made a formidable defender), but the only sports offered for girls back then were swimming, softball, basketball, and field hockey. And cheerleading, if you consider that a sport.

"Mom, I think you worry too much about the Juvie kids," Robyn says. "There's only so much you can do."

"Lots of kids use drugs," Ali says, taking a bite of salad. Tonight we're having spaghetti and meatballs with what our friends call "Ketcham salad," which is just red leaf lettuce with cheddar cheese sprinkled on top and Walla Walla sweet onion and peppercorn dressing from Klickers, the local farm stand.

"What kind of drugs?" I can't help myself. Robyn shoots Ali a look, which I interpret as "Don't get her started."

"You know," Ali says. "Alcohol and marijuana usually. That's all."

I remember what Janelle, age thirteen, had said in the detention group a few weeks back. "People keep asking us why we use drugs. You know, really, it's kind of a stupid question. We use drugs because they're there and because they make you feel good, or at least different for a while. I don't know anyone who hasn't used drugs."

The candles look so pretty on the table. We light candles with every dinner, whether we're having tuna fish sandwiches or my "famous" (because it is my only fancy meal) lemon chicken with roast potatoes and carrots.

"But Robyn's right, Mom," Ali adds with a concerned look on her face. "You worry too much."

"I know I do," I admit. "It's just that these kids start so young—eleven, twelve, thirteen years old—and their brains are so vulnerable because they're still developing."

I look at Pat, who is listening patiently. I read his silence as assent to keep talking. "Like today, I talked to a fifteen-year-old who started smoking cigarettes and marijuana when he was eleven, and now he's deep into cocaine and prescription pills. His probation officer is trying to get him into treatment, but first he has to get an assessment, and there's a three-week waiting list. They can't keep him in detention for three more weeks, so they'll let him out and he'll use again, and then he'll get put back in detention, and on and on it goes."

Robyn and Alison look uncomfortable, probably because I tend to get emotional when I talk about the problems the youth are facing in Juvie. Ben doesn't appear to be paying any attention. He holds his fork with all five fingers and lowers his face to his plate rather than lifting the fork to his mouth. One of these days, we'll have to work on his table manners, but he's only twelve, plenty of time ahead to worry about proper etiquette. Pat and I are not the least bit formal, but at least we try to follow the rule my father set with his five children: "All I ask is that you keep your feet off the table."

I switch the subject, and we talk about school, soccer, weekend plans. I know my family is growing weary of the Juvie stories, but this is my life now, and I want to share parts of it with them. I want them to understand, through the stories, that kids locked up in detention are not so different from them. I think about Eric, a gang member, who has a tattoo that reads, "If You Could Only See Inside Me." When I asked him why he had those words permanently engraved on his chest, he said, "Because people don't see the real me—they only see the outside. You got to know me from the inside, too. You know what I mean?"

I want my family to see what I see on the "inside" of these teenagers—the same hopes, dreams, and fears they have, we all have. I never discuss names or identifying details but talk instead in generalities about the problems the youth are facing: people who judge them because they use drugs, labeling them losers, lost causes, or just plain "bad kids"; the lack of resources in our community for treatment and recovery support; the difficulty finding doctors, mental health practitioners, and other health-care professionals who are educated and knowledgeable about addiction.

I want to talk about how dramatically things have changed in the adolescent drug world, how young people have access to so many drugs—super strong marijuana (not the marijuana I used in college, which the Juvies laughingly call "brown" or "dirt" weed), over-the-counter drugs, alcohol, inhalants, prescription drugs, cocaine, crack, even heroin. Heroin! Who would ever have thought that twelve- and thirteen-year-olds would get hooked on heroin? It's cheap—much less expensive than buying prescription drugs on the street, and kids don't have to inject it because the drug is so pure these days that they can snort it.

And meth. Shit. Meth.

~

Colleen is in group the next week, dressed in an orange jumpsuit. The meth circles have faded a bit as time, rest, and good food begin to drain the toxins from her body. Her eyes are bright blue. She smiles at me.

"I remember you," she says.

I smile back. "I remember you, too."

We sit in a circle on hard plastic chairs—four boys, two girls, and me. I ask them to tighten up the circle, explaining that I like my circles "close." Someone always hangs back a little—usually one of the kids next to me—and I assure them I won't bite. They think that's funny. For some reason they trust me. The circles help, but I think there's another reason. I'm far from perfect: There's the "old" thing (I'm old enough to be their parent, even their grandparent). And I'm kind of goofy. They laugh at my funny faces and old-fashioned expressions. *Yuck! Holy cow. Are you nuts?*

And then there's my voice. I have a funny voice. When I speak, I sound slightly nervous, somewhat tentative, not completely sure of myself. I think that obvious imperfection makes me human to the kids in Juvie. It levels the playing field. They never ask me about my voice; if they did, I'd tell them about the rare neurological disorder that makes my vocal cords tighten when they should be loosening up. They are polite and don't want to pry, and so they just conclude that I am old, vulnerable, a little quirky. I make funny faces, I swear sometimes, I don't talk too much, and I'm a good listener because, as I often remind them, I want to hear their stories. My voice is just part of who I am, and they accept it.

I can't say for sure that's what they are thinking, but for whatever reason, they open up to me.

"You can sit on the soft chair," one of the boys says, pointing to a red armless chair pushed up against the wall. Only kids wearing blue or green jumpsuits are allowed to use the soft chairs. Maybe one out of ten kids has earned the privilege, as most are in the orange or yellow jumpsuits. Red jumpsuits are "on security" and not allowed to attend the group.

"No, thanks," I say. "That wouldn't make us equals. If you're sitting in plastic chairs, I'm sitting in a plastic chair."

They nod their heads solemnly. Colleen looks at me with her shoulders slightly turned away from the circle, signifying she hasn't bought into this "equal" stuff.

I always start the groups by telling them a little about myself. "My name is Kathy. I write books about addiction and recovery. But I'm the student here, and you are the teachers. I'm here to learn from you."

"You write books?" a boy with bright red hair and freckles interrupts me. Three small black dots—gang tattoos—adorn the soft fleshy part between his thumb and index finger.

"Will you write about me? You can use my name. I don't care." Probably the youngest person in the group, he looks from side to side, grinning, seeking approval from his older peers.

"I'd like to write about you," I say, looking around the group. "But I'm mostly here to listen. I want to hear your stories. I want you to teach me so I can help other people understand what you're going through, what your struggles are, what you dream about for your lives."

We go around the circle and I ask them to tell me their first name, age, and drug of choice. "You don't have to talk if you don't want to," I tell them. "Listening is equally important. The only rule I have is that we listen and don't interrupt when someone else is talking."

"No cross-talk," says Ryan, age seventeen, obviously proud of his knowledge gleaned from previous experience in groups. He has four tattooed designs on his face—one on his forehead, one on his chin, and one on each cheek. Pointing at the curtained observation window, he adds, "But they can hear us."

"This group is confidential," I assure them. "The detention staff know that if they listen in, I can't come here anymore."

"Why?"

"Because then you wouldn't trust me."

They nod their heads. Trust is a word they all understand.

I don't tell them I'm tired of writing after twenty years, eight books, thousands of hours of research, and more fifteen-hour days than I can count. I'm tired of the deadlines—that word *dead* always does me in. When I'm in Juvie, I can let go of the whole "expert" thing and just listen. And learn. Because what is going on here, behind these concrete walls, is beyond anything I ever could have imagined.

It's as if another door (I think of those thousand-pound doors I have to pass through to enter here) has opened into a terrifying new world. Just months ago, I didn't know this detention center existed—a low, one-story concrete building in a part of town I rarely visit, not far from the courthouse and the county commissioners' offices, a few blocks from Kentucky

Fried Chicken and several other fast food restaurants. Inside this nonde-script building, I listen to stories full of loss, grief, guilt, and shame, and the sheer weight and number of them overwhelm me.

I had no idea that so many kids, children really, are using so many drugs and progressing so quickly into addiction. The old model of alcohol addiction I wrote about in book after book—a relatively slow progression from early to middle to late stage, with problems usually appearing in the twenties, thirties, or forties—simply does not fit these kids. Most of them start using drugs in middle school, but some start drinking or smoking cigarettes or marijuana in elementary school. As the weeks and months go by and they keep using, marijuana often doesn't do the trick anymore, because their tolerance has increased. They start experimenting with other drugs, hoping to find that perfect high. If they're hanging around other kids who are using, the chances are they will be offered "harder" drugs such as cocaine, crack cocaine, and prescription pills. Over-the-counter drugs are popular, too, especially cough and cold medicines containing dextromethorphan, which they gulp down by the bottle or take pills by the handful (the most I've heard about is sixty pills at one time). The list goes on and on—inhalants (glue, paint, gasoline, nail polish), "sherm" (embalming fluid), PCP, ecstasy, LSD, mushrooms . . .

What kills me is how young they are when they first start using. For each group, I keep informal records that I take home and store in a locked file cabinet. The average age of first use is eleven or twelve. By age fourteen, most of the kids are using two, three, four, or more drugs, not always and not all the time, but most use what I call the "regulars"—alcohol and marijuana. Marijuana tends to be the everyday drug, and "waking and baking" is a normal daily activity.

I bring my mind back to the group. "If it's okay with you, I'll take notes, but I'm the only one who ever sees them," I say. "I want to remember what you have to say because in this group you are the teachers—and my memory isn't as good as it used to be. But, again, if you don't want to say anything, that's fine. You can listen, like me."

They all want to talk. "I'll go first," says the boy to my right, the one with red hair and gang tattoos. "My name is Chris, I'm thirteen, and weed is my drug of choice. I started using when I was ten. Then I started drinking, taking prescription pills—hydrocodone, oxycodone, morphine—and heroin. Oh yeah, and cigarettes."

Matt is seventeen. His drug of choice is weed. He started using when he was eleven; when he was fourteen, he got hooked on meth. "Well, actually," he corrects himself, "I guess I have two drugs of choice—weed and meth."

"Meth is ridiculous; people go crazy on meth," Ryan says to Matt, who surprises me by nodding his head in agreement. "I stick to weed, alcohol, and prescription painkillers."

"Where do you get prescription drugs?" I ask.

Ryan laughs. "They're easier to get than alcohol," he says. "Just look in somebody's medicine cabinet. Or walk down the street, and in minutes, you'll find somebody selling hydros or oxys. Or you get on the phone to someone—'Hey, you got some pills?'"

It's Colleen's turn. "I'm fifteen," she says. "I started using weed when I was twelve. I also drank alcohol, and then I started stealing pills. When I was thirteen, I started using cocaine. And then crank.

"Crank is meth," she says, looking at me, "in case you didn't know. That's when I stopped going to school because I was so tweaked out on crank."

"I'm fifteen, too," Holly says in a soft, shy voice. "I love pills. I started with cigarettes and marijuana around twelve, meth about fourteen, and then pills."

"What kind of pills?"

"Oh, anything, really, but I like hydros and oxys best."

Last in the circle is Junior, age fourteen: "I started smoking weed when I was seven. I've tried lots of other drugs, but mostly I just use weed and alcohol. And cigarettes."

"You were seven when you started?" I can't quite comprehend it—seven years old?

"Yeah, my brother is a coke addict. And my dad is an alcoholic. We've always had lots of drugs in our house."

~

We talk about drugs, but that's just the beginning. What we really talk about is life. I could stand up and lecture about this drug's or that drug's effect on the brain, the signs and symptoms of physical dependence, the risk of overdose and even death, but most of these kids know all those facts, and their eyes turn to glass if I start pontificating. So I don't lecture; I listen. Sometimes, usually after they admit that drugs are "doing me bad" but insist they can handle them, I stand up and hit my head against the concrete wall (not too hard, because those walls don't give). I want a visual for their stubborn refusal to see what the drugs are doing to their lives. To their families. To their bodies and their minds.

And their souls. What I have come to realize is that most of the youth in detention—perhaps most of us, everywhere—are struggling with spiritual dilemmas. *Spiritual* sounds like such a heavy word, but I think of it this way: Human beings thrive on connection and communication. Drugs cut us off from the people we love, but they also sever the connections to our values and the deepest yearnings of our soul. *Soul* is also a bit of a quirky, controversial word, but it makes sense to me when I imagine the soul as the repository of all those intangible realities that give meaning, purpose, and value to our lives—honesty, empathy, kindness, love, awareness, acceptance, courage, trust, forgiveness, and simple human decency. Where else do those values rest and find a home if not in our hearts and our souls?

I ask questions that guide the discussions to the things that really matter to them. "What's hurting you?" I ask. Their answers are honest and revealing. I don't have to draw the connection between the drugs and the loneliness they feel. They know what causes the disconnection.

"Having everyone I ever get close to leave me eventually."

"Being alone most of the time."

"Not feeling loved."

"Being abandoned."

"Knowing that I'm hurting my loved ones."

"Not being able to help my family."

"Disappointing my parents."

"People telling me I'm worthless."

"Not being trusted."

"People who judge me."

When I ask them to tell me what they really want, the answers range from "be off probation" to "get a job" to "I want my Grandma's cooking." And, often, they answer with one-word responses: "Peace." "Happiness." "Health." "Forgiveness." "Respect." "Education." "Control." "Freedom." "Sobriety." "Help."

Ashley, age seventeen, wrote a long list of the things she wants:

1. I want all the things people say I will never have.
2. I want my faith to be strong.
3. I want to help other people.
4. I want to be a good role model.
5. I want a healthy family life.
6. I want healthy friendships.
7. I want to be loved.
8. I want to be trusted.
9. I want to travel the world.
10. I want God in my heart.

~

One day in group, I read a note from Sara, age sixteen.

> People see us as bad people because we have drank
> alcohol or smoked, people don't take the time to study
> us, look past our actions. I may act tough sometimes
> and act like I don't care, but the truth is I do care and
> I have a very soft heart. I just am that way sometimes
> because I have to put a wall up so I don't get broken
> down and beat on.

When I finish reading, Megan, age seventeen, starts to cry. "I've ruined my whole life caring too much," she says. Wiping her tears away, she looks around the group and smiles, almost apologetically. "I don't know what just happened to me; I hardly ever cry."

I think I know what happened—Megan saw herself in Sara's story and, realizing that this was her story, too, she knew she was not alone. Someone else—a stranger, a person she doesn't even know—feels the same way she feels. This person has built a wall to protect herself, just as Megan has done. And although Megan acts tough and pretends she doesn't care, just like Sara, she has "a very soft heart."

∼

Sometimes we talk about shame—little shames, big shames. Vanessa, who is sixteen, tells a story about throwing French fries at an old man at a McDonald's restaurant. "I was high on weed," she tells the group. "I was showing off for my cousins, trying to be cool, talking bad stuff about old people—you know, how wrinkled and weak they are. And I threw French fries at this old man. I feel so sad about that day. I look back, and I feel so bad about the way I acted and what I said. I know that might sound funny because maybe it seems like a little thing, but I think about getting old and having young kids treat me like that, and I know I'd feel really bad. Maybe that's what growing up and becoming responsible is about—you think about the other person's feelings before you say or do things that might hurt them."

"I did a lot of stupid things on drugs," says Emily, age thirteen. "I used alcohol, cocaine, and crank, but weed was my drug of choice. I had blackouts all the time. Once I stripped in front of a whole bunch of people. I was just crazy, way out there. And when I used, I felt so dirty. My body felt like it was just sprinkled, covered with dirt. Your soul feels like that, too—just filled with dirt."

Tony, age seventeen, is having trouble telling his story. His voice is all choked up. "I was drunk, so drunk I could hardly walk. And I saw this homeless guy just sitting there, not bothering anybody. He had a dog. His dog was probably his best friend. Maybe his dog was all he had. I started throwing rocks at him. I don't know why. I was drunk; that's my only excuse. I threw rocks at the dog, and the homeless guy started crying. He was begging me to stop, but I kept throwing rocks, and I hit the dog in the head with a really big rock, and I think I killed it. The man put his arms around his dog, and he just cried and cried. I got the hell out of there. But I can't forget that. I can't believe I did that. I will have to live with that memory for the rest of my life."

"I've done so many terrible things to so many people I love," Joe, age seventeen, says, hands clasped together, eyes on the floor. "I stole from my parents. I cheated on my girlfriend. I punched my best friend and broke his nose. I got my brother high, and he's only seven years old."

Samantha is crying. "I hated the way I was. There was no me. I was a horrible person who was mean to everyone. I cheated, I lied, and I stole from people. I even stole from drug dealers. Everyone thought I was so sweet and innocent. People just couldn't believe I would do drugs. But I did. I was shooting up meth. And I thought I was pregnant. I didn't care. How could I have done that? What kind of a human being am I?"

I am convinced that if we can unearth that shame, as searingly, scorchingly painful as it is, we can help these young people understand that they fit and belong in a world that seems to have turned its back on them. They want—they need—to talk about these private agonies. They need to know that others also feel shame, that we all feel shame for what we have said or done. If we open up the wound, bring it into the light, air it out, it is not so unbearable. Because it is shared. Because every human being on this planet lives with the shame of their mistakes, misdeeds, and imperfections.

~

One day after group, Colleen asks if she can talk to me for a few minutes. We spend more than an hour together. She tells me she wants to quit using drugs, go back to school, get a job, and help her grandmother, who is getting older and unable to take care of herself.

She sighs and looks at me, hoping I will understand. "I'm just so tired of the drama. People say I'll never change. I want to prove them all wrong and get clean."

Something fierce is growing inside this tiny young woman. I can see it in the determined look in her eyes and hear it in the intensity of her speech. She wants to live a good life. She wants to be a good person.

After Colleen is released from detention and placed on probation, we stay in touch. She stops using, goes back to high school, graduates, gets a job, takes classes at the community college. Today, eighteen years after I first met her, she has three children and continues to take care of her grandmother. She worries about her old friends who still use drugs, and she mourns the friends who have died.

The day before Mother's Day, Colleen calls to tell me a story: "A good friend died a few days ago. Another damn overdose in this town. I should have known. I tried to contact him a few months ago, but he didn't call back. I should have kept trying."

She is talking so fast and crying so hard that I have to ask her to repeat herself.

"I know what's next. I'm going to lose more friends; there's nothing I can do about it. Unless we have some type of help. All people need is other people who care, who are genuine, and who are sober. We need to show people love and stop being so scared of them."

She sighs, gathering her thoughts. "I'm just so frustrated. Six months ago I wrote a letter to a friend who died of an overdose, telling him what a good person he was and how much I would miss him. I'll write another letter today. But that's enough. I don't want to write any more letters to dead friends."

All people need is other people who care.

A story comes to mind. I first heard this story from my great friend and coauthor Ernie Kurtz, who taught me about spirituality, storytelling, and what it means to be human—which means to be imperfect, yet long for perfection, to be broken, yet crave wholeness. Ernie liked to talk about "beyond" and "between." What lies beyond us, beyond our ability to possess or claim it, or even wholly understand it? What lies between us that sustains and supports us, allowing us to put one foot in front of the other, even after we stumble, even after we fall? Most important of all, Ernie encouraged me to think about how those two are connected—the beyond and the between—how hope and despair, helplessness and faithfulness, lack of control and embrace of community complement and complete each other.

Of all the hundreds upon hundreds of stories Ernie gave me, this is my favorite.

I recently heard a story of someone asking a monk,
"What is your life like as a monk?"

The monk replied: "We walk, we fall down, someone
helps us up. We walk some more; someone else falls
down. We help them up. That's pretty much what we do."

This is why I bring the Juvie stories home with me. I want my children to understand that we are here on this earth to help each other. Because we will fall and we will fail—there's no way around it. Bruised and bloodied, we will need someone to reach out and help us get back on our feet. We need others who will walk with us, steadying us along the way.

We may look different, but inside we are pretty much all the same.

We are all searching.

We are all afraid, at times.

We all build walls to protect ourselves.

And we all need to know that whatever we have done in the past, there is a pathway leading to a different future.

3

the hole inside

1999–2000

One day, in October of her senior year, Robyn sits down on the sofa next to me. I'm working on a proposal for a column in our local newspaper, writing down ideas in a steno notebook. "How are things going, Mom?"

"Good," I say, turning to smile at her. "I'm working on this column idea. What if I title it 'Straight Talk About Drugs'? Do you like that?"

"Yeah, that's great," she says. "So, can I talk to you about something?"

"Sure," I say, closing the notebook and turning toward her. "What's up?"

"You've changed, Mom," she says softly. "It seems like you're always sad."

"Always?" I smile, but for some reason I want to cry.

"Well, not always. But a lot. I'm worried about you."

I sit with her words for a while, reflecting on them. She's right. I am sad. I cry a lot, sometimes for no good reason. This tightness in my chest is new—almost as if I'm holding my breath and suddenly I take a deep, long gulp of air and let it out in a rush. Not good—I know that from all those yoga classes I've taken over the years. "Don't forget to breathe!" the teachers always say. That instruction sounded so silly to me when I first heard it—like, what am I going to do, not breathe? But then I realized how easy it is to hold my breath, almost in anticipation, as if I need to be prepared for the moment that is surely to come, ready with baited breath to jump in so I don't miss anything.

Maybe I am a little depressed, I think. I ask myself, over and over again, what am I doing with my life? An even bigger question: What do I have to give to this world? I'm "unemployed" again, as writers often are when they finish a book or some other writing project. Having time on my hands feels good for the first few weeks, but then I get bored and distracted. All the everyday activities just don't take up enough time—there's nothing like writing a book to eat up the hours of the day—and I find them endlessly tedious and repetitive. I don't like grocery shopping, for example. It seems like the silliest activity—walking up and down the aisles, putting all kinds of stuff in a cart, only some of which I really need, standing in the checkout line with all the lines around me moving much faster, so I switch lines and watch the line I used to be in speed up. Finally, the checker starts pushing my stuff through, fills up the bags, loads up the cart, which I roll to the car to unload everything, drive home, lug the bags inside the house, unpack them, and put all the stuff away. More often than not, I have to rearrange the refrigerator to fit the gallon of milk, yogurt containers, and bags of salad, while tossing out smelly old leftovers and limp carrots.

Then begins a whole new round of endless activity as I search through recipe books for meals to make with the groceries I have on hand—swearing and stomping my feet because, as usual, I forgot to choose the recipes first and make a list of exactly what I needed at the store. Always, always, it never fails, I forget something—chicken broth, soy sauce, crushed Italian tomatoes, an onion. The whole exercise seems so endlessly futile, because even after I go through the mess and drama of cooking and serving, I have to put the dishes in the dishwasher, run the garbage disposal, wipe off the counters, put the clean dishes in the cupboards. On and on it goes.

I don't know what I'm complaining about. Pat does almost all the grocery shopping. He actually likes it, which is so interesting because he's the introvert; yet, he always comes home with stories about who he ran into that day—friends, colleagues, students. Often he ends up chatting with the same people week after week. I wonder if maybe, for some people, grocery stores are second homes: colorful, crowded places to see and be seen and to feel part of a community. I'm always amazed when people in line ahead of me are so patient when the price doesn't come up automatically, the checker apologizes for the delay, and the person shrugs his or her shoulders and says, "No worries, I'm in no hurry at all."

Pat also does at least half the cooking and cleaning up—more than half when I'm working on a deadline—while I putter around trying to be helpful by emptying bags of salad into bowls and grating cheese on top.

Then there's the laundry . . . and the beds to make . . . and the shoes all over the floor . . . and the coats tossed over the chairs and sofas. Our children are anything but neat and tidy (I might even call them slobs, but that word contains more judgment than I intend). The bathroom counters are filled with makeup and hair products (Ben is into hair gel these days), and every one of the kids steps out of the shower sopping wet, so the bath mat is always damp, the tile floor is slippery. Underwear, T-shirts, and dank towels are strewn all over the floor, and every cupboard is open, just waiting for a hip or a knee to catch an edge.

I get kind of a kick out of the mess, to be honest, because this is how I grew up—five children born within six-and-a-half years living in a three-story house in suburban Westfield, New Jersey, with every one of us running from swim practice to school to more practices—softball, football, baseball, cheerleading, and church choir—run, run, run. No wonder Mom sat in front of the TV most of the day, smoking one cigarette after another (Tareytons) and working on some needlework or crewel project. She created a smoky little corner of the house where she watched her favorite TV shows (*The Fugitive* topped the list), and she was perfectly content there, all by herself.

Thinking about the big old three-story house where I grew up fills me with an aching sense of nostalgia. I think about time passing, all that once was and is no more, and it is as if I have a hole somewhere deep inside. Life whistles through that empty space without filling in its creases and crevices. Lately, I seem preoccupied with the mysteries of life and the inevitability of death. The phone rings and, in a second, the world is upside down. Shortly after my fortieth birthday, my father is diagnosed with idiopathic (meaning "who knows where it came from") pulmonary fibrosis. I'm convinced the pills he took for colitis destroyed his lungs, and that bizarre connection—soft bowels to hardened lungs—disturbs me. Maybe it was the flu shot his doctor convinced him to get that sent him into respiratory failure, although everyone says that's not possible. But still, *what if?* He didn't drink, he didn't smoke, he exercised every day, he filled his life with love and laughter, and he died at age seventy-four.

In his hospital room, we gathered around his bed and watched the heart monitor beep down, counting out the remaining minutes of his life. Somewhere around forty-five or fifty beats a minute, my mother leaned down, kissed him, and whispered in his ear. His blood pressure shot up ten or twenty points, before settling back down again.

"What did you say to him, Mom?" I asked, bewildered by the blood pressure spike.

She gave us a Mona Lisa–type smile, half-shy, half-pleased with herself. Holding my father's near-lifeless hand, she lifted it to her lips. "I said, 'Frankie, you always were a great screw.'"

We had never, not once in our lives, heard our mother say anything like that. With all the tears in that room, there was laughter, too.

Five years later, my mother is brain damaged in a car accident, but, stubborn Scot that she is, she bounces back to live on her own for several years before emphysema grabs her and takes her away. Those damn cigarettes.

Ruthanne, one of my best friends of all time, has breast cancer. Her son, Gregory, was born a month before Ben, and they are great friends, too. I take Ben with me to visit Ruth in the hospital, just days before she dies. She is asleep, and I lean over to kiss her. Ben asks if it would be okay to kiss her, too, and in the darkened room, on tiptoes, he gently places his lips on her cheek.

One of Pat's favorite students dies suddenly of an epileptic seizure. The boy's mother—a good friend and the principal of the elementary school our children attended—dies a few years later of brain cancer.

Robyn is leaving for college in the fall. I find myself thinking about what it will be like to have her so far away, to see her only every few months, to sit down to dinner without her. First there were five, and soon there will be four, then three, and finally just the two of us again. Life fills up and then empties out.

Robyn is right. I am sad. Time is moving so swiftly. Not so very long ago, it was a slow-moving stream, with gentle eddies and playful pools. I think about mishaps and catastrophes coming so unexpectedly, with no warning. I hear, just a dull roar, the rapids ahead and feel the waters churning underneath me, deep and dark, as I'm carried along, no longer in control but pretending to paddle my way along as if I know what I'm doing. As the wind and water pick up speed, I hear in the distance, growing louder, the steep, bottomless waterfall that will claim us all.

I'm not afraid of death—I'm fascinated by it. The only true terror is the thought that one of my children might die before I do, which is why I love the story about the holy man who stays overnight with a farmer and his family. Before the holy man continues on his way, the farmer asks him for a blessing. A moment passes before the holy one speaks: "Grandfather dies, father dies, son dies."

"That's not a blessing!" the farmer sputters indignantly. "That's a curse!"

"Would you want it to happen any other way?" asks the monk.

I'm addicted to reading obituaries. I scan them quickly to see if all is right with the world, meaning that those who died had their fair share of years on this earth. I read the first names, which are often dead giveaways—Rowena, Roland, Prudence, Parley, Eunice, Eugene, Gertrude, and Godfrey have most likely lived a good long life. I feel so happy when I read lines like this one about Willard, born in 1912, who met "the most beautiful woman he'd ever seen" while playing league baseball. I wonder, was she in the stands watching, thinking he was the most handsome man she'd ever seen? Was it love at first sight for both of them? Willard traveled to Missouri nearly every summer "to visit family, swim, float, or shoot fireworks over the Current River."

Really, can life get much better than that? One day, every person on the obituary page was at least eighty-three years old. I read that page with a smile on my face, feeling a sense of peace knowing that the dead had a good shot at life. Those late-life obituaries make me feel good. Death is not a happy thing, but it comes to us all, and, like the blessing bestowed on the farmer and his family, we can only hope that it comes in the right order.

When someone dies before, say, age fifty, I start sniffing around the edges of the words, obituary hound that I am, trying to figure out if alcohol or other drugs were somehow involved in the death. Rarely are drugs ever mentioned, so it takes some sleuthing, but if a forty-five-year-old dies with no mention of the cause of death, I get suspicious and try to hunt out the facts by reading between the lines. These deaths weigh heavy on my heart, because if alcohol or other drugs are involved, I can't help wondering if something could have been done to prevent them. If only addiction weren't so stigmatized, if only people weren't afraid to face the truth, if only treatment weren't so expensive, if only people understood how many obstacles stand in the way of people trying to stay clean and sober. Lately there have been too many obituaries about young people dying in their twenties and thirties—even in their teens. I read these obituaries and feel a deep sense of loss, knowing that their families are grieving for them, too often in silence and in shame, and that losing a child is a grief that never, ever ends. As one mother whose son died of a heroin overdose told me, "I'm still breathing. That's all I can say."

On another day, I open the paper to find two obituaries, side by side, almost exactly the same size. On the right is Neoma, eighty-eight years old, who married "the love of her life" and "in her younger days enjoyed sewing, golfing, bowling, snowmobiling, knitting, painting." Neoma had seventeen great-grandchildren and seven great-great-grandchildren.

The obituary on the left describes the short life of Sierra, age twenty-one, "a brave girl, full of courage," who loved soccer and volleyball, dancing, music, funny television shows, cats, and being with friends. The photograph shows a beautiful young woman with a big smile and sparkling eyes. She died two weeks shy of her twenty-second birthday.

I look from one picture to the other—Sierra so young and lovely, with her broad happy smile, to gray-haired Neoma, with the kind, patient look of one who has lived long and well. Carefully, I cut out the obituaries, my heart tight in my chest. I grab some toilet paper and wipe at my eyes, dry my nose. I can't help wondering what happened to take Sierra from this earth and her family. I can't help thinking that the trajectory of her short life could have been changed, if only we had the resources, if only we could have offered the family more help, if only we understood more, knew more, cared more. I feel the old outrage inside, the loss of this life, the pain of this family, the sister who is left behind, the grief that goes on and on and on.

~

I wonder what I believe in. Every so often in the detention groups, we talk about God, a discussion that is stimulated by an exercise I hand out that lists eighteen "Life Qualities That Make You Happy"—faith, family, freedom, friends, fun, God, happiness, health, honesty, love, loyalty, possessions, pleasure, power, respect, responsibility, trust, wisdom.

"Okay," I say, "here's what you need to do. Circle the top five qualities that are most important to you."

"I can't pick just five," someone always says.

"That's all you get," I say. Slowly, thoughtfully, they make their selections.

Then, one by one, they have to eliminate one choice. "You got arrested and spent a week in detention," I explain. "So you have to take away something."

They argue with me. "I can't get rid of anything. Why can't I keep them all?" Reluctantly they put an X through one of their choices.

"You were caught at school selling drugs. Take away one more."

And on it goes—they ran away from home, take one away; they overdosed and had their stomachs pumped, take away another.

At the end of the exercise, they have only one "life quality" left. Three out of four kids choose "God." The other favorite is "Family."

One day Michael, age sixteen, circles family, God, honesty, respect, and love. Rather than crossing anything out, he draws a line from God to each of the circles. When he hands the sheet of paper to me, he says, "God is every one of these. As long as I have God, I have everything."

Every once in a while someone in the group will ask if I believe in God.

"I'm not sure," I answer honestly.

"How can you not believe in God? What's the matter with you?" It seems they are truly concerned about me.

"I believe there is a force for good in the world," I say. "But I'm not sure there's a white-bearded person up in the heavens. If God exists, I think He or She is most interested in what goes on here, between us, on this earth, in the way we care for each other and take care of each other. I think God might be right here with us in this room, listening when we tell our stories, interested in what we are thinking and feeling about life and our struggles to be a good human being."

They look at each other, some more skeptical than others, but they don't argue with me. It's a new perspective, and they are open to thinking about it. I keep thinking about it, too—what do I believe in?

~

I continue to work on the newspaper column idea, turning words around, creating a file of ideas, crafting a few sample paragraphs, then setting everything aside, afraid to jump back into writing. It's always a push-pull sort of thing, because writing is plain old hard work, nothing glamorous about it. I have grave doubts about whether I am good enough or smart enough to keep putting words on paper and expecting people to read them.

I hear my mother's voice: "Chin up! Stiff upper lip, Kath!" A deep sigh. I pick up my pen and write the first column.

> Drugs. Addiction. Drunk drivers. Courts. Prison. Gangs. Suicide. Violent crime.
>
> Is this what you want to read about in your newspaper's "Food & Family" section every other Tuesday evening?
>
> I hope to convince you in this and future columns that these are the subjects we should be discussing as our families gather around the kitchen table. For these are the subjects that affect every individual in this community.
>
> If you are 13, 40, or 75, male or female, rich or poor, college professor or migrant worker, your life is both directly and indirectly affected by what is euphemistically called "the drug problem."

Our children are exposed to alcohol and other drugs on
a daily basis—at school, on the streets, in the parks and
recreation areas, and in their own homes. More than half
our nation's middle and high school students drink alcohol.
Fifty-four percent of 12th-graders have tried an illegal
drug such as marijuana, cocaine, methamphetamines, or
heroin; 25 percent have used in the last 30 days.

After promising to write about gangs, prisons, drunk driving, preven-
tion, education, treatment, twelve-step groups, spirituality, current
research, the stigma of addiction, and real-life stories about people,
young and old, in recovery—really, is anyone going to want to read
this stuff?—I end the column with more talk about the dinner table.

Drugs and the problems they cause—for you, for me,
for our community and our nation—are not the stuff of
normal dinner table conversation. I believe that's a big
part of the problem. I hope this column will be part of
the solution.

Ugh. I read those paragraphs and wonder why anyone would want to
read this stuff. My own family is sick and tired of these dinner table
conversations; why do I want to inflict them on my community?

Seconds later, I answer my own question. People need to know
what is happening beneath the surface, beyond their awareness—in
detention centers, county jails, juvenile institutions, and prisons.
Behind closed doors, in church meeting rooms, in treatment centers
and homeless shelters. These are not just other people's children. They
are our children, our neighbors' children, our teachers' children, our
ministers' children, our children's friends and fellow classmates. They
are not "losers" or "lost causes." They have taken a wrong turn, and
they need our help to find their way back.

I remember what Matthew, age seventeen, said in group: "Don't
look at kids and say they're bad. Everyone is a good person. They're
just lost. They've taken a detour."

"Yeah," Evian, age fifteen, added. "Don't give up on your kids. Never give up."

~

The Juvie stories are ripping me apart. They are just kids—children. Maybe they had family problems. Maybe they were abused or neglected or introduced to drugs at an early age by their parents, siblings, cousins, friends. Maybe not. But still, before drugs, they were just kids. After drugs, everything changed, inside and out. Life went to hell, and all thoughts of childish things evaporated.

I hear their longings, and they mirror my own. "I want to be nice, not mean." "I want freedom." "People who listen." "People who care." "People who understand me." "Gratitude for what I have." "I want to be with my family." "I want to be left alone." "I want a fresh start." "I want to listen to music." "I want to go fishing."

I am too deeply connected to their grief and their longing. I'm absorbing it; it's becoming part of me, part of my own experience. I watch my own children reading books, playing with the dogs, jumping on the trampoline, throwing the Frisbee, on vacation at the beach; then, hours or days later, I am in this other world, listening to boys and girls their age talk about the things that are hurting them. Feeling worthless. Hurting other people. Being judged. Life.

I don't know how to reconcile those two worlds—one full of joyful events and unconditional love and the other a place of loss, fear, grief, guilt, and shame. As my own children grow up and became increasingly independent, I find myself gravitating toward the Juvie world, where I feel I am needed and can make a difference. I want to give Robyn, Alison, and Ben space to be independent, because that is clearly what they need and want. Even Ben is gently pushing away, with school, sports, friendships, video games, and books (the Fear Street series is his current obsession) filling the bulk of his days.

I can't hold on to them forever. I wish I could. I remember when the kids were little, and Pat and I would go away for a weekend, leaving them with a trusted babysitter. Within hours, my hands would hurt—literally, ache—because I missed touching them, holding them, hugging them. Now they do not want to be touched so much, although they let me hug and kiss them, and we always say goodnight with the traditional Ketcham ritual, "Hug, Squeeze, Big Fat Mooch."

"But face it, Kathy," I say out loud. *They are leaving you, and you better find something to fill your time, people to care for who need or want at least part of what you might have to offer. Buck up. This is life. Figure out where you fit and belong. How you can be productive. How you can help. What you want to be when you grow up.*

I'm having a spiritual crisis, no doubt about it. It feels like a thickness in my throat, as if I have an obstruction there, making it hard to breathe. My chest hurts. My eyes ache. I walk in circles; I go to the kitchen to find something, stand there, turn around, ask out loud, "What am I looking for?" I go back to the living room, remember, "Oh yeah, scissors," go back, hold them in my hand, and wonder why I needed them. All my senses are clouded, dulled. I'm all fogged up.

I remember, it seems like just yesterday, walking Robyn in the stroller when an older woman, probably my age now, stopped me. "What a beautiful baby," she said. "How old is she?" In my memory, Robyn was a newborn, just eleven or twelve days old. The woman reached out to touch my hand. "Hold onto these moments," she said with great intensity. "Don't let them just slip by."

At the time, I thought this was an odd encounter, a stranger approaching me and offering me such heartfelt advice—in words that I had heard so many times before, they qualified as a cliché—but I haven't forgotten one detail of that moment. We were walking past the prescription counter in Payless Drugs. Robyn was wrapped up in a blanket in the light purple stroller, a baby shower gift. I was wearing jeans and sneakers; in my mind, I can still imagine the rubber soles squeaking on the store's freshly waxed linoleum floor.

It was such a happy time. Pat was taking classes for his PhD in geology at the University of Washington. That evening, Robyn and I would pick him up at the bus station. We lived in an old one-bedroom farmhouse on ten acres that we rented for $200. Nellie, our golden retriever, had twelve puppies when Robyn was four months old. A rickety barn on the property was filled with owl pellets, which Pat, ever the paleontologist, picked apart to unearth the tiny bones of field mice, moles, and an occasional squirrel. Horses and coyotes shared the neighbor's field, and my sister Billy's dog, Blue, would sometimes romp around in the tall grass with them. It all looked like good fun—but I was afraid the coyotes would turn on her. They never did, though they did feast on two newborn lambs early one morning at a nearby farm. We had a wood-burning stove and spent hours splitting wood and chopping kindling.

Hard as I tried, as many photographs as I took (dozens of albums stuffed full), the moments, months, and years blew by, and here I am in Walla Walla with the girls in high school and Ben in seventh grade. I'm off-center, out of balance. I try to figure out what's wrong with me, why this gloomy melancholy when I have so many good, wonderful, amazing things in my life—my writing career, my gentle husband, our three healthy children, lots of good friends. We live in a beautiful house in the country with big windows and views of the Blue Mountains, pheasant and quail wandering through the backyard, and doves cooing in the spring and summer when Pat and I drink coffee on the back patio. We have all the books I could ever want to read, all the roses and flowers I could ever dream of having (and, I have to admit with a hefty amount of guilt, neglecting).

I coauthor books with people I respect and even, over the two or three years it takes to finish a book, come to love. Reviewers, for the most part, like the books, and from the online reviews, it seems that readers appreciate the information. People have told me that the books saved their lives. I've probably heard that a hundred times. Pat read *Under the Influence* just after Alison was born, when he was thirty-two, and decided to quit drinking because he knew he had a genetic predisposition from his father's side of the family—his only symptom was a high tolerance (he could drink a lot and still function) and a real love for the stuff. After reading the facts about the disease, he didn't like his odds, so he stopped, just like that.

I make money writing books—advances, foreign sales, and small royalty checks coming in twice a year—although I couldn't support a family on my income. *But it's not about material possessions, is it, Kathy? It's not about prestige or reputation or moving ahead in this world. It's about connection, community.* I hear Ernie Kurtz's voice and remember the words we wrote almost a decade earlier. *Get beyond yourself!*

He's right. I've been thinking too much about myself. I pick up our book, *The Spirituality of Imperfection* and search for a favorite passage. It's easy to find because of the flagged page.

> Spirituality is that which allows us to get *beyond* the
> narrow confines of *self* . . . to get beyond the self to a
> place of interior peace where we are not obsessed with
> thoughts of material possessions, to get beyond the
> immediate concerns that dissipate us, we must first
> learn to put up with—to accept—our selfish, impatient,
> often recalcitrant human nature.

I am impatient, for sure. Recalcitrant, stubborn, obstinate, headstrong—absolutely. Selfish . . . well, that is harder to admit and accept, but yes, okay, I can definitely be self-centered. Am I obsessed with thoughts of material possessions? Crap, I hate this. Yes. I had to have the big house in the country with the view of the mountains. I like cars, and even though we can't really afford them, I talk Pat into getting a new car every three or four years. Toyotas and Hondas are fine with me, but once we bought an Acura SUV, which Alison then rolled in a ditch trying to avoid a coyote and her pups walking across the highway. The car served its purpose—it saved her life. I buy more rose bushes than I can possibly take care of, more groceries than I can possibly eat, more clothes than I can possibly wear.

The thing about spirituality—at least this spirituality of imperfection that Ernie immersed me in—is that it forces you to look at yourself honestly, without flinching or trying to escape the truth of yourself. It hurts as much as it heals, and it seems it heals in large part because it hurts. I keep thinking about the line from William James's book *The Varieties of Religious Experience*, in which he talks about "a form of regeneration by relaxing, by letting go. . .

It is but giving your little private convulsive self a rest, and finding that a greater Self is there."

I wonder if that is what is missing—a greater Self. But if I am to believe William James, before finding that Self, I have to give my "little private convulsive self a rest." I don't know how to do that. I don't like the image of "convulsive," but there is truth there, too, for I am restless, constantly squirming, shifting, and relocating. It's rare for me to walk into a restaurant and be led to a table without requesting a different spot, maybe by the window or in a quieter corner of the room. I knit scarves that I never finish. I read four, five, six books at a time. I keep switching seats in movie theaters and channels on the TV. I skip steps in recipes, often forgetting key ingredients and botching the whole deal. I go to weddings, baptisms, and funerals, sit down in one chair, feel uncomfortable, and move to another. And sometimes another. Pat knows to wait before he sits down, standing off to the side a bit, hands in his pockets, until I'm settled.

I can feel the energy building inside as the restlessness roams around, looking for a place to settle and sink in. The Juvie stories keep building up inside me, seeking an outlet, a home, and one morning I wake up and know what I need to do—I need to write a book about them, be their mouthpiece, tell their stories. People need to know about the drugs out there and the threat to our children—not just other people's kids but our own as well. If the drugs are "everywhere," as the Juvie kids tell me, and even elementary school children are exposed to them, then parents need to be educated about the threat. I'll call the book *Teens Under the Influence.* Maybe it will make a difference. Maybe it will help even one child, one family.

I have hope again.

4

vampire dreams

1993–2001

One warm, sunny day in the spring of Ben's seventh-grade year, I pick him up at school after tennis practice, as I always do. He walks to the car with his head down and gets in the back seat. I wonder why he doesn't sit in the front seat as he always does. I look at him in the rearview mirror. He's crying.

"What's wrong, Ben?" My heart feels tight and squished in my chest.

He hunches over, his head close to his knees, and starts sobbing.

"Benny, tell me, please, what's wrong?"

He can't stop crying. I drive home, my hands tight on the wheel. Ten minutes later, we are sitting on the sofa. I put my arm around him, and he leans into me. The story comes out slowly, unevenly, in bits and pieces.

"They took my backpack. Tripped me. Hit me."

"They?"

"The baseball kids."

"The kids who play baseball?" *Good athletes*, I think. *Good kids.* "They pick on the tennis kids?"

He shakes his head.

"Just you? They just pick on you? Why you? Didn't anyone notice, didn't anyone do anything? Where were the coaches?"

He keeps shaking his head, as if to say, *I don't know, I don't know, I don't know, I don't know, I don't know.*

"But these are your good friends—you grew up with them; you've known them for years." I'm suddenly, furiously angry. "You have the right to protect yourself, Ben. I know we taught you to be kind, not to hurt others, to talk things through, but if someone hurts you, you have the right to defend yourself."

He looks at me, and in his eyes, I see confusion and despair. The question he asks has no answer: "Why would one human being inflict harm on another?"

That conversation embarrasses Ben now when I remember it. He thinks it puffs him up too much, makes him seem kinder or wiser than he really is. But he said those words, and they struck me with such force that I wrote them down in my journal: *Why would one human being inflict harm on another?*

The bullying didn't start in seventh grade. A boy with red hair and freckles who refuses to fight back and is quickly moved to tears is a vulnerable target. In second grade, we moved him out of Mrs. Locati's class, where four of his good friends, the "popular" kids destined to be great athletes and magnets for the pretty girls, teased and taunted him. They liked Ben, they invited him to overnights and birthday parties, he played soccer and YMCA basketball with them, but he never quite fit in. He wanted so badly to be part of the popular group, and the wanting to be something he was not tore him apart.

Many years later, he told me about a recurring dream he had over the years. He called them "vampire dreams." The details are striking, the colors vivid, as he described being on a field trip with his first-grade class. They stopped at museum after museum, and Ben was always a few steps behind the crowd, afraid to be left behind, hurrying to catch up.

At the last stop, the students gathered in a dark room lit only by a red glow. Coffins lined the walls. The teachers wore Dracula capes, billowing robes lined with red satin with crisp, wide collars. All the popular boys stood in a single file. Ben joined them at the very end of the line. As he watched, each boy would step forward, like a robot, turning their heads to expose their necks and allowing the teachers to bite them. No one flinched or yelped. As each boy stepped forward and the line shortened, Ben's heart beat faster and faster.

"Don't be afraid," said Mrs. Dutton, his first-grade teacher, with a beckoning look in her eyes. "It won't hurt, and soon you'll be like everyone else."

He bared his neck, she leaned forward with her mouth wide open, and at that point in the dream, he always woke up.

Ben knew what the dreams meant. "Although I didn't realize it until many years later, baring my neck and becoming a vampire in the dream was the first step to admitting that I didn't want to be myself," he told me. "I didn't want to stand out. I didn't want fucking red hair or freckles. I didn't want to be the kid who couldn't help crying when he got hurt or worked up emotionally. I wanted to be a robot vampire like everyone else."

When we switched Ben to a multi-age classroom, he thrived and quickly became a member of the "Midget Patrol," a group of fun-loving, not-particularly-athletic-just-shy-of-popular kids with lively imaginations who thought up all sorts of adventures, including sneaking out at night to the graveyard a mile from our house. Their plan was to meet at 11:00 p.m., just an hour before midnight, at a particularly gnarly grave that was haunted, they'd been told, by a witch. They never did make it to the graveyard, but just thinking about the escapade thrilled them as they imagined what it would be like, with the owls perched on the headstones, the moon making shadow pathways between the stones, and the specter of a real live witch hiding high up in the trees, perhaps knowing they were coming, waiting for them.

Multi-age was all about imagination and creativity. First-, second-, and third-graders worked and played together in project-based learning, including units on rain forests, medieval times, and ancient Egypt. In the ancient Egypt section, the students mummified a chicken, which they called King Chickakufu, and buried it in their teacher Mr. Wood's yard, setting a date to come back in eighth grade to dig it up. Mr. Wood introduced Ben to the Goosebumps books, which Ben read nonstop. We filled an entire bookshelf with Goosebumps books (*Monster Blood, Night of the Living Dummy, Say Cheese and Die!*). It was right about then that Ben discovered Teenage Mutant Ninja Turtles—the "cool nerds." They became the great passion of his life for years to come, as he collected dozens of the toy figures and staged momentous battles. Raphael, the "hotheaded" member of the group gifted with "berserker strength," was his favorite.

One day, Mr. Wood sent home a note, letting me know that Ben had been unkind to his friend Andy, a first-grader. Ben adored Andy—our families were close friends, we celebrated holidays with them (the "ugly cookie" contest, birthday celebrations, Fourth of July swimming parties), and even vacationed with them at Priest Lake in northern Idaho. I couldn't imagine that he would be mean to his good friend, so I wrote a long letter to Mr. Wood, defending Ben, even expressing some indignation that he would accuse Ben of picking on anyone, especially Andy.

I feel such shame now about that letter and my refusal to acknowledge that Ben might bully other children, just as he had been bullied. I just couldn't imagine that sweet, sensitive Ben would mistreat another child. I wish I could find Mr. Wood—he moved a long time ago—and apologize to him. If I could go back—if, if, if—I would listen carefully and respectfully to the teacher and use that incident as a teaching moment, both for myself and for Ben. I would be certain to hear both sides, and I would refuse to take one side over the other, because the truth is always somewhere in between. But whatever the facts might be, I would insist that Ben apologize to Andy. And I would let Ben know, no matter what happened between him and Andy, that as much as it hurts to be tormented, over time, it hurts even more to be the tormenter.

I failed Ben in that moment. It was not the first time, and it would not be the last.

~

In fourth grade, Ben became good friends with John Quaresma, a quiet, handsome kid with a goofy sideways smile. Ben idolized John, in part, I think, because they were complete opposites—John was everything Ben wanted to be. Where Ben was impulsive and hotheaded, John was calm and cool. Ben loved to talk and make people laugh, while John was the quiet observer. Ben yearned to be accepted by the popular kids, while John couldn't have cared less. Ben wore "preppy" clothes, while John had holes in his jeans and kept his shirt untucked. John was a great athlete, excelling at every sport, while Ben, in those early years, was awkward and self-conscious.

I remember a middle school football game when John zigzagged down the entire length of the field, avoiding every tackle, to score a touchdown. He did it again. And again. "That kid is going to be an All-American," Pat said with a touch of awe in his voice. In that same game, Ben stood awkwardly at the defensive line, unsure what to do with himself. When he finally landed a tackle, he looked at us on the sidelines as if to ask whether he did the right thing. We watched as he extended a hand to the player, helping him up and patting him on the back. "I didn't like that feeling of knocking someone down," he told us after the game.

I wonder how life might have turned out for Ben if John hadn't continued to play football in high school. I wish . . . but I try to stop myself right here, with those two words, for that is magical thinking, an attempt to control what cannot be altered. Still, I can't help myself. I look at the past and imagine I can manipulate it, in the same way I might shift the trajectory of a story in a book. A moment here or there, a right turn instead of a left turn—how different our lives might be.

My best friend from elementary and middle school, Judy Crum, told me a story that has stayed with me all these years. Her father was walking down a New York City street on his way to work when a sudden blast of wind blew his hat off his head. He went back to retrieve it, and seconds later, right where he had been walking, a huge plate glass window crashed down from a high-rise building under construction.

A moment here or there. A right turn instead of a left turn. A gust of wind. Thousands of tiny moments, most unrecognized and uncounted, and in each one, our lives may hang in the balance.

~

"What am I going to do if all my good kids are using drugs?"

Ben's middle school principal, a good friend of mine, is close to tears. I can hear the strain in his voice as he clears his throat and tries to control his emotions. Over the years, we've talked a lot about "the drug problem" in our community and how so many kids are starting to use at such early ages. We struggle to understand the reasons kids use drugs. Boredom? Anxiety? Depression? Peer pressure? Gangs? Family problems? We brainstorm ways to help them. But this time, it's Ben.

I hold the phone to my ear, but I feel as if I am standing outside myself, listening to the conversation, thinking, *Is this really happening?*

As the story unravels, we learn that Ben and three of his friends—all "good" kids from "good" families (that word *good* always made us believe we were inoculated somehow)—bought a forty-dollar bag of marijuana. One of the boys brought the marijuana to school ("to be cool," Ben says later), and one friend told another friend, who told somebody else, and eventually word got around to a teacher who took the news to the principal. Called into the principal's office, the boy folded under pressure and, as Ben told the story with not a little disgust, "ratted everyone out."

Something about that phrase—"ratted everyone out"—bothers me, but I ignore it for now. We talk. We listen. We try to listen more than we talk, but I'm not sure we do such a great job. We're sort of shell-shocked. I try to keep in mind the advice I've heard from the kids at Juvie. Every so often in group, I ask them, "What suggestions do you have for parents raising kids these days?" They're taken aback, confused, for they're accustomed to taking advice from older folks, not giving it. So they sit for a while, thinking. Then, tentatively, one person offers an insight from his or her own experience, and then another builds on those words. Then, as so often happens in these detention groups, suddenly everyone has something to say.

"Try to talk to your kids more."

"Yeah, express yourself to your kids as a human being. You can yell at them, or you can talk to them. It's much better just to talk to them."

"Listen to what we have to say. Don't assume you always know what's going on."

I think that last bit of advice may be the smartest of all—don't always assume you know what's going on.

"We were just trying to be cool," Ben says, teary-eyed. The tears seem genuine. We ask him where he got the money, and he answers, truthfully we are sure, that he took ten dollars' worth of quarters from the change jar on the upper shelf of my closet. Pat and I exchange a look—time to get rid of the change jar. We ask if this was the first time, and Ben swears it was. He also promises he will never, ever use drugs again. "Definitely not worth it," he says miserably.

Ben and his friends are charged with an MIP (minor-in-possession) charge, which goes on their juvenile criminal record to be expunged with good behavior when they turn eighteen. They are all required to go through the diversion program at the Juvenile Justice Center. There, they participate in education classes; complete written assignments, including apology letters; attend the DUI Victim's Panel, required by the State of Washington; and act appropriately ashamed of themselves.

Pat and I organize a parent meeting. It's my idea, and we host it at our house. Eight parents, four boys. Firmly but not unkindly, we set down the rules, creating a home contract that each boy signs.

I think that we did a good job and that the whole thing turned out pretty well. The boys are remorseful and willingly accept the consequences, which are significant (especially that MIP charge on their juvenile record), and the parents are united not only in their opposition to marijuana use but also in closer monitoring of their children's activities. We all figure the kids were just experimenting and posturing, showing off for their friends, having fun smoking a little weed, and probably coughing their lungs out. They got caught, they were forced to face the consequences of their actions, and they have learned a lesson.

I actually feel grateful for the whole experience and wonder what might have happened if Ben hadn't been caught. Would he have bought another bag of weed and another? But I quickly backtrack from that thought. Not our Ben.

~

But why not our Ben? That question nags at me. Once again, I hear the Juvie kids talking.

"Parents are so stupid; they believe anything you tell them."

"If parents would just open their eyes, they'd see what's right in front of them, but they don't want to see."

"When your kid has red eyes, leaves empty Visine bottles lying around in his room, laughs or gets mad at the stupidest things—what do you think is going on?"

Ben has the genetic predisposition. He's a passionate boy prone to emotional outbursts. He hates his red hair and freckles. He can be impulsive, hypersensitive, anxious, moody. He wants to fit in with the "in crowd," to "be cool." Aren't those warning signs?

I look back through my books, all in a row in my office—all those books I wrote before I started working at the Juvenile Justice Center, when Ben was a little boy, even before Ben was born. The word *families* in the subtitle of one of my books draws my attention: *Living on the Edge: A Guide to Intervention for Families with Drug and Alcohol Problems.* I pull the book off the shelf and look at the publication date—April 1989. When I started working on the book with coauthor Ginny Gustafson, Ben was ten months old. I was thirty-seven.

I open the book and am surprised to find the pages are yellowing and stiff; as I turn them, searching for passages that might be useful, they start to pull away from the binding. *That's weird*, I think. This book is only eleven years old, and I've hardly looked at it since I wrote it. I put my nose to the pages, an old habit from the days when I read every one of my mother's Nancy Drew books, kept in a box stored in our attic for decades. I expect to drink in the smell of an old book, that sweet, musky smell—similar to the vanilla-y smell you get when you scratch in the thinning places between the bark of a Ponderosa pine. But this book has no odor—except, perhaps, of neglect.

I turn the pages slowly, searching. On page 22, I find this passage:

> Families are fooled by addiction, in part because
> society misunderstands and misdiagnoses it. It takes
> years, we think, to become a *real* drunk or a *real* addict;
> if we watch carefully, it won't happen in our family.

But it doesn't take years to become a "real" addict, I know that even better now from my time with the kids in detention. Still, with Ben, we're not talking about addiction—he's only used once. *Kathy.* I hear the warning voice. *Don't be stupid. You know that for every time someone is caught with drugs they've probably used dozens of times.* Just like drunk drivers—how many times does someone drive drunk before they are finally caught?

On pages 51–54, I find some interesting—*aw shit, be honest, Kathy*—disturbing information:

> "How could this have happened without warning?"
> parents and relatives wonder when their children
> are suddenly in big trouble with drugs. It seems that
> the drug problem appears—massive, overwhelming,
> terrifying—out of thin air. But drug problems don't
> happen overnight. If we look back and think clearly,
> there were warning signs. There are *always* warning signs,
> if we know how to recognize them.

And then this:

> Many adolescent drug users express amazement at how
> deaf, dumb, and blind their parents are to the drug use
> going on right in their own homes. . . . Too often, an
> adolescent's drug problem is ignored or mishandled
> because the family members have come to blame
> themselves. The adolescent's problems are perceived
> not as a progressive, insidious physical disease but as
> a statement of parental failure. The early symptoms
> of trouble are pushed away, excused, rationalized, and
> covered up because most of us have been taught that
> addiction is a disease of unhappy, psychologically
> maladjusted adults that takes years to develop. We just
> can't believe it could happen to a thirteen-, fourteen-, or
> fifteen-year-old.

Ben is not addicted, I keep reminding myself. I would be able to see it, even in its early stages. I know what addiction looks like. Still, I turn with shaky hands to the pages where Ginny and I include an A-to-Z list of symptoms with one-paragraph descriptions, intended to help parents in their efforts to assess their child's drug problems. I go through the list and try to honestly check off those symptoms that might—just might—indicate that something worse than experimentation is going on. I put a little arrow next to Ben's symptoms.

Anger <
Bloodshot eyes
Change in physical hygiene
Defensive
Emotional highs and lows <
Fear <
Getting secretive
Hardheaded <
Inadequacy
Joylessness
Keeping to himself
Legal problems
Money problems
Nervousness <
Oblivious
Possessions sold or missing
Quirky behavior
Resentments
Smell
Temper tantrums <
Underachiever
Violent episodes
Weight changes
Xenophobia
Yammering
Zany

Okay, so everything I checked off has been part of his personality since he was a toddler. I remember those awful tantrums when he was two and three years old, when he would scratch and bite and bang his head against me. I'd hold him tight, like a straightjacket, until he calmed down. He's a passionate boy, prone to anger and emotional ups and downs, occasionally anxious and nervous. But none of the other "symptoms" fit him—oh, except the one and only legal problem. Which was an anomaly, his bad luck to get caught and our good luck to address the problem before it got out of hand.

I shut the book and put it back on the shelf, feeling a little better about things. Ben is just going through normal adolescence, the typical ups and downs all teenagers experience and all parents can expect. *Drugs are everywhere.* Of course he was going to be exposed to them, and because he wants to fit in, be part of the crowd, even "be cool," as he phrased it, it's no big surprise that he tried them. As I walk away, I think to myself how lucky we are to have three healthy, happy children. I even feel a little smug about it.

∼

At the end of eighth grade, Ben and his classmates write letters to themselves. The teacher keeps them, little time capsules full of information about life as it is now and life as they imagine it will be four years in the future when they graduate from high school. She mails the letters to her students in their self-addressed, stamped envelopes, and they arrive a few days after high school graduation. Ben's letter (I smile at the misspellings) is dated June 11, 2001; the postmark is June 6, 2005.

> Well, this is for myself in the feauture. Everything is good right now. I have a girl in mind right now and I'm not sure whats going to happen with that. Her name is Nichole. I'm really into tennis and I'm thinking about getting into a couple of tournaments. I also made a new friend named Colby and he's going to be a great

influence on me to help keep me off drugs and stuff. I used to like doing drugs at school, but now I love swimming, riding bikes, and playing with fireworks and tennis. I like Slipknot, too, Nirvana, Pat Benatar and a lot of Pop and rap. My sister Robyn is in college, Alison is going to be a senior, I'm going to be a freshman, my dad is working at Whitman, and my mom is still writing. By the way, Robyn is going to be a sophmore in college. The world is pretty peaceful. We had that dispute with China about them not giving our pilots back, but other than that it's ok. A dream I have is that I will eventually go out with Nichole because I liked her from the moment I met her. In highschool I will acheive all my goals which will come to me, after highschool I'll go to the University of Washington. For a job I will work at Bon Appetite catering service or yard work for Dave Beebe. I will do language, photography, tennis, etc. My friends will be who they are now plus more. I would probably ask Nichole for a dance to. The world will still be peaceful. I really hope I can go out with Nichole because I'd be nice and respect her.

Ben Spencer

When the letter from the past arrives four years later in 2005, just a few days before his high school graduation, Ben reads it, chuckles a few times, and tosses it aside. Maybe he mumbles something about Nichole or not being able to spell very well. Really, I don't remember.

Here's what I do remember: Picking up the letter after he leaves the house, smoothing my hand over the page, almost as if I can feel his fifteen-year-old hand holding a newly sharpened pencil, almost as if I can see him, concentrating hard, writing a script for his life four years in the future. I want to hold that hand again, to feel the child-like smoothness of it, to remember how happy it made me to hold his small hand in my own.

A teacher once told me that during the days when it was her duty to stand outside the entrance to Garrison Middle School, welcoming kids to school for the day, she liked to watch Ben kiss me goodbye. "He wasn't embarrassed at all," she said. "He would just lean across the seat and give you a hug and a kiss." She hoped that her son, now a toddler, would do the same thing when he was in middle school.

I run my hand one more time across the page Ben wrote, as if I can feel the pressure of his pencil on the paper. Then I staple the envelope to the letter and put it in a folder titled "Ben 2001" so I will remember the way he used to be.

5

who made you god?

2001–2003

"John and I are talking about going out for wrestling."

Wrestling? I am flooded with memories of my high school friends and boyfriends trying to "make weight," wearing those tight one-piece suits, hip bones jutting out, and the funny-looking helmets, soft and form-fitting, specially designed to prevent "cauliflower ear." *Cauliflower ear!* Gross.

I remember watching Joey Wiendl and Jeff Thiel, both state champions, picking up their opponents and throwing them to the mat with a bone-crushing boom, then jumping on top of them as they thrashed around on the sweaty mat, neck tendons stretched, shoulders straining as they struggled to escape the pin. I would look up at the stands, searching for the mothers, wondering how they were dealing with the gruesome twists and torques. They wore varying expressions of fear, excitement, anguish, triumph. *What a stupid sport*, I thought. I even talked with my wrestling friends, asking them if it was a good idea to lose (or gain) so much weight, wondering what it was about wrestling that they found so exciting, wishing they wouldn't subject themselves to the torment.

"Wrestling," I say to Ben. "That sounds great." Pat and I are careful not to repeat the mistake we made a few months earlier when Ben asked if he could try out for the swimming team. We (especially me) hemmed and hawed—we had both been swimmers, both national champions in fact (for a few minutes, until the records were broken yet again), and we'd had enough of chlorine, early-morning practices, stopwatches, and heart-pounding moments on the starting block before the official fired the gun. Ben eventually gave up the idea. I felt a little guilty about my lack of support (and, of course, given my perennial "what-if-ing," have wondered since if swimming might have led him down a different path in life), but in truth I was relieved.

"When does wrestling start?" I ask.

"After John is finished with football," Ben says, a big smile spreading over his face. "John told me today he wants to hang out with me a lot more after football is over."

I smile. "You like John a lot, don't you?"

"I love John," he says, adding with pride, "he's my best friend."

"Nothing better than a best friend," I say softly, running my hand through Ben's red hair and kissing his forehead. I adore this boy who is so close to his emotions and so willing to express them. I'm also relieved that he's found a devoted friend. John accepts Ben for who he is—a goofy, somewhat awkward, overly sensitive teenager who has difficulty controlling his exuberant and, at times, explosive emotions.

Yin and *yang*, sort of like me and Pat. I think about the book I coauthored on the five elements of traditional Chinese medicine. Ben and I are most like the passionate energy of the fire element, with some of the ambitious, competitive nature of wood thrown in (wood feeds fire, which, in our lives at least, often leads to passionate outbursts). John and Pat, it seems to me, are mostly water—reflective, resourceful, steadfast, fearless, and eminently capable of adapting to changing circumstances. Fire types can definitely use the cooling, dependable water energy to balance them, while water types are attracted to fire's blazing emotional energy.

Whatever the attraction, Ben idolizes John, who he views as his trustworthy guide and loyal protector. Nobody will pick on Ben for his red hair and freckles with John by his side. Watching the two of them together, I get the sense that Ben is finding his "fit" in life, discovering a safe place where he is comfortable being himself and accepted by a friend who likes him just the way he is.

No more vampire dreams for Ben.

~

Was it days later? Weeks? The memories are all jumbled up.

Alison comes home from school, her face red and blotchy from crying.

"Something bad happened to John," she says, her words choked with tears. "In yesterday's football game. He's really hurt."

"Hurt? How? What happened?" I'm thinking maybe John broke his leg or his collarbone. Maybe it's a concussion. Something fixable. With a strong, healthy fourteen-year-old, what isn't fixable?

"I heard he's in intensive care and unstable. I guess he walked off the field feeling dizzy and then just collapsed. Someone said that he was having a seizure, but I don't know if that's true." She starts to cry again. "People are saying he might be brain damaged."

I'm holding my breath, and I remind myself to breathe in, breathe out, stay calm. This report is most likely just high school drama, rumors gone wild. But when I think about Ben, my eyes fill with tears.

"What about Ben? Does he know?"

"Yeah, it's so sad. He broke down at school; he was just sobbing. He left with Mario and Ross and those guys." I reach out and pull her into my arms. "I'm just so afraid for Ben. He loves John so much."

Ben comes home a few hours later. "John isn't doing too good," he says, collapsing on the sofa with his head in his hands and breaking down in convulsive sobs.

I put my arms around him and hold him tight. I can feel his heart beating against my chest. Ali sits next to him and puts her arms around both of us. I wish Pat and Robyn were here with us. I wish I could turn back the clock to yesterday, to before the game, switch things around, keep John on the bench for one or two plays. I wish he had had the flu and missed the game altogether.

Between sobs, Ben tells us that John is in the intensive care unit. He says the kids at school are walking around saying that John is going to die. Some are saying they hope he does die; if he lives, they worry his brain is so damaged that he will never be John again. A bunch of John's friends are angry, talking about how stupid football is, how John never liked the sport. Teachers are acting weird, keeping their voices low, trying to calm students who are crying in the classrooms and hallways. The principal announces that grief counselors will be available for students who might need them.

"I don't know what to believe," Ben says. "Johnny can't die. If Johnny dies, a part of me will die, too."

Only family members are allowed to visit John in the hospital. "Why can't I see him?" Ben keeps asking, a frantic tone in his voice. "I need to see him, to tell him I love him and everything will be okay."

Over the weekend, the news gets worse, but we don't know how to separate rumor from fact. We hear that John was tackled hard and hit his head on the ground. We hear he was running full steam—just like John would—and rammed his head into an opponent's leg. We hear he was sandwiched between two players, collapsed on the field, walked off on his own, and then had a seizure. Someone said he went back into the game even after he was badly hurt, but we wondered if that was just a John legend—after all, he was not the kind of athlete to sit on the sidelines with a game going on.

Wednesday morning, October 31, Ben is in his first-period math class. Alison is in a pottery class across the hall. Her teacher leaves the room for a few minutes and returns, red-eyed, to tell Ali's class she has an announcement. Ali doesn't wait to hear what the teacher has to say. She runs out to the hallway and stands at the door of Ben's classroom, trying to get his attention. Finally, he looks up and sees her, leaves the room, and, as she remembers it, "just sort of fell into me." They are both crying. Everyone is crying. Ben's math teacher, who is also a football coach, comes out to the hallway and hugs Ben, holding him tight. Ali and Ben walk to the counselor's office and ask if they can go home. Ali has her arm around Ben's shoulder, and he is leaning into her.

"John was his best friend," Ali says, and the counselor, whose eyes are red from crying, says yes, of course, they can go home.

"I can't believe he's gone," Ben keeps saying, over and over again. We're sitting on the living room sofa again, the three of us. His eyes have that distant look of grief, as if all his senses are engulfed in a fog of dense, impenetrable sorrow. He looks dazed, staring off into space, wide-eyed but unseeing. His shoulders slump forward, and he is so still and silent that I wonder if he is breathing.

There is a right-here-ness about this kind of grief. It is all-encompassing, wrapping us in a shroud so that we feel encased and enclosed, separated and disconnected not only from each other but also from the world we inhabit. I remember after my father died, my sisters suggested we take our children to Toys"R"Us on New Jersey's Route 22. I sat in the back seat of the car, listening to the cars passing us on the highway, feeling shrunken and terrified. In the store, I was blinded by the bright lights and vivid colors and sat down in the middle of the floor, my hands covering my eyes. In tears, I begged my sisters to leave, ignoring the cries of our children as we dragged them back to the car. My heart longed for silence and solitude. For darkness. For peace.

The essence of sorrow, of suffering, is that it must be endured. There is no escape. I look at Ben, and I see in him the embodiment of the term "torn-to-pieces-hood," William James's brilliant translation of the German word *zerrissenheit*. He is broken within and without. In a very real sense, he's lost his home, the safe place John created where Ben felt at peace with himself, with his friends and his family, with his world.

"I don't know what to do," Ben cries. "I need to do something, but I don't know what to do."

Stories. Maybe it would help Ben to write about John, telling some stories about their friendship. When I suggest this, he looks at me for a moment, as if he can't quite make sense of my words, and then he slowly nods his head. Ali and I sit on the sofa with Nessie, our golden retriever, and Sophie, our springer spaniel, holding them tight. They look at us with big, sad eyes, as if they know something terrible has happened and understand the grief we feel for John, his family, and Ben. We keep looking up at the second floor where Ben is typing on my computer. An hour later, he walks down the stairs and hands me what he has written.

> John meant the world to me. We had the funniest times
> and had so many good experiences together. One thing
> I was really proud of John about were his muscles. I
> remember one time at Oasis Water Works, he was looking

so buff, and I was so proud of him and I wanted him to
show my sister his muscles, but he was too humble to do
that. He was so humble about his muscles and he would
hardly ever show them to me even if I asked.

It's really strange, it's like I can't even breathe because
he's gone. I feel so much for Laure and Jerry and Amy
and Whitney and Jamie because they loved him so
much. I remember the day before he was injured how I
went over to his house to study and he and Marquel and
Spencer and Mario and Josh were talking and laughing
together. I just sat by myself with Ross. After that I
walked over to them and John came over by me and he
said, "You wanna go inside?" I felt like that was cool
cause he left his other friends and just came over with me.

John really never was very emotional or sentimental.
I remember once that Spencer hit me in the head with
a cowbell and I started crying and went outside and
Clinton came out with me and was comforting me and
John came out, looked at me and decided to go back
inside. Later, I was outside with Spencer, and John came
out and he was wondering what we were doing and then
Spencer said talking about sentimental stuff and John
said sentimental stuff sucks and went back inside. People
always called me a follower of John cause wherever he
went, I was close to follow. I really don't care because
I loved him and I always will and I will forever be the
Sam Gamgee of John Quaresma.

I remember one time we went snowboarding together
and went down a run that looked fun that was through
the trees. We got in and started wrestling, John kicked my
ass really bad and at first he just creamed me and gave me
white washes. Then when he thought it was all over I dove
at him from about ten feet up the hill and hit him good
but then he gave me another whitewash. We got down
to the bottom and got stuck in some small brambles. I

kept trying to escape and right when I was about to, John
jumped from afar and smashed me but then helped me
out of the bushes. If I would have escaped no way would
I have helped John. Right before this incident happened, I
was talking to John about wrestling. We were planning to
start hanging out a lot more and working out on Tuesdays,
Thursdays and Saturdays.

    I believe in a God somewhere but any god that
would steal my John from this earth so very early in
life is no god that I would like to know. I know that
there is a better place than this world, that doesn't have
worthless sports like football, and I know my beloved
Johnny is there waiting for the day when I will return to
him and we can share another life time of memories. I
wanted to say one more thing, John and me always had
this thing since Mr. Reid was our sixth grade teacher.
Mr. Reid would say "Benny and the . . ." and I would
say "Jetts." Me and John have done that ever since. But
I just wanted to write this letter in Johns memory and I
know he would be scolding me for being sentimental, but
I just wanted to say this like I always will until I see you
again, I love you Johnny, and I will always remember you,
no matter what.

I have read those words dozens of times, and every time I end up
in tears. I love the way Ben admired John's muscles. How he talked
about John's humility. How he didn't care if people called him a
follower of John's because that's exactly what he was—"the Sam
Gamgee of John Quaresma." How proud he was to play that role of
the loyal sidekick. How he questioned his faith in God but in the next
sentence expressed his belief that he would meet John again in a better
place where they would be able to share more memories together.

    But my favorite part is at the very end, when he writes as if he is
talking to John. "I just wanted to say this like I always will until I see
you again, I love you Johnny, and I will always remember you, no

matter what." I imagine, reading those sentences, that John will always be alive for Ben and that, as different as they were, they will forever be kindred spirits. I imagine John shaking his head with that shy smile of his, letting Ben know that it's okay to be true to who and what he is because that's what John would want for him. That's what John would expect of him.

~

"I'm worried about Ben," Ali tells me a few weeks after John's memorial service. "Sometimes I look in his classroom, and he's just sitting there, his head in his hands, or he's just staring off to space."

She hesitates a moment. "Plus, a bunch of older kids are reaching out to him—kids I don't trust."

"Why don't you trust them?"

"I don't know. They're nice and all, and I think they really want to help Ben, but I know they use drugs. He's hanging out with them a lot, and I'm afraid he might be using with them."

Pat and I talk to Ben, and he assures us that he doesn't ever want to get in trouble with drugs like he did in seventh grade. "That was it for me," he says. "I'm just making some new friends, and I'm careful. They're good guys, and they watch out for me."

He spends a lot of time reading and devours every Stephen King novel he can get his hands on. His favorites are *It*, *Pet Sematary*, *The Stand*, *Desperation*, *Firestarter*, *Skeleton Crew*, and *Needful Things*. He finishes one book and starts another and then another. One day I ask why he likes the horror genre so much—first the Goosebumps books, then the Fear Street series, and now Stephen King.

His brow furrows as he considers the question. "It's the 'what if' part of the whole thing," he says pensively. "All this stuff Stephen King writes about may not be real and may not even be possible, but what if? I love the 'what if?' questions."

"What's your favorite book so far?" I ask.

"*It*," he says without a moment's hesitation. He tells me the book is about a group of nerds and outcasts who call themselves "The Losers'

Club." When each of them comes face-to-face with IT—an extra-terrestrial shape-shifter that has terrorized the town for hundreds of years—IT becomes the monster of their imagination, the thing they fear the most.

Maybe that's what Ben is doing. Facing his fears. Traveling the "what if" road. Wondering why life is the way it is.

He spends hours drawing warrior figures with blood dripping from their swords. The images—thickly outlined in pencil or black pen—concern me. One character, which he titles "J8-04," is an alien-type figure with antennas coming out of a tiny one-eyed head. The creature wears a neckpiece with skulls dangling off a chain at each end, and his big-muscled arms hold a serrated sword in one hand and a gun in the other. His stomach is "ripped," as Robyn and Alison might describe Mark Wahlberg's physique, and his feet have claws for toes.

That drawing gives me the willies.

But Ben seems happy. We talk about John sometimes, though Ben tends to keep his feelings to himself these days. Maybe he's remem-bering John's words that "sentimental stuff sucks." Every so often, he wears a shirt that Laure, John's mother, gave him a few days after John died; it's the same shirt John wore in the photograph I took of him and Ben at their eighth-grade graduation. After John died, I enlarged the picture and framed it. They were so happy, two growing boys ready for summer and then high school, arms around each other, big shit-eating grins on their faces.

Ben's grades are good, all A's and B's, and his teachers describe him as hardworking and respectful. "He's having a great year so far. He's on task, working hard. His writing is good; he's a good listener," his history teacher says in November at the fall conferences. "His reading comprehension is top-notch. He's really good at interpretation," his English teacher says. The only B he gets is in his PE class.

Winter, spring, and summer go by, and then Ali is off to the University of Montana to start her freshman year. Robyn spends the fall of her junior year abroad in Australia, and Ben begins his sophomore year in high school. We see less and less of him as he hangs out before and after school and on weekends with his friends. As it should be,

Pat and I reassure each other—and, to be honest, the time we have together now, after raising three children born within four and a half years of each other, is something of a gift. When Ben is home, he spends hours playing video games in the basement. *Grand Theft Auto III* is his favorite. One day I ask him why he likes the game so much.

"You can do anything," he says, when I can get him to stop playing for a few minutes. "Drive cop cars and chase down the bad guys, beat people with baseball bats, rob banks, steal cars, put bombs in houses and blow them up, shoot helicopters out of the sky. You can go anywhere, be anyone you want to be. It's a whole world I can disappear into."

Disappear. That's the word. It's a slow process of withdrawal, beginning in the spring of his sophomore year and turning into a full-on vanishing act by the middle of his junior year. He withdraws into his video games and horror novels and spends every moment he can with his friends. A few new boys and girls have joined the group, but for the most part, these are kids he's known since elementary school. As the months go by, he gets increasingly surly and uncommunicative. He even looks different. His eyes are huge, bulging out of their orbits, as if he is constantly startled or frightened.

I wonder if he has a thyroid problem—it looks to me as if his eyes are popping out of his head—and ask his doctor to check. His thyroid is fine, but he seems depressed, so the doctor suggests an antidepressant, which he takes for a week and then throws in the trash. He agrees to try a different antidepressant, gives that a few weeks, and then tells us he's not going to take any more stupid pills. "Why are you trying to drug me?" he shouts at us as he heads out the door.

He skips dinner, choosing to eat at his friends' houses. He takes two or three showers every day. He is angry, all the time, irritated with us, annoyed with any request to help with chores, pissed off at his teachers, irate when his friends don't call him, fed up with life in small-town Walla Walla.

We ask him to sit down with us to talk. Within minutes, we're arguing with each other. Pat and I practice what we will say, promise each other we will stay calm, try hard to be good listeners, but Ben is impatient and annoyed with these conversations. His knees jump up and down. His fingers tap the table. He gives us one-word answers. It's clear that he doesn't want anything to do with us.

The F-bomb starts flying. "This fucking teacher." "What a fucking load of crap." "I'm tired of this fucking school." "I hate this fucking town." Then, a switch, seemingly overnight, and it's in-our-faces personal. "Fuck you and the fucking dogs and the fucking girls and this fucking family. FUCK you! Fuck YOU!"

Doors slam. He punches a hole in the bathroom wall and, a few weeks later, bashes his fist through the living room wall. We tell him to fix the holes, and he refuses. "Who cares about your fucking walls?" We leave the holes where they are, hoping he will feel some sense of guilt or shame, but he seems beyond remorse.

We confront him, almost on a daily basis. Or rather, I should say, I confront him. Pat dislikes conflict, which, paradoxically, is causing some heated disagreements between us. Pat grew up with an alcoholic father, and the way he avoided physical and emotional abuse was to clam up or walk away and wait until the storm had passed. My way is the complete opposite—if there's a problem, I confront it head-on, try to get to the bottom of it, and fix it. I grew up with four siblings, two older brothers and two younger sisters, all of us born within six years and all fiercely competitive. We used to have swimming races in the living room, diving off the wall radiators onto the carpeted floor and rug-burning our skin as we "swam" to the opposite side. We fought our way through our disagreements, sometimes drawing blood. But when the storm was over, we forgot all about it.

"I need to talk to you about something," Pat says one night when we're reading in bed. He places his book on the bed next to him and turns toward me.

Oh, shit, I think. I've done something to upset him. I feel like I'm always doing one thing or another that irritates him. And I'm annoyed with him, too, because it seems as if he keeps putting me in the Bad Guy role, the parent who typically initiates the conversations and does most of the talking. I don't want to be the confronter—I want to stand quietly on the sidelines while my husband puts on the gloves and steps into the ring.

His voice is calm. Steady. Like a rock. Like him. "Today you asked me to talk to Ben, and I said I would. Then you got impatient. You wanted me to talk to him on your timetable. And you started telling me what to say and how to say it—don't get angry, keep my voice down, tell him I love him, stuff like that."

I don't say anything because he's right. I'm impatient and impulsive. And bossy. Screwing up left and right.

"I think if you want to say certain things to Ben," he continues, "and especially if you want to say them in a particular way, then you should talk to him. Don't ask me to talk to him on your behalf."

I want to say, *Well, why don't you talk to him without me having to ask you to talk to him?* But I don't.

"I guess I just don't understand why you have to keep stirring things up," he says.

"Things are already stirred up!" I snap. My emotions are all roiled up. I'm just so sick and tired of the fighting, the stress and tension in the house, that awful feeling of needing to tiptoe around to avoid irritating or upsetting anyone. I'm walking on eggshells in my own home—a cliché if ever there was one. Actually it feels as if I'm stomping on glass shards, but to stick with the eggs cliché, what I'd like to do is take a whole carton of eggs, ten cartons of eggs, a truckload of eggs, and smash them one after another after another. I could throw them at a wall or stomp on them—it doesn't matter. I just want to break something, anything. Eggs, dishes, windows, mirrors, anything that makes a mess and a bunch of noise.

I'm mad and I'm sad and I'm frustrated. Something is wrong, and what good does it do to ignore it, pretend it doesn't exist, wait for it to pass?

"Kathy," Pat says, taking me in his arms. "I'm sorry."

It takes me a moment or two, but finally I say, "I'm sorry, too. I just want this to be over."

"Me, too," Pat says, his voice breaking. "Ben isn't Ben. He's not the boy we raised. Something is happening to him."

"Drugs," I say.

"Yeah," he says. "I think you're right."

~

One afternoon, when Ben comes home from school, I ask him if we can talk. He glares at me but sits down at the dining room table.

"Something is wrong, honey," I say. "I don't know what it is, but Dad and I are concerned about you. We want to help."

"Why do you always think something is wrong? Nothing's wrong."

I take a deep breath. "We've got holes in our walls, you seem angry all the time, and you don't want to be anywhere near us. It's as if we're your enemy, and you can't even stand to look at us."

"I'm sick of you," he says through clenched teeth. "I'm sick of all your questions. I'm sick of your attitude, the way you act as if you know everything. You're always criticizing me; you're always on my back."

"If I'm on your back, it's because I love you and something is wrong," I say, willing myself to stay calm. "You're not happy. You're not yourself."

"What does that mean? Who do you think I am?"

I ignore the question. "We think you're using again," I say, stating it as fact.

He stands up, red-faced and furious. "It's always drugs with you, isn't it? You always assume the worst. You lump me with your Juvies. You think I'm an addict just like you think everyone else is an addict. Who made you God to make that conclusion about everybody?"

And then he's out the door with a slam that shakes the windows.

6

cielo/inferno

2002–2003

The leaves are shining orange, yellow, and red on this sunny fall morning, but I barely notice because I'm rushing to get to a staff meeting at the Juvenile Justice Center. I'm volunteering several days a week with both detention and probation youth and meeting with family members individually and in weekly groups. I even have a title: "Youth and Parent Advocate."

Ben is in a hurry, too. He says he has a math test this morning.

I can't find my keys. Sometimes I put them on the back of the sofa by the front door. Sure enough, they're wedged in between the cushions. As I lift up the cushion, Ben's wadded up gym clothes fall off the couch and out roll a marijuana pipe and film canister. The pipe is green and blue, glazed ceramic, a pretty little thing. I hold it up to my nose and smell marijuana. Not such a bad smell, really. I look in the film can. It's almost empty.

Ben comes down the stairs, taking two steps at a time. He lands on the wood floor with a big thud, all 180 pounds and 72 inches of him. I stand there holding the pipe, looking at him. His face gets red, and I see flashes of anger, betrayal, fear.

"I'm going to quit," he says, reaching for the pipe. I back away from him and put the pipe in my jacket pocket.

Ben is pleading with me. "Give it to me," he says. "I'm taking it to school to get rid of it. Look in the film can—there's nothing in it. I'm done. I swear, I'm done."

"We need to talk," I say, trying hard to stay calm and focused. "But you need to get to school, and I'm late for work. Tonight we'll talk—you, Dad, and I."

He follows me out of the house, walking past the 1993 Honda Civic we bought for him last year. I thought it was perfect because it has a driver's side airbag. I want him to be safe.

I open my car door and put the pipe next to me on the passenger seat.

"Mom," he says, holding the car door open. His voice is shaking. "I'm done. I swear I'm done."

"We'll talk later," I say, putting the keys in the ignition and trying to close the door. But he's stronger than me.

"Give me that pipe," he says in a low, angry voice.

"No way," I say, because now I have evidence. Proof positive that he is using at school, on the way to school, after school—who knows when. Before we just had our suspicions, but the pipe tells the story.

"Give it to me."

"No," I repeat. Suddenly he reaches over me to grab the pipe. I pick it up first, holding on as tight as I can, but he grabs it from me and wings it at the garage door, where it smashes into a dozen pieces.

He glares at me, defiant, as if to say "I won," but there are tears in his eyes. "I mean it," he repeats. "I'm done."

I stare back at him, jaw dropped. I can't speak. Who is this boy? Where is my son?

~

My mind scans backward through the years, seeking explanations. I remember the day of his birth, June 18, 1986, and the monitor signaling oxygen deprivation, the prolapsed cord, the emergency C-section. The tantrums when he was three—not the terrible twos, like most children. The school psychologist at the preschool screening, who told me that Ben's fine and gross motor skills were a little underdeveloped. The bullying. John's death.

Blame and shame. I must have done something wrong. My sisters think I "coddled" Ben, and I suppose it's true. I was always extra protective of him, maybe because of his traumatic birth and my never-at-rest fears that something might have happened to his brain in those six minutes when his oxygen was depleted. Maybe that's why he had tantrums; maybe that's why his hands shook when he held a pencil; maybe that's why, as a young boy, he was a little clumsier than some of his friends.

When Ben was six months old, lethargic and flushed with a high fever, I rushed him to the doctor, who tested his reflexes and looked concerned. For some reason, perhaps hoping for reassurance, I mentioned the prolapsed cord and emergency C-section. I will never, ever forget what the doctor said in a strange syntax: "I can't tell you not to be worried." What was that, a double negative? Cancel out the negatives? I can tell you to be worried? Was he telling me, without wanting to actually say the words, "I'm worried, something is wrong"? But what—what was wrong?

"What do you mean?" I asked, somehow able to say the words, for the fear and panic were right there; my voice felt strangled, choked off. I could barely breathe.

He took another step back. "Well, I can't tell you not to be worried," he repeated.

I started to cry. Sob. Panic, memories, denial flooded through and over me. The doctor looked terror stricken, finding himself shut up in a room with a hysterical mother. Seconds later, he disappeared and his nurse stood next to me (I've wondered since if the doctor had a panic button), put her hand on my shoulder as I held my child tight, protecting him.

"Shhh, shhh, it's okay," she said. "Everything will be okay."

"What did he mean?" I asked.

"You have a sick child with a high fever." Her voice was so soothing, it was almost as if she were singing me a lullaby. "Don't you worry—everything will be alright."

Well, really, I have no idea what she said, because there wasn't one thinking brain cell in my body. I had to escape. I wrapped my arms tighter around my baby and somehow made it to the car, strapped him into the car seat, drove home. We had a minivan then, a maroon Plymouth—or was it blue?

Pat was riding his bicycle on the way from home to his office. He must have come home for lunch. I stopped the car.

"The doctor thinks something is wrong with Ben," I said, my voice choked with tears. "He said, 'I can't tell you not to be worried.' I don't know what that means. Do you? Does he think Ben is brain damaged? He did these tests, reflexes . . ."

Pat leaned his bike against the car and kissed me. His eyes softened as he looked in the back seat where Ben, his face flushed with fever, was asleep in his car seat.

"He's still our boy," he said softly. "He'll always be our boy."

~

That night at the dinner table, Pat, Ben, and I talk about the pipe incident. Ben is contrite.

"I meant what I said," he tells us. He is folding and unfolding his hands and keeps his eyes focused on the table. "I promise, I'm done. I'm sick of drugs."

"Mom said she found the pipe and film canister rolled up in your gym clothes," Pat says. "So you've been taking the drugs to school? Smoking before school? After school?"

"I told you, I'm done with them. Can't we just forget about drugs for a while?"

"No," Pat says firmly. "We can't forget about drugs."

"Your brain is still developing, Ben," I say, automatically reverting to my default position, the know-it-all expert. "And drugs interfere with normal brain functioning. Marijuana is not a safe or harmless drug for adolescents."

I want to read him these paragraphs from *Teens Under the Influence*, the book I've been working on with Dr. Nicholas Pace:

> The short-term effects associated with regularly smoking marijuana can have devastating consequences. Anxiety and panic attacks, depression, and suicidal thoughts can disturb social relationships and personal growth. School performance and grades often drop due to the effects of marijuana on memory, concentration, and the ability to solve problems.

Chronic marijuana use leads to decreased activity in the temporal lobes, which are involved with memory, understanding language, facial recognition, and temper control. Problems in this area can lead to temper tantrums, rapid mood shifts, memory and learning problems, and a sense of being out of balance, out of control, and generally confused.

The look on Ben's face stops me. "Do you think I haven't heard this before?" he says, practically spitting the words at me.

I don't want to get in another fight, so I don't respond. Pat is silent, too.

"Okay, yeah. You're right," Ben blurts out. The tendons in his neck are strung tight. "I'm using. Every day, sometimes multiple times a day, sometimes before school, always after school."

We just stare at him. We had no idea.

"Weed makes me forget about shit." His tone is belligerent, challenging. "It makes me feel good. I can control it."

Pat takes a deep breath, gathering his thoughts. "Mom and I made an appointment with your doctor. We're concerned about your health, and we want you to talk to the doctor about your drug use."

Ben is trapped. He fell down a dead-end rabbit hole, and now we're shining a blinding spotlight on him.

He rolls his eyes and sighs heavily. "Whatever," he mumbles.

∼

A week later, Ben and I are in the doctor's office. Ben says he's okay with me being in the room with him. "You're the one with the concerns," he shrugs. I wonder what he is hiding, what emotions—anxiety, fear, panic—he is covering up. He looks calm, almost bored.

I've been looking forward to this appointment, seeing it as our chance to have an expert, a respected physician Ben has been seeing for a few years, give him the hard facts about teenage drug use. He's heard enough details and statistics from his mother. Pat has also often shared with our children his reasons for quitting drinking in his early thirties, including his genetic history, his high tolerance, and the fact that he liked to drink often and much. It's time, perhaps even past time, to get a medical professional involved.

The doctor walks in, shakes Ben's hand, and smiles and nods at me. "How can I help?" she asks.

I had practiced what I wanted to say, repeating the words over and over again so I had them carefully ordered in my mind. I wish Pat were with me, but he has a geology lab and faculty meeting this afternoon.

"We're here because my husband and I are concerned about our son's drug use," I say. "We've discussed our concerns with Ben, and he agreed to talk to you."

She points to a plastic chair in the corner of the room, indicating that I should sit down. Her voice is very soft as she talks to Ben, who is sitting on the examining table. Her back is to me, blocking him from my view. I fight the urge to move my chair but remind myself that this is his appointment and his doctor. I'm just an observer.

She listens to his heart and his lungs, takes his blood pressure, tests his reflexes, looks in his ears, eyes, nose, throat. As she examines him, she asks how he is doing, does he have any concerns to discuss, is the school year going well, does he enjoy his classes, is he happy with his grades? Good, no, good, yes, yes. She asks if he has any health concerns—fatigue, chronic cough, anxiety, depression. He shakes his head no to each question.

She consults his chart. "You're seventeen, just a few months shy of eighteen? Are you thinking about college yet?"

"Yeah, but I'm only a junior, so I still have lots of time to think about college. My parents kept me back a year before starting kindergarten," he says, in part as explanation and in part, it seems to me, as accusation. Ben has told me more than once that he wishes he had started school with his preschool friends. We held him back because his teacher thought it was a good idea. We thought we were doing the right thing.

Ben and the doctor chat for another five minutes, and I'm feeling pretty good about this meeting. She's taking her time, gaining his trust.

"So, we're here today because your parents are concerned about your drug use. Is that right?"

"Yeah."

She asks if he uses drugs. Yes, he says. How often? Marijuana once or twice a week; alcohol on the weekends, but not every weekend; and cigarettes once in a while.

Liar, I think, shifting in the chair. Should I tell her the truth, which he just confessed to us, that he uses marijuana every day, often before school, always after school?

"Well," she says, still with her back to me. "Physically, everything looks just fine. As for the drugs, I'm not concerned with occasional marijuana use. Alcohol and nicotine concern me a bit more."

He repeats that he only drinks and smokes cigarettes once in a while, mostly just on weekends, but I'm not really listening. I'm stuck on that part about not being concerned with occasional marijuana use. I can't believe she just said that. Does she have any idea that she has just given him permission—a doctor's permission—to use marijuana "occasionally"? I feel the heat rising inside me and wonder if I'm having a hot flash. I take off my scarf.

I don't know what to do. He's giving her half the story, not even half the story, minimizing his drug use as people with drug problems often do. Surely she can see through him. I want to stand up, walk over to Ben, and say in as calm a voice as I can manage, "Why don't you tell the doctor what you told us about smoking every day, sometimes multiple times a day, sometimes before school?"

But I don't, because I can't get my thoughts under control. My heart is beating way too fast, and my throat feels like it's being squeezed from the inside out. Ben is not telling the truth, and she seems to be accepting his version of reality. But still, even if he were being honest, the fact remains that he admitted to using three different drugs every week, sometimes multiple times a week. That's not healthy, that's not unconcerning. She should be talking to him about the risks, the fact that adolescents who use drugs before age fifteen are five times more likely to become addicted, that one in six teenagers who use marijuana become physically addicted to it, that the risk of schizophrenia and other psychotic illnesses is six times higher in marijuana users. I wonder if she knows about all those research studies or the ones showing that regular marijuana smokers often suffer withdrawal symptoms, including cravings, sleep difficulties, mood swings, and significant increases in aggression, anger, anxiety, and irritability.

I'm not making up these statistics; they're spread all over the scientific literature. The teen brain is vulnerable—it's still developing, and it doesn't stop maturing until the mid-twenties. Throw drugs into a developing brain—even "just" marijuana once or twice a week and "occasional" alcohol and nicotine use—and you've got an explosive chemical experiment on your hands. And then there's the genetics piece—people with a family history of alcoholism or drug addiction are four times more likely to develop the disease. Ben's father, grandfather, and great-grandparents all struggled with addiction. Why doesn't she ask about his family history? Doctors do that with all other diseases and disorders; it's one of the first questions they ask. Why the hell doesn't she ask if he has relatives who have this disease of addiction?

I want to ask the doctor straight out if she understands the word *disease* in the context of alcohol and other drug use. Addiction isn't a choice; it's not a moral failure, a maladaptive lifestyle habit, or a developmental learning disorder. It's a brain disease that is both chronic and progressive, beginning in an early stage that looks nothing at all like a life-threatening illness, proceeding into a middle stage where mental and emotional problems begin to appear and intensify (and that, I think, is where Ben sits). If the drug use continues, it steadily marches on into later stages when physical and psychological problems become apparent and undeniable.

But all this knowledge and all these statistics do me no good, because here sits Ben, a big healthy boy whose heart, liver, lungs, and other vital organs are working as they should and who exhibits no outward signs of mental or emotional problems. So, the doctor has apparently concluded—they're chatting about sports now—that Ben is just experimenting with drugs, like so many other adolescents. As time goes by, he'll grow out of this phase, go to college, establish his independence, and discover who he is and what he wants most in life.

Maybe. Maybe. I hope so. *Hope*—that word sounds so positive and upbeat. But it doesn't seem real to me; it feels ephemeral and nebulous. Hope isn't going to help Ben. I imagine comforting myself with thoughts of what his future might hold—college graduation, a good career, marriage, children, good health, a happy and fulfilled life—and I want to kick myself in the shins and yell, "Wake up!" I don't know what the future holds, but I'm fully aware of what's happening to Ben right now, right here, and something is really, really wrong.

I want to kick the doctor in the shins, too. She should know better. If parents are concerned about a child's drug use—concerned to the point that they make an appointment to discuss it—wouldn't it be a good idea to include them in the conversation? Or has she written me off as an overprotective, overwrought mother? I don't know, maybe I am, but that doesn't mean I don't have valid concerns.

My mind suddenly switches gears. *Give her a break,* I think to myself. Maybe she's being sensitive and respectful to Ben by talking to him directly, counseling her patient, treating him as an individual and not a young child who needs his mother's involvement to manage his care. Maybe I am a panic-stricken, hovering-helicopter mother who needs to back off and let her child—almost an adult—live his own life, make his own decisions.

I'm suddenly flooded with self-doubt. I had set my expectations for this appointment too high, hoping she would see Ben through my eyes, understand that he is in harm's way, and join with me in my efforts to help him. But her perspective is clinical, detached—she sees a healthy, respectful teenager who (he says) is moderate in his drug use, maintains his good grades, and plans on going to college. Her job is not to comfort me, see my pain, or presume my needs—Ben is her patient, not me.

Back and forth I go, thoughts and emotions careening off the insides of my bony skull like pinballs ricocheting around in an absurdly complicated machine. I'm angry. I'm frustrated. I'm close to tears but hold the emotions in, trying hard to appear calm and collected when what I want to do is shout at her, *He's in trouble. Why would we be here if there weren't a problem?* She doesn't see me shaking inside, the trembling of my muscles, the fibrillations of my heart, the tension in my gut. She doesn't know what led up to this meeting. She hasn't seen the holes in the walls. She hasn't heard the swearing and shouting. She can't understand the depth of my fear and desperation. She wasn't there to see my hands shaking as I dialed the clinic's number to make the appointment. She has no idea how much value I put on this meeting, seeing it as an opportunity to get through to Ben by enlisting the help of someone he respects, if only because of the MD after her name—someone with knowledge and insight, perhaps even with wisdom.

She shakes his hand as we leave the office, thanks him for coming in, and tells him to call if he ever has any concerns he'd like to discuss with her. Ben and I don't say a word to each other the whole way home. His legs are jumpy, and his fingers tap tap tap his jeans. I imagine what he's thinking: *Wow, glad that's over! Time to get high.*

I'm flushed with anger and not a little shame. I didn't speak up. I didn't force myself into the conversation and rationally discuss my legitimate concerns. I was intimidated by her. I was hoping, right up to the moment when she shook Ben's hand and told him to call if he ever needed to talk, that she would offer a warning of some kind, just a few words of caution about the dangers of using drugs when you're young and your brain is still changing and maturing.

She doesn't know that if she had only said, "So, Ben, using these drugs regularly can harm your developing brain and make you more vulnerable to mental health problems, anxiety, depression, and suicidal thoughts," she might have gotten through to him. Or she could have kept it simple and said, "If you're using marijuana twice a week and alcohol and cigarettes once a week, that's definitely not good for your health." I don't know what words she should have said, but holy shit, she should have said something.

I needed an ally who would be willing to look at the situation from both the parents' and the son's perspective and realize that the truth, if there is in fact a truth to be found, is not black and white but multiple shades of gray.

But I didn't do my part. Once again, I failed him.

~

Over the next few weeks, I think a lot about the "what if's." What if Ben had something visible like a tumor or a blood sugar anomaly or an abnormal thyroid test or a seizure? Would the doctors take an in-depth history, do some tests, write referrals to specialists, perhaps listen to the parents' perspective? Certainly they would be concerned. But here's the problem: The early stages of drug addiction don't reveal themselves with surefire "objective" evidence of disease—all organ systems and blood work tend to be normal, and signs such as dilated pupils, shakiness, and lack of energy can be overlooked or attributed to other causes. The "subjective" symptoms are easy for family members and close friends to recognize but, again, are often attributed to other problems and are easily hidden from outsiders.

What are the early signs and symptoms of adolescent drug problems? (I might as well use the word *problems* so nobody thinks I'm exaggerating or overreacting.) I'll tell you what they are: Relationships going sour. The F-bomb flying. Anger. Anxiety. Depression. Irritability. Behavior changes. Denial. Rationalizations. Resentments. Blame. Shame.

And that's only the early stage. That's only the beginning.

~

I am filled with what seems like useless knowledge. I know how to talk and listen to other people's children, and when I talk, they listen to me. But I don't know how to listen or talk to my own child. I read the books I have written over the years, and my words sound preachy, pumped up, pathetically full of themselves.

The only book that makes sense to me is *The Spirituality of Imperfection*. After writing maybe fifteen drafts of that book with Ernie and reading and rereading it dozens of times, I still find passages that take my breath away. I pick up the book and open to a random page.

> To deny imperfection is to disown oneself, for to be
> human is to be imperfect. *Spirituality*, which is rooted in

and revealed by uncertainties, inadequacies, helplessness, the lack and the failure of control, supplies a context and suggests a way of living in which our imperfections can be endured. Spiritual sensibilities begin to flower when the soil is fertilized with the understanding that "something is awry." There is, after all, something "wrong" with us.

I open to another random page.

Saying "I'm sorry" and having the apology immediately accepted; listening to another speak of pain and seeing your own pain for the first time; hearing the words "I love you," when you have just done something unforgiveable—these are universal experiences. As so often in the realm of spirituality and its antithesis, addiction, "alcoholic" means simply *human being* writ large.

I email Ernie to apologize for being out of touch. I feel guilty because I haven't been much help with the book on shame, which we've been struggling to get into shape over the past few years. Guilt and shame seem to permeate my life, but I just cannot put pen to paper or fingers to keyboard in a detached way.

"I really do not know what is going on with me," I write in the email. "Poor Pat. I keep picking on him, wanting him to be positive all the time, laughing and uncritical. I love him just as he is, but I seem to need him to be something else right now. It is difficult. Our Ben is using marijuana and being defiant, and that spins us against each other and slightly (completely?) out of control."

"Thank you for your trust of me," Ernie emails back. "I am not a parent, but from my observation and perspective, the most important thing is that Ben knows deep down that you care about and love him. We do what we can do, but in a very real way, all any of us can do is 'trudge on.' I am not sure whether youth or age does that better, but we have really no choice, at any age."

Trudge on, Kathy.

I turn for advice to my expert friends—treatment professionals, intervention specialists, addiction psychiatrists, friends in long-term recovery. Listening carefully to the facts and the timeline—alcohol and marijuana use starting in seventh grade, legal problems, admission of daily use, a genetic history of addiction, trauma (bullying, John's death), combining drugs (alcohol, marijuana, nicotine, and who knows what else), out-of-control anger, punching holes in the walls, personality changes—they agree that Ben may have a serious problem. In this little circle of experts, I feel no shame. Just fear.

~

One day in the detention center, we talk about tattoos. Nine of ten kids in these groups have some kind of tattoo. Maybe not a professional tattoo—no big-winged eagles with sharp beaks and talons digging deep into writhing snakes. These are hand-drawn for the most part. The ones that make me cringe are the bowl burns.

"We just get really, really high," Susie says, smiling sweetly. She is fifteen ("almost sixteen") and has dyed blonde hair and braces. "Then you don't feel it, or maybe you do, but it feels, I don't know, good, I guess."

"It" is the bowl of the marijuana pipe, burning hot after dozens of hits, the rim offering a perfect circle of red hot metal. Turned upside down and placed on flesh—teenage flesh, soft, fresh flesh—it creates a perfect ring for those who let it burn long enough. Like branding. I think of cows, roped up, and the red-hot iron applied to thick hairy flesh, animals screaming in pain as they are branded and forever after belong to someone, freedom denied, a possession to be bought, sold, milked, butchered.

I shake the image out of my head. These kids love their tattoos. The tattoos mean something to them, by commemorating an experience, remembering a loved one, symbolizing a stage in life, paying homage to God or family or friend. Engraved with pain, the tattoos are worn with pride and a sense of personal power—living, breathing reminders of life's experiences and even, perhaps, life's meaning.

"I have tattoos." Manuel has been sitting back a bit in the circle, watching but not contributing to the discussion. His hair is long, and he combs it over his eyes, like a curtain that he can close when he wants to shut out the world.

"Two tattoos. One on each shoulder." He pulls aside his orange jumpsuit to show us the words, which are written on the top of his shoulders in a graceful, looping script.

"Cielo" is engraved on the right.

"Inferno" is inscribed on the left.

"Cool," someone in the group says. We're sitting in our customary Wednesday morning circle in the juvenile detention center. Four boys and two girls, ages fifteen to seventeen, all in orange jumpsuits.

The look on Manuel's face is hard to read. It's not pride, I realize. He's not showing off for the group. No, there's something deeper etched into the lines around his mouth as he looks at me.

I might call it an invitation. He is asking me to understand. For on his shoulders, it seems that Manuel has outlined a battle of polarities, the push and pull of good and evil, the moral struggle between right and wrong.

"Why did you choose those words?" I ask him.

Some of the kids in the group smile. Like, "Isn't it obvious, you know, heaven, hell, angels, devils, life, death?"

But Manuel understands why I'm asking the question. These are his tattoos to decipher, no one else's.

"Because they remind me," he says, looking down at the floor.

"Of what?" I ask.

"Of what is inside me."

"What is inside you?" I know these questions sound silly, even stupid because the answers seem so obvious. But I don't want to assume anything. This is, after all, his story to tell.

"Good," he says solemnly. "And evil."

The other kids lean forward in their chairs. Good and evil are subjects worthy of attention.

Manuel smiles and softly pats one shoulder, then the other. "I know I have a choice," he says. "I can choose to be good. Or I can choose to be bad."

"If I'm good," he adds after a moment, "the goodness doesn't last. I have to keep doing good. If I do something bad, something evil, it also doesn't last. But I can learn from my mistakes. I can lean toward the good."

I nod my head, and he sits back again, signifying that he has said what he wants to say. After a respectful silence, the rest of the group continues to talk about their tattoos.

I want to know more. I want to understand the deeper meaning and significance of tattoos. I email my friend Nick, who is heavily tattooed, and ask him to explain what tattoos mean to him.

"Even the most random or seemingly meaningless tattoos," Nick writes back, "are imbued with a story. That story might be just the actual experience of getting the tattoo. I can remember the day, the shop, the artist, the conversation, jokes people made, the music that was playing, what I ate, what I did before or after, and the pain. All of that is a story behind the tattoo. Some of my tattoos are favorites not because of what they look like but because of how they remind me of an amazing time or day or place. And that place may be painful and unpleasant."

"What about a bowl burn?" I ask Nick. "Do they also have meaning?"

"They are also imbued with memories of times when someone was just messing around while high and wanted a dumb tattoo," he writes. "From one perspective, it may seem sad that people damage themselves in this way. But for them and their friends, these marks showcase a life lived."

Stories. Showcases of lives lived. We humans are a mix of polarities—right and wrong, heaven and hell, good and evil, broken and whole. *Cielo/inferno*. Manuel understands this tug of war and tries to lean toward the good. But I imagine drugs and addiction pulling him—as they are luring Ben—in the other direction. I cannot erase the image of addiction as a monstrous force that challenges our best instincts, subverting the good and threatening the very essence of who we are and what we believe in. Addiction widens the schism between good and evil, and in that ruptured space, we encounter unfathomable suffering.

As the great mythologist and teacher Joseph Campbell wrote in *The Power of Myth*, "The demon that you can swallow gives you its power, and the greater life's pain, the greater life's reply." Both Ben and I swallow the demon. I see it as enemy. Securely under its power, he sees it as friend, consoler, protector. My goal is to destroy it. His desire is to embrace it.

7

438,000 minutes

2004–2005

A few weeks before the end of his junior year in high school, I write Ben a letter. Letters are my safe haven, giving me the distance I need to express my thoughts and feelings in a coherent way. If I sit down and talk to him, I turn into a blubbering idiot within minutes.

I've become a coward, a weakling. My self-confidence is shot to hell. I'm frightened of his anger and the way he turns everything back on me. I get so confused. He sets my head spinning, like the girl in *The Exorcist*. And this is really baffling to me. If he has the demon inside, why am I the one who feels so possessed?

My friend Julie, a family counselor, gives me the best advice ever. "When you're in a conversation with Ben, and it starts to go south," she advises me, "bite your tongue."

"Why?" I ask. I want detailed instructions. "Bite my tongue" seems easy enough, but these days I find myself wishing I had a little tape recorder I could put in my ear with some wise person's voice telling me exactly what to say. Maybe it would be the same words to repeat, over and over. And that would be okay, because I wouldn't have to think or maybe even feel. I could be a robot Mom.

Julie explains the downhill slide that so often happens when parents try to talk to their drug-using children. "When an adolescent feels attacked and up against a wall—maybe they're scared, nervous, guilty, ashamed—they will most likely attack, change the subject, or flee. Parents get frustrated and interpret this as denial, which they see as a major red flag signaling trouble. They get scared and want to fix the problem, so they start lecturing, which makes the adolescent feel even more attacked. Things spiral out of control to a bad place, often ending in a power struggle between parent and child, which tends to let the kid off the hook and undermines the parent's ability to bring the conversation back to the original problem—concerns about drug use."

That makes sense to me, and I even practice biting my tongue—biting my lip is easier, actually—but in the heat of the moment I get riled up. Julie is right about the dynamic; as soon as I start talking about the fact that Ben seems unhappy or depressed, often not even mentioning the drugs, he gets defensive and turns the conversation around so that I'm the one with the problem ("you think you know so much," "you don't listen," "you just assume you know what's going on with me"), which makes me feel guilty and confused. Then the conversation ends with one of us (usually Ben) leaving in a huff.

So I write letters. I am half-mad with love and fear for him, and the panic takes me to this feverish place of worrying that if I don't do or say or try something and some terrible event befalls him, it will all be my fault, and I will live with regret and remorse for the rest of my life. I may even lose him, and the thought of life without him is too much for me to bear. I could never face myself again if I did not keep trying to reach him.

May 24, 2004

Dear Ben,

I am writing this letter because I miss you. . . . I miss the Ben I know so well, the gentle, kind, considerate boy with a great sense of humor and an ability to recognize when he makes a mistake and say he is sorry. I think of all the great qualities you have, Ben, your kindness and sweetness are the most important.

I've watched for the past year as you have changed. We thought it was adolescence—the ups and downs of trying to figure out who you are amidst all the growing pains and changes that are taking place in your world.

Then we thought it was a stage. Then we realized you were using drugs.

After we'd fight and then talk and try to work things out, things would get better for a while. But then they start to go downhill again. I don't know if you see the changes yourself, but I think I see them pretty clearly. I see your personality changing. I see you become angry and I hear you say hateful things to me and Dad. I see you punch holes in the wall and kick things. I see you get quiet and withdrawn. I see you become more argumentative at times, as if you are trying to provoke a fight. For what reason? I don't know. I feel bewildered, sad, helpless.

I ask you to think about one thing, Ben: Is this really who you want to be? Do you want to be someone who you are not?

I want so much for you to be free and to love life and to love people and to spend your days doing productive things, helping others, learning, growing, laughing, loving. I want you to feel connected to the world and to others.

That is my dream for your life, Ben. What is your dream? What do you want? How will you work for those dreams, for those desires?

I pray that you will find your way, Ben. But I fear that if you keep using, you will lose your dreams.

Life hurts. Sometimes it hurts so much it is unbearable. But the pain is where we grow—the pain is a reminder that we are alive.

I love you.

Mom

Two weeks later, on a sunny June morning, I sleep in. I love that luxurious feeling of soft sheets against warm skin, waking up from a good night's rest, fluffing up my pillow, turning over to doze a bit more, dreaming about the day ahead. After all, it's Saturday and the beginning of summer.

I stretch and smile, thinking about spending the day in my garden with my roses. I have over four dozen rose bushes. Two dozen red, double knock-out roses line the front split-rail fence, creating the most breathtakingly beautiful summer hedge. Another thirty roses grace the front and sides of the house. I've never had enough time to spend with my roses—given how many I've planted, it's no small wonder. I'm forever apologizing and talking out loud to them. I talk to myself, the dogs, and my roses because I spend so much time alone, writing in my upstairs office; it feels good to hear a voice, even if it's my own.

"I'm sorry," I say to my Double Delight, as I deadhead an abundance of blooms that I overlooked. They still hold a fragrance that smells like heaven to me, something of this earth yet beyond beautiful, beyond anyone's ability to create or design, beyond our control. Who could make a perfume that matches the swooning scent of a Double Delight rose? Which reminds me of a story Ernie told me. "Who knows the fragrance of a rose?" the Master asks his students. All of them know. "Who can put it into words?" All of them are silent.

Stately Mister Lincoln, widely reputed to be a hardy, proud rose with an astonishing fragrance, has grown too tall and spindly. When I put my nose to his spare red velvet blooms, I smell musty decay. Most rose growers love Mister Lincoln, but he does not like my garden—or maybe he doesn't like me.

"Why aren't you happy here?" I ask him, as I chop off his dead branches.

Ingrid Bergman isn't content either. I planted her under a vigorous crabapple tree, not realizing (amateur rosarian that I am) that the tree roots eventually would choke the life out of her. Years later, I dig her up and throw her out, disappointed in her, not realizing (or more likely not admitting) that it was my fault for planting her there. I dig up Veterans Honor, too, and Peace and Chicago Peace—I neglected them too long, and they are dead to the world. I ask Pat to throw them in the back of his pickup and take them to the dump. It hurts my heart to look at them, their black branches stiff and inflexible, their lifeless roots dangling.

I spend a lot of time in the garden feeling bad. Most of my roses look beautiful, despite my neglect. They work so hard to bloom and make me happy, and I don't nurture them the way I should. Today I decide I am going to devote hours to them. I am going to trim them and talk to them and love them, and they will respond with gratitude and their unique, forgiving grace.

Pat is already up and about; I can smell the coffee brewing. I walk into the kitchen, and he gives me a morning hug.

"Guess what?" he says. I can't quite read the look on his face, but something momentous has occurred.

"What?" I ask, holding my breath.

"Ben was arrested last night."

I tighten both fists, raise them in the air, and offer a small shout of gratitude. "YES!" Pat is smiling, too, because here is the answer to our prayers. What was hidden is no longer concealed. What was unspoken—*better left unsaid*—is out in the open. No more secrets. Best of all, Pat and I now have unlikely allies in the law—Ben will be held accountable for his actions by individuals and institutions who wield both power and authority. This is the break we've been waiting for. It feels as if we've won some kind of lottery. The Police-Finally-Arrested-Our-Son Sweepstakes. How could we ever have dreamed that this moment would be a cause for celebration? How could we ever have imagined that this would be a scene in the script of our lives?

In the next moment, I feel that old push and pull between my personal and professional lives, asking myself what kind of mother I am, what kind of human being I am. The paradox of me strikes deep. I dream about talking to my roses, apologizing for my negligence, and in the next moment, I'm celebrating my son's arrest on a drug charge. I wonder if the two are connected. Do I talk to my roses because I can't talk to my son? Or do I neglect my roses because I spend too much time worrying about Ben?

We learn the details later that day. Ben was arrested at a party on a minor in possession/consumption (MIP/MIC) charge. When he mouthed off to the police, he was handcuffed and charged with obstructing a law enforcement officer. Because it's his second arrest, with the first back in seventh grade and still on his record, he will go through the diversion program a second time, which requires that he complete a drug evaluation with a chemical dependency counselor, complete twenty hours of community service, attend the DUI victim's panel again, pay fines, write apology letters, and follow all treatment recommendations.

Ben is lucky. He's still a juvenile, with just eight days left before he turns eighteen. If he'd been arrested after his birthday, his case would have been processed through district court; if convicted, he would have had a criminal conviction that would become part of the public record—in essence, a sentence for life.

Several weeks later, we receive the chemical dependency evaluation.

Chemical Dependency/Mental Health Evaluation

Identifying data/current status: Ben is an 18-year-old Caucasian male who is currently a senior in high school. He lives at home with his parents. He has two older sisters who are in college, but home for the summer. This is Ben's 2nd MIP/MIC. The first was while in the 7th grade.

Referral source: Juvenile Justice Center, the Diversion Program.

Client's statement of the problem: "Alcohol isn't really a problem for me. My using marijuana wasn't a problem. My grades have gone up. It hasn't really affected me. My priorities are to get into a good college. I get my homework done before I use. I'm excited to see what the next few months will be like not using."

Mental Status: No hallucinations, illusions, or delusions. Mood and affect are appropriate. Thought content is within normal limits. He is dressed and groomed appropriately. He appeared open and honest. Denies suicidal thoughts or attempts.

Substance Use:
- **History:** Ben states he had his first drink at the age of 12. He reports his last drink as being about three weeks ago. He reports that over the last year he drinks on average four times a month. It takes 5–6 drinks to feel buzzed/drunk. Marijuana use began in the 7th grade. He reports using almost daily for the last year. He has experimented with a couple other drugs, but only used a couple times.
- **Relapse history:** reports that after approximately 18 months of being clean and sober (after last MIP) he realized he wasn't going to get a UA so began using again.

The next part of the report is "Diagnostic Impression," which contains lots of mumbo jumbo about Axis I, II, III, IV, and V. I read through this section quickly, looking for useful nuggets of information and then skip ahead to the counselor's summary:

> Based upon the clinical interview/evaluation, and the diagnostic testing that was administered, it is my professional opinion that Ben meets the criteria for Cannabis dependence, moderate stage; Alcohol dependence, mild stage.

So, there it is in black and white. Ben is "moderately" dependent on cannabis and "mildly" dependent on alcohol. I feel vindicated reading this report written by a chemical dependency professional—I knew it; I *knew* it. While "dependence" is not technically the same as addiction, the terms are often used interchangeably; furthermore, I know from conversations with treatment experts that counselors and health-care professionals often use the term *dependence* to reduce the stigma and soften the blow of a diagnosis of "addiction." Somehow it may seem kinder or safer in the sense of not jumping to conclusions to diagnose someone as "dependent" rather than "addicted," because nobody in their right mind would want to carry that addicted label around for life. And addicted individuals are well known for switching from one physician or therapist to another if they are advised to stop or cut down on their drinking or using.

But addiction *is* for life. A diagnosis of addiction is based on tolerance, the need to use more of the drug to experience the same effects, and withdrawal symptoms, which vary from drug to drug but always involve some level of physical and psychological anguish. Addiction is evident when someone gradually loses control over drug use; continues using despite obvious physical, emotional, or mental harm to oneself and others; and experiences increasingly severe cravings and compulsion to use, sometimes after months or even years of sobriety. People with active addictions don't just want the drug, they need it, which is why they fight back with teeth bared (the demon emerging) when someone threatens their continued use. When *want* becomes *need*—that is, when there is a physical demand to get the drug into the body to relieve the progressively painful and distressing withdrawal symptoms—the disease is obvious and undeniable.

The only piece of that addiction/dependence puzzle that I can't know for sure is whether Ben experiences uncontrollable cravings. If he does, I'm sure he won't admit it to anyone, most of all to his parents. "I can control it!" he keeps telling us. I'm convinced that this insistent, repetitive claim of control ("I can quit anytime I want," often followed by the predictable, "I just don't want to") is actually a red flag signaling possible loss of control. Every addicted person can control their drug use to some extent until the final stages of the disease, when they lose control. Loss of control—that's the image we carry in our heads of an alcoholic or drug addict, epitomized by the Skid Row drunk lying under a park bench clutching a brown bag or the heroin addict nodding off in the corner of a seedy motel room.

Crap. Here I am again, spouting my knowledge to myself, finding some kind of comfort in the distance that creates, as if I can step outside myself and calmly, clinically sort out the problem. This is my son—my son!—who is under the microscope, being analyzed and dissected. And at age eighteen, he is addicted—I'm not afraid to say the word—to two drugs and, who knows, maybe more. Addiction is a bad disease. Addiction is for life. Addiction can be, and often is, deadly. Addiction is misunderstood, stigmatized, thought to be caused, in part at least, by personal or moral weakness. Addicted individuals are labeled "abusers," as if they choose to destroy their own lives and the health and well-being of the people they love. The people who love them and try to help them are called "enablers," as if we somehow allow this disease to happen. As if we consent to it. As if we smooth its progress, aid and assist it, support and facilitate it, agree to its demands.

Does anyone realize how much these words hurt, how they add to our guilt and shame and make us hide in fear and self-loathing from the very people who might be able to help us? I want to erase the words *abuse, abuser, enable,* and *enabler* from the addiction vocabulary. And we might as well toss out *codependence* too, with all its hurtful, harmful connotations of weak (or rigid) boundaries, people pleasing, obsessive fantasies, problems with intimacy, and perfectionism. Throw the labels away and find the human being inside, struggling to find his or her way.

I hate addiction and all the misery, ignorance, and fault finding that accompany it everywhere it goes. But if Ben has this disease, I will fight for him to get the help he so desperately needs without having to hide his head in shame.

The chemical dependency professional concludes her report with these comments:

> "Ben is resistant to the idea of needing treatment at this time."

> "Because most of Ben's friends also use, he is at higher
> risk of relapse."

> "While he has good family support, friends will
> potentially be a concern. He does state that he does not
> feel that remaining clean during high school will be a
> problem. He does not want to have any more problems
> or create difficulty in getting into college."

Friends will potentially be a concern. I see the faces and hear the voices of Ben's friends, all universally considered "good" kids from apparently happy families, all dedicated or at least decent students, active in theater or sports, popular with their classmates and teachers, polite and considerate to their friends' parents (most of Ben's buddies give me a big hug when they stop by). Pat confides, however, that a few of Ben's friends remind him of fawning Eddie Haskell from the old TV show *Leave It to Beaver*, who mercilessly picks on Beaver ("Hey, Beaver, you gnaw down any trees today?") but shows an entirely different face to his parents ("Gee, Mrs. Cleaver, your hair looks real pretty today"). We laugh, which feels good, but we're both wondering how we keep Ben away from his friends when "most" of them, according to the report, also use drugs.

I sigh and keep reading. Recommendations for treatment include "total" abstinence from alcohol and other drugs, outpatient treatment, self-help recovery groups, and chemical dependency counseling. Ben starts attending Alcoholics Anonymous (AA) meetings, but because he has a summer job, working with his tennis coach to lead summer camps for elementary and middle-school children, he asks if he can schedule regular private counseling sessions rather than attend outpatient treatment. The counselor agrees.

His apology letter arrives in the mail.

Dear Mom and Dad . . .
I feel horrible about what I did mostly because of how it has affected you two, Robyn, Alison, and me. Believe me, if I could take my actions back, I would, but I can't, and that is what troubles me. That it is not just me in trouble, but it also affects you. It's weird how an experience like this can teach you so much about how your actions affect those around you.

The consequences I have received are most definitely not to my liking, but I think, on the positive side of things, that at least they will keep me busy and out of trouble. I'm pretty surprised that I didn't learn the first

time around, but after a while, in adolescence, you begin
to think that you are invincible.

I love you guys and I thank you for how you have
been there with me through this whole experience,
however painful it was. I love you and I am happy that
you are my parents.

Hmmm. I can't help wondering if he would still feel "horrible" if he
hadn't been caught.

Finally, the diversion program requires that all participants with
alcohol or other drug-related issues read my just-published book,
Teens Under the Influence, and write a book report. "When I was initially given the assignment of reading my mother's book, I was a little
skeptical," Ben writes.

I had never given thought to reading one of her books,
because of the fact that it would be awkward reading
something and knowing the person very well who wrote it.
However, I was extremely surprised. I guess the thing that
intrigued me most about this book is the stories and the
commentary about different drugs.

For the most part, I was under control of my actions
when I drank or smoked weed. I was known as a nice guy,
and the only thing that would trigger me to do something
stupid like fighting was if my friends or family members
or other people I cared about were threatened, and I was
rarely put in that position.

I will be the first to admit that drugs are extremely fun.
You can have the times of your life, and doing normally
boring things can be intensified by drug use. But drugs are
like gambling. Reading this book has made me wonder if
having that much fun is really worth the risk of being busted
by the police and going through diversion, treatment, or
whatever else is in store. I'm starting to think it's not.

Reading Ben's words, I'm skeptical, too—sounds to me like he's shining us on. I wonder how much of the book he read, especially since he never mentions the fact that I quoted him in two places. First, on page 103, when he talks about the time he got stoned with his friends and watched the movie *Half Baked* ("I laughed so hard I could hardly breathe, it was like laughing myself clean") and again on page 241, in the section on the importance of listening to your children ("My mother is a good listener, but then she always ends up giving me advice. Sometimes I just want her to listen and not say anything. Just listen. Can parents do that?").

On August 22, a week before Ben starts his senior year in high school, I write him another letter. We just had a blowout argument over the stupidest thing in the whole wide world. I had asked Ben and his friend David—an adorable, sweet boy whom Ben has known since his preschool days—to help me move a large, heavy rug in the TV room. David leaned down and started to pull on the rug, while Ben stood next to him, laughing, telling him what a great job he was doing. I asked Ben to help. I even said "please." Ben crossed his arms against his chest, laughed again, and said David was strong enough to move the rug by himself.

David looked embarrassed. I was sure I could read his mind—*I would never treat my mother like that*—and my emotions just boiled up and over.

"Ben, stop being lazy and help your friend," I said.

"Lazy?" he turned around to face me, his face flushed with anger. "Is that what you think of me? You think I'm lazy? What is it with you? Everything has to be done on your timeline. You can't give us five minutes to move your fucking rug? You need this. You need that—it's always about you. I hate this fucking place. I can't wait to get the hell out of here." And with that he walked out of the house with David, eyes glued to the floor, following close behind.

I was wildly pissed off—my heart pounding against my chest wall, muscle against bone. I'm fighting myself, bloody flesh hammering against an unyielding skeleton. I can't crack those ribs, and my heart muscle is bleeding and bruised, tired and old, thumpingly, achingly exhausted.

But within minutes—seconds?—I'm "shoulding" all over myself.

I "should" have been patient. I "should" have given him two minutes or five minutes (why not ten?) to finish what he was doing. I "should" have removed myself from the situation, gone upstairs to my office, or walked outside to talk to my roses. I "shouldn't" have called him lazy. Should should should. Shit shit shit.

I felt the familiar, debilitating rush of shame—shame about my inability to stay calm, shame because I never know the right thing to say at the right moment, shame because I am incapable of talking to Ben face to face, shame because I fear his anger, shame because my own son hates his home, shame because he can't bear to be with me. What kind of mother am I to have instilled such loathing in her own child?

So, I write another letter.

Dear Ben:
I really don't know how to start this letter to you. I even wonder if anything I say makes any difference to you. I feel that we have grown apart in so many ways, and that causes me great sadness.

We still have 10–12 months together. What can we do to make this time productive, constructive, happy, fulfilling for you, for me, for our family? I ask you to think about that question. 10 months is a long time. 24 hours in a day, 60 minutes in an hour, I come up with something like 438,000 minutes. Most of those minutes you will not spend with us, but there will be a few thousand that you do.

Our love for you has helped us through all the tears and struggles. Love is healing; hatred and anger are poison. I cannot tell you what to do with your anger, but I hope you will find a way to turn it into something positive and constructive.

You have many gifts. My hope is that you will see them and feel gratitude for them and smile more and love more and give more of yourself to others.

Life is too short. Thank you.

Mom

I file a copy of the letter with my other letters, emails, and notes. Tucked in between the pieces of paper, I notice a colorful birthday card Ben had given to me a few months earlier. He made the card out of green and blue construction paper, pasting orange and green stripes on the front with a drawing of a birthday cake and five candles. Five candles—maybe five for the number of people in our family? Or five for my fifty-fifth birthday? I open the card to find a picture he drew of himself, smiling with slightly crooked teeth, his eyes big and round with enlarged pupils, his hair long and scraggly. He looks happy in the drawing. He drew himself happy.

> Happy Birthday Mom! I hope that it was great and what you expected. This next year is going to be great for Me, you & Dad (our last before I go to college). Your the best mom.
>
> *Love, Ben*

I read the card again. I look at the picture, and it reminds me of something he might have created in elementary school. I imagine him now, just turned eighteen years old, stoned out of his mind, cutting strips of paper and gluing them to the page, engrossed in a repetitive childlike task. I read the words again and again. "This year is going to be great." "Your the best mom."

I start to cry, and then I am on the floor, sobbing, holding that green and blue card to my chest, hugging the goofy drawing, reading and rereading the words "Your the best mom," wanting him back, wanting the son I once had who loved me but who now seems to despise me. That's how it's been these past few years—love, then hate, then love, then hate. I feel so bruised and battered and bloodied that my tears burn my cheeks because I am starting to feel the hate. It is in me, too—the hate and the love, the love and the hate. I do not know which way to turn, which path to take, whether to go by way of anger and resentment or compassion and forgiveness, tossed and turned and set upside down, not knowing how to right myself or twist myself back into shape.

I want to lie down and sleep. I want to wake up somewhere else, on an island or a lake or a mountaintop—somewhere, anywhere that is quiet, peaceful, removed from real life.

Part of me wants to go to sleep and never wake up.

lost

2004–2005

t's Ben's senior year. He meets with the chemical dependency counselor twice a week and has random urinalyses (UAs) to test his urine for the presence of drugs. He passes all of them. He can't drive because this is his second offense and his license has been revoked, but if he completes all the requirements of the diversion program, he'll be eligible for early reinstatement after one year. He fulfills the requirement of twenty hours of community service by volunteering at the Rising Sun Clubhouse, a nonprofit, grassroots organization with the mission of providing "daily activities, job skill-building, and camaraderie to those with mental illness."

The clubhouse board president writes a letter to the Juvenile Justice Center, praising Ben's service.

> Ben was helpful and such an interesting, kind, young man—I wanted to let you know what a pleasure it was to have him at the food drive. Ben also volunteered additional hours at the clubhouse and helped put up a lot of Christmas decorations, served lunch, and even cooked! He was genuinely friendly and interested in the Clubhouse members and spent time with each member.

I read this note over and over again, my mind hovering over the words *helpful, interesting, kind, genuinely friendly*. This is the Ben we used to know. The note fills me with hope that he is coming back to us, breaking free of the darkness, the demon, that has held him prisoner for all these months. Maybe this is all it takes, a few months free of the drugs to clear his mind so he can see what he was like when he was using and decide that being his authentic self, his sober self, is the pathway he wants to take in life. I'm so deeply, inordinately, unbelievably (I can't find the right adjective) grateful to the legal system—the police officer who handcuffed him, the detention staff who detained and questioned him, the diversion program that required the chemical dependency evaluation, the random UAs, community service, weekly counseling, and Twelve Step meetings—they are all holding his feet to the fire.

This entire chain of events is what I call the "velvet hammer" we need to get through to him and hold him accountable in this fragile early stage of staying clean and sober. "What if" is once again the question that haunts me. What if he hadn't been caught at age seventeen, before he turned eighteen, when he would have been processed and tried as an adult? What if he kept using all summer? What if he got drunk or high and drove his car, filled with his friends, into a tree? I think about my old boss Bill Asbury—his blackouts, DUIs, and the thin line between life and death—and I shudder with gratitude. Oh, thank you, thank you, whoever you are, whatever you are, wherever you are—*whether* you are—thank you for helping us keep him safe and sound.

As the months go by, hope builds. We wonder if maybe, just maybe, we've made it through the worst days. Maybe it really was just youthful experimentation combined with normal adolescent anger and frustration and the universal pushing away from the people you love the most in order to establish your own identity. Robyn and Alison needed their distance, too, but they were quiet about it, almost secretive, mostly keeping their thoughts and feelings to themselves. Ben never has been able to keep things to himself; he is forever asking questions—the same "what if?" questions I find myself asking. Maybe his anger and resentment are related to an existential angst, not so uncommon in teenagers, about the meaning of it all. *Who am I? Where do I fit? Why am I here on this earth?*

Who knows? I try not to spend too much time analyzing the positive changes in Ben's attitude and behavior. Honestly, I think a good part of the reason he's staying away from drugs are the random UAs and the fact that he doesn't want to get caught again. More than anything, he wants to get out of Walla Walla, go to college (University of Washington is his first choice), and be on his own. The more time he has clean, the better his brain is going to function; the healthier his brain is, the better his decisions will be. A healthy, functioning brain is what matters most to me.

We settle into a comfortable routine, daring to believe that the dark days are behind us. Ben spends hours looking up colleges and universities in the *Fiske Guide to Colleges 2005*. He has a lot of fun memorizing college mascots—hundreds of them. Some of his favorites are the Wake Forest Demon Deacons, the Santa Cruz Banana Slugs, the University of Delaware Fightin' Blue Hens, Idaho State's Benny the Bengal, the Texas Tech Red Raiders, and Louisiana-Lafayette's Ragin' Cajuns (a costumed chili pepper). Pat and I play a game, looking up the most obscure mascot names, but no matter how hard we try to stump him, he has the names down cold.

He looks healthy. He acts healthy. He no longer erupts, suddenly and seemingly without provocation, stomping out of the house. He seems happy to come home after school or tennis practice, have dinner with us, tell stories about his friends, teachers, classes. We disagree, even argue at times, but he's reasonable and respectful.

His fellow students elect him to the homecoming court. His grades are good, and at fall conferences, his teachers tell us what a terrific student he is—polite and responsible, a bit of a jokester ("You might want to speak to him about toning that down in class," his math teacher says), and popular with both the boys and the girls. "When Ben walks in the room," one of his teachers confides, "the girls are all eyes."

In October, he auditions for the school musical, *Guys and Dolls*, and gets a small part in the chorus with a few speaking lines. One of his closest friends lands the lead role of Sky Masterson but loses it when he's caught drinking at a party. With just three weeks to go before the first show, the director offers the part to Ben.

"But I can't sing," Ben protests.

The director pats him on the back, smiles, and says, "You'll learn."

Weeks of intense rehearsals, including dozens of extra hours in singing lessons with the choral director, follow. Ben practices by singing in the shower and in the hot tub, singing before and after school, singing at breakfast and dinner, and singing in his bedroom an hour or so before he goes to bed. He's a singing fool.

He's smiling again, and there's a playfulness about him, a tender goofiness. He talks to us about the scene where he kisses a pretty girl who plays Sergeant Sarah Brown, a sister at the Save a Soul Mission.

"She gave me the tongue!" he says, his eyes big with amazement. "She's a Mormon in real life, and she gave me the tongue! She's pretty cute, don't you think?"

"She's adorable," I agree. We laugh together, and I think how handsome he is, with his big smile and his flashing brown eyes.

Watching him on opening night, I'm in tears—good tears, happy tears. My sisters and Ben's cousins make the five-hour drive from Seattle to cheer him on, hooting and hollering every time he appears on stage, knowing what a big moment this is in his life and how far he has come from the troubles of the past. We are all so darn proud of him for standing on that stage in front of hundreds of people and singing his heart out.

In the spring, he's cast as the King in the *The Three Musketeers*, and his days are once again full of rehearsals. And then the capstone event of his high school career: the day he opens the acceptance letter from the University of Washington. He's officially a Husky. All is right in Benny's world.

With less than a month left in school, the play over, college decided, he spends more and more time with his friends. He still doesn't have his license, so he's dependent on his friends for rides and spends most of his afternoons and many of his evenings with them. It was the same with Robyn and Alison—in high school, their friends were the center of their universe—so we're not too concerned. On nights when he comes home after we've gone to bed, he always comes upstairs to let us know he's safely home.

But the doubts start creeping in. We can't pin it down, exactly, because he's polite and respectful, but he lacks his usual energy and enthusiasm. He's difficult to engage in conversations and mumbles one-word answers to our questions. In the mornings, he sleeps through his alarm clock and grumbles about having to go to school. "What's the point?" he asks one morning, adding, "I can't wait to get out of this stupid town." That seems to be the gist of his conversations with us—school is ridiculous, and Walla Walla is the pits.

One day I take a photograph of Ben hugging Sophie, our springer spaniel. It's a close up, and I can't miss the heavy, red-lined eyelids or the bloodshot eyes. When he leaves the house, I actually get out a magnifying glass to look a little closer. There it is—the same faraway, glazed look in his dark brown eyes, even as he looks straight at me and smiles for the camera. He's using again.

The demon is clawing its way back into our lives.

～

On May 9, 2005, I write in my journal:

> I am sick at heart about Ben. He is lost and I don't know how to find him.
>
> Tonight at dinner he talked about being a stoner and how his old friends—David, Riley—talk about him. "I don't care," he said. "I *am* a stoner."
>
> I drop him off at a friend's house and he says, "I care about marijuana more than I care about you and Dad. More than I care about my sisters."

The rest of the pages in the journal are blank, along with my memory of the next few months—except for one event, sometime that spring.

Ben is still on probation, and rather than drive him to the Juvenile Justice Center, we decide to give him random UAs at home.

Pat and Ben are arguing on the landing of the second-floor stairway. I'm in the kitchen making coffee.

"I'm not peeing in that fucking cup."

I walk to the bottom of the stairway. Ben has his fist raised to Pat's nose.

"You want to hit me?" Pat says in a quiet voice. "Is that what you want to do?"

Ben grabs the plastic UA kit out of Pat's hand and throws it at the wall, just above my head. He bounds down the stairs and out the door.

I walk up to the landing and put my arms around Pat. He's sobbing, his shoulders heaving. I can feel his tears falling on my cotton shirt. He is a man of few words, a private man who keeps his thoughts to himself. When I ask what he's feeling, he says just one word: "Despair."

We talk about calling Ben's probation officer but decide against it. Just one more month and he will graduate from high school. Just six more weeks and we'll drive him across the state to the YMCA's Camp Seymour in Gig Harbor, Washington, where he'll spend the summer as a counselor. My brother Mike is the camp's executive director, and Ben's cousins Will and Casey will both be campers there. Casey is in a wheelchair; she is slowly dying of a rare neurological disease, and this might be the last time Ben will have with her. Summer camp—a healthy place, a safe place where Ben will be surrounded by family and water and woods and young campers who need him to be responsible and take care of them.

Then he will be off to college, called to task by his professors, out from under his parents' worries and demands, living the independent life he seems to crave. Perhaps these coming months will reveal new worlds to him and give him the space and time he needs to fit into his own skin and to find that it isn't such a bad place to be.

To be honest, one reason we never call his probation officer is because we want Ben out of our house. Any obstacle standing in the way of graduation, summer camp, or college threatens our own future happiness. It does not make us happy to admit that, but it is the truth.

∼

"What do you want to major in?" the academic adviser at the University of Washington's Advising and Orientation session asks Ben. It's just a week after his high school graduation.

"I don't know," he says, a bewildered look on his face.

"If you pick a major now, you'll be on pace for graduation in four years," she explains. The room is full of students, and she seems to be in a bit of a rush. "Otherwise, it might take a few extra quarters to get your degree."

"Well, I like to write," he says. "And I love to read. Maybe English?"

She suggests that he take four English classes, they work out a schedule, and he logs onto the computer to register online. I call Pat while Ben is registering and tell him about Ben's schedule.

"Four classes in the same subject?" Pat sounds completely flummoxed. "That doesn't make sense to me. How is he supposed to know what he wants to major in before he's even taken a class?"

When we get home late that night, Pat talks to Ben about the possibility of changing his schedule and selecting a more balanced set of courses, but Ben is overwhelmed with the whole process. "If I need to drop or change a class, I can do that later," he says, in a seriously annoyed tone of voice. "Right now, I just want to be done with all this shit."

A week later, we drive to Gig Harbor to drop him off for counselor training at Camp Seymour. He stands apart from the group of counselors, most of whom seem to know each other, looking lost and out of place. This is his first job as a counselor, and he'll spend the entire summer here. He's been a camper before, but only for a week at a time, and I wonder if he might be feeling a little homesick. That would be weird, I think, after he's spent the last few years counting the days until he could get away from us.

Back home, life settles itself into a new routine—early morning coffee on the patio with Pat and Alison, who is home for the summer; weekend visits from Robyn, who is working with children with autism in San Diego; taking the dogs for long walks; golf; gardening (the roses that I haven't killed are coming back to life). It's a relatively quiet, peaceful summer. Ben sends playful letters home about his first skinny dipping experience and confesses that he has a serious crush on one of the counselors. He calls her "Q."

"I think I'm in love," he writes. "And she really likes me."

Three hundred miles away, we breathe a sigh of relief, knowing that he's in a serene, peaceful place surrounded by pine trees and salt water, far away from drugs and the "people, places, and things" that might pull him back into using. It feels so good not to worry about him every single moment of every single day. Walla Walla without Ben is a new experience—we can breathe. He sends more letters about "Q," telling us how amazing she is and how much he loves her. "And she loves me, too." Once again, we have hope—he will find his way; he's a good, kind, sweet person (when he's not using drugs); he has new friends; and he's in love. Camp romances are notoriously short-lived—I had several of them myself back in the day—but still, I find myself heartened by his newfound happiness.

I tell a close friend that Ben is in love. "Hmm," she says, looking at me with a little sideways smile. "Love? Or is it just infatuation? He's only known her for a few weeks." Her words—and especially that knowing little smile—make me cranky.

"Teenagers can fall in love," I say with an edge to my voice. "I have friends who fell in love in seventh grade, and they've been married for forty years."

But Ben? I think I hear the questions she doesn't ask. Ben who has had so many problems, Ben who gets sober for a while and then falls into the same damn hole again and again, Ben who hasn't had a chance to deal with his emotions or with life itself because of his drug use? She knows the trouble he's been in; although she doesn't say the words, I'm sure she thinks we're deluding ourselves. I realize later that she's worried about me—she doesn't want my heart to be broken once again. In the moment, though, I am hurt and irritated. Why can't she be happy for me, for him? Why does she have to let the past rule her thinking about the present?

I want to live in hope, float in it, get carried away by it. I don't care whether we call it love or lust or a summer camp crush; what matters is that Ben is happy right now. I need this break. I need to believe that everything will work out now that he is away at camp and soon to be in college and on his own. Pat and I are reclaiming our lives; slowly, surely, we are beginning to think about ourselves again. After a quarter century of tending to our children and after nearly six years of on-and-off-again worrying about Ben, we can begin to focus on our own lives.

Toward the end of summer, Ben calls to tell us a story. In the dining room after lunch, he stood up and told the roomful of campers and counselors that he wanted to make an announcement. Then he walked over to Q's table, got down on one knee, and sang "I've Never Been in Love Before" from *Guys and Dolls*.

As he's describing the scene over the phone, I'm smiling ear to ear. I want all the details. What did she say? What did she do? Did his campers kid him about it afterward? I want to be there in the dining hall, listening to him sing his heart out. I need this story in the same way I need oxygen, and I breathe it in with gratitude, letting the images settle in my heart where I can pull them back into memory when I need them.

~

When the summer ends, Ben moves to Seattle and decides to join a fraternity. We debate whether we should put our collective feet down and insist that he live in the dormitories instead. Then we think maybe it will be okay; he'll have "brothers" who will make him feel more at home in a huge university. What control do we have, anyway? He's nineteen years old—old enough to vote, old enough to go to war, old enough to get married and have children, get a job, become a tax-paying citizen. It's time, maybe long past time, to let him go, give him space, allow him to make his own decisions, even if we disagree with them. And live with the consequences.

In October, three weeks after the quarter starts, Pat drives over for a Husky football game. He and Ben have a plan to meet for coffee, go to the game, and then have dinner together. It's a day for father and son to be together, just the two of them, and a big deal for Pat who, like Ben, is a diehard Husky fan.

When Pat arrives in Seattle, he calls Ben's cell phone. Ben doesn't answer. Pat tries a few more times before going to the game, where he calls Ben perhaps a dozen times. Ben never answers. Pat calls home to ask if I've heard from him. I haven't. Pat drives back home without ever seeing or talking to Ben. When he tells me about the phone calls and not being able to reach his son—or find him with 65,000 people or so in the stadium—he has tears of anger and frustration in his eyes.

We know then that Ben is in trouble. We look through the cell phone bill, which lists all our calls broken down by phone numbers; my hands shake as I leaf through the pages. From September 8 to October 7—twenty-nine days—Ben made or received 696 phone calls, an average of twenty-four calls a day. On just one day—Tuesday, October 4, a school day—he made thirty-nine phone calls.

We look at Ben's bank account statements for the past month and notice a suspicious pattern of withdrawals of twenty or forty dollars every two or three days. In one week alone, he withdrew $173.00. At the beginning of the quarter, we had deposited $500.00 dollars into his account, figuring it would last through the quarter, since most of his needs—books, food, lodging—were already covered. He blew through that money in less than six weeks.

Pat types a three-page email to Ben, starting off with a few chatty paragraphs about how the new semester is going, classes he's teaching, the upcoming installation of Whitman's new president, progress I'm making on my book, and a hunting trip with Sophie and Murphy, our seven-month old springer spaniel puppy. Nessie, our golden retriever, had died almost exactly a year ago.

Then he jumps into the hard stuff.

I am sitting here looking at our most recent phone bill. I don't think I have made 696 phone calls in the past 10 years (but I'm not, as they say, a phone person). I can't understand how anyone could possibly get anything done in the course of a day with that many phone calls.

What really hurts is that of those 696 phone calls, maybe a handful were to us, and of those that were to us, a smaller handful were of the type where you wanted to let us know what your life is like. Most were of the type where you told us you needed more money. We aren't asking for the world here, nor are we asking for you to divulge your secrets or the details of your life. Nor are we trying to tie this to money. It isn't about money. We are simply interested in communication with our son as he enters this newest phase of life, and we aren't even getting that.

Our relationship has been out of balance for some time now. Is there some way that we can agree on how to bring the balance back? I ask you—what can we do? What have we done that has resulted not just in your total silence, but in your refusal to even pick up the phone or to answer an email? All we want is to know that you are OK and that your life in college is going as smoothly as a first-year student can expect.

Love, Dad

Ben writes back less than an hour later:

Dude, write to me like im your son.

Pat responds:

Dude, respond to my (many) emails like I'm your father.

Half an hour later, Ben sends another message:

Sorry dad, I do have other commitments, like the shitload of schoolwork I do every day, frat stuff, a

girlfriend who I really like, and a social life. I'm getting
fucked in my English class, and I haven't checked my
email in 2 weeks so just understand if I can't sit down
and write back all the time.

Later that afternoon, Pat forwards the emails to me with this note:

I give up. I don't know what to do. I have written him
letters over the past two years about his choices in both
friends and activities. In return, I have gotten lies and
false promises. I sat with him twice in Pioneer Park,
trying to help him understand what it means to take
responsibility. I looked him in the eye after one of those
talks, which was the result of us finding a bunch of
paraphernalia in his (our) car and listened to him as he
said, "I'm done with all that." I have written him emails
with the tone of a father who wants to know what his
son is up to, asking for nothing more than letting us
know whether or not he is alive and still in school. For
my thoughts, efforts, and love, I get these responses. Oh
well. At some point in his life, he will understand why I
have done those things.

We call our friend Stan, a professor in UW's geology department, and
ask him to check up on Ben. Ben tells Stan that he hates his classes
(they're "horse," he says, which is apparently short for horseshit). So
they look through the course catalog, selecting classes he can take next
quarter. Ben says he's really interested in landscaping. Maybe art. Possibly geology.

Then—silence. A week passes with our phone calls and emails
unanswered. Finally, on a Saturday early in November, six weeks into
the quarter, Ben calls.

"I'm lost." He's sobbing. "I can't remember anything."

"Lost? Where are you?"

"I'll call you back," he says and hangs up.

When he calls back a few minutes later, his voice is low, his words choked off by tears. "I lost my backpack, I don't know where I left it. It has all my homework in it, everything. I lost everything."

I take a deep breath and put my hand on my heart, willing it to slow down. I ask the obvious questions—Where were you? What were you doing? Is there anyone who might be able to help you remember?

"I don't know, I don't know, I've got to go." He hangs up. I dial his number several times, but he doesn't answer.

He calls back that night. "I fell," he says.

"You fell?" I am reduced to repetitive comments and questions.

"On the bridge. Going to the football game." Staccato sentences. "I was running across the bridge. I slipped and fell."

Ben is talking in a monotone now, slow, emotionless. He tells me he fell, twice. A woman on the bridge saw him hit the concrete, identified herself as a nurse, and told his fraternity brothers to take him to the hospital. I ask if he went to the hospital, and he says no, he blacked out. He came back to consciousness in the middle of the UW stadium, covered in mud from the falls. People were staring at him. His fraternity brothers kept asking if he was okay. A friend from Walla Walla took him back to her sorority.

"Something is wrong. I can't remember anything."

"Go to the hospital, Ben. You need to see a doctor." I feel desperate.

"I'm not going to a hospital here," he says. "I need to come home."

Q comes home with him the next weekend, but it's clear their relationship is falling apart. He's brusque and dismissive with her. She tries to hug him, and he pushes her away. One night, he leaves her at home with us while he goes out with his friends. He complains of headaches, difficulty concentrating, exhaustion, trouble sleeping, and a general feeling of being "lost" and confused. He's irritable as hell. After much pleading, he agrees to go to the emergency room. The CT scan is clean, but the diagnosis is "severe concussion with post-concussive disorder." I research the diagnosis on the Mayo Clinic website:

> Post-concussion syndrome is a complex disorder in
> which various symptoms—such as headaches and
> dizziness—last for weeks and sometimes months after
> the injury that caused the concussion.
>
> Concussion is a mild traumatic brain injury,
> usually occurring after a blow to the head. Loss of
> consciousness isn't required for a diagnosis of concussion
> or post-concussion syndrome. In fact, the risk of post-
> concussion syndrome doesn't appear to be associated
> with the severity of the initial injury.
>
> In most people, post-concussion syndrome symptoms
> occur within the first seven to 10 days and go away
> within three months, though they can persist for a year
> or more.

I keep focusing on the term *traumatic brain injury* and the fact that symptoms can last for weeks or months and may persist for a year or more. If Ben fell twice and hit his head hard both times, does that double how long the symptoms will last? Does it make a "mild" concussion a moderate or severe brain injury?

Before he leaves, Ben has a confession to make. "I used with my friends this weekend," he says with no emotion in his voice. "I know I'm addicted. I know I can't control it."

I'm confused about how I should feel, what I should think. For the first time, he admits he is addicted and has lost control. Did using with his friends while he left his girlfriend home to watch TV with us fill him with shame and lead him to the realization that he is addicted and out of control? Or did he use with his friends, knowing that he couldn't control his drug use and just not giving a damn? Maybe he's offering us a throwaway statement, trying to divert our attention and make us think he's learned something from this experience, while fully intending to go back to his old ways. But he's scared; I can see it in his eyes.

We ask him what we can do to help. He says he doesn't need us anymore. He has his friends back in Seattle who will help him. "If I didn't have my friends," he says, "I'd shoot myself."

When Ben leaves, Pat breaks down. "I've never in my life experienced the kind of sadness I'm feeling right now." He puts his head in his hands and cries. "I am beyond anger and frustration. All I want is my son back."

Holding him tight, I feel hollow inside. I hear the blood rushing in my head, a whooshing sound as if I am holding my hands over my ears, as if I am under water. All I can hear is that internal roar, and I panic. I can't breathe. I am sinking, drowning, lost.

A childhood memory comes back to me. I'm five or six years old, and we're at a family picnic at Echo Lake Park. I wander away and walk up a pathway into the trees. I feel brave and happy, and I keep walking, maybe I am even singing—I used to love to sing. But when I stop and look down the hill, all I can see is smoke. Indians! I panic and keep walking up and up and up. It's getting dark, and the trees are big and scary. I start crying. I can't see through my tears.

"What's the matter, honey?" Two men are kneeling down next to me. I tell them about the Indians and how all I can see is smoke and I don't know where to find my family.

"Don't you worry," they say. "There are no Indians here. We'll help you find your family." One of the men puts me on his shoulders, and they sing and laugh as we walk back down the hill. I feel safe with them.

"There they are!" I yell. The man lifts me off his shoulders and sets me safely down on the ground. I start crying again and run up to my mother, hugging her knees.

"What's wrong, Kath?" she says with a little laugh. She didn't even know I was gone.

~

Get a grip, Kathy. Pull yourself together. Stop whimpering. Get strong. Be brave. I can feel my hands reaching down, pulling myself up, out of the dark place, onto a different path. *Get moving. Do something.*

I send emails. I write letters. I make phone calls. I turn to the experts I know, people I have worked with over the years, professionals whose advice I trust completely. My friends Jeff and Debra Jay, both highly respected clinical interventionists, respond to my email within hours. I ask if I should make an appointment with a psychiatrist. They advise that I should only do so if the psychiatrist is extremely experienced in addiction, meaning he or she has had a close relationship with a treatment facility. I agree with them—a psychiatrist or psychotherapist who doesn't have experience with addiction is likely to focus solely on Ben's irritability, anger, impulsivity, anxiety, and depression and arrive at a psychiatric diagnosis that calls for antidepressants or antipsychotics. Over the years, Ben's doctors prescribed three different kinds of antidepressants. But after trying each one for a few weeks, he would refuse to take them, insisting they made him feel even worse, agitated, irritable, out of control, "crazy." I wonder now, after hours and days and weeks of research on the Internet, if Ben's reaction to the antidepressants might have been a red flag signaling that he might have a mild form of bipolar disorder. Research report after research report shows that antidepressants can trigger or intensify both manic and depressive symptoms, even leading to psychosis and suicidal ideation.

The problem is that we can't get an accurate diagnosis because the drugs Ben is using—marijuana, alcohol, nicotine, and, I suspect, others as well—are exacerbating or even perhaps causing whatever mental health problems he might have. The most skilled psychiatrist in the world can't accurately diagnose a mental health problem when a brain is poisoned by drugs. It is important to eliminate the drugs, give the brain time to clear (weeks, perhaps months), and then go to an addiction medicine specialist/psychiatrist for a diagnosis.

Jeff Jay emails with suggestions of several treatment centers he respects—Wilderness Treatment Center in Marion, Montana, is at the top of his list. The minute I get Jeff's email, I give him a call. We talk for a long time as I sit on our front steps, watching the sunset. I take a roll of toilet paper out with me because as hard as I try, as much as I bite my lip and take deep breaths, I can't stop crying.

"You can only support Ben in his recovery, not in his addiction." Jeff's voice is low and calm, soothing. "And it's his addiction that is calling the shots now. He thinks he can control it, but it's controlling him."

"I know." I wad up a bunch of toilet paper and wipe the tears off my face.

"You need to let go."

"Let go?" How many times had I said those words, written those words? But in this context, on the receiving end of the advice, I can't make sense of them. "Jeff, what do those words mean? How does a parent let go of a child?"

"Let him fall. Let him fail. Don't try to protect him."

"But he's had two bad falls. He hit his head. He's not thinking right. He feels lost." I think about Ben wandering around Seattle streets, dizzy, confused. "He might get hit by a bus. He might die."

"Kathy, life is unpredictable." Jeff is choosing his words carefully. "Ben might get hit by a bus no matter what you do. How much control do you really have?"

He might get hit by a bus. He might die. I nod my head, unable to speak. I imagine Ben, drunk, walking across a busy street. It's dark outside and rainy. It's cold, so bitterly cold. I want to yell, to scream, but he can't hear me; he is too far away. I hear the brakes squealing, and I see him lying on the ground, as if he were sleeping. The sobs come up from deep inside me, waves of fear and despair, swelling and breaking, never ending.

I can't control whether Ben lives or dies. I want to throw out a net, to pull him close. My fear extends to Robyn and Alison. How far can I throw the net? What can I do to protect them? I hear Jeff's words in my mind, repeating them over and over—*let go let go let go let go.* I know then that I do not have the power to save Ben, to save any of them. Once upon a time, I lived under the illusion that I could keep them safe. Now I know the truth.

I call the treatment centers Debra and Jeff suggest, fill an entire notebook with handwritten notes, spend hours comparing costs and programs. Should we send him to Sundown M Ranch in Yakima, Washington, just two hours from Walla Walla? I love Sundown—we've sent dozens of detention youth to the adolescent program there, and I'm close friends with the executive director, Scott Munson.

"One thing to remember," Scott says, "is that no amount of knowledge you have about this disease can change the pain it causes." Those words strike me as so wise, I type them into an email and send them to myself.

Sundown, it turns out, may not work out for Ben because, at nineteen, he's too old for the adolescent program. Although the adult program is a possibility, it only lasts twenty-one days.

Scott agrees with Jeff and Debra that Ben, like most adolescents with serious drug problems, needs months in treatment, not weeks, and that Wilderness Treatment Center may be our best option. Pat and I get on the phone and set things up. Wilderness has a "bed" for Ben, and our insurance will cover about half the cost. We can't decide if we should let Ben finish the quarter—just five more weeks—and plan an intervention in mid-December. But then he'd be in treatment over Christmas, and we can't imagine Christmas without all of us together. And what happens after treatment? Ben can't go back to UW, because all the triggers to use are ready and waiting for him, and he can't come back to Walla Walla for the same reasons.

"Okay, okay," we laugh uneasily. "We're skipping ahead of ourselves." *Stay focused. Be in the present. One step at a time.*

Thanksgiving is in less than two weeks. We'll be celebrating in Seattle with my brother, Mike; my sisters, Debbie and Billy; and their children. We'll have fun. It will be a great time. Then we can decide. Then we will know what to do.

9

kodak moments

November 2005

*S*ometimes I wonder what we were thinking, bringing our drug-addicted nineteen-year-old son into my sister's home with a dozen relatives—aunts, uncles, cousins—all watching, waiting, wondering why we didn't "do something." They didn't speak the words, but I knew what they were thinking in the looks they shared—those quick-don't-get-caught side glances. I knew by the sudden intake of breath, the jaw drops (and quick recoveries), the raised eyebrows, pained expressions, rapid-fire shifts in conversations.

Better left unsaid was the rule. I knew all this because I felt it in my gut—the pain, the shame, the fear and the frustration, the desire to scream *I don't know what to do! Help me!*, the tears burning behind my eyelids, the sick sense of helplessness. My fear-turned-anger-turned-heartsickness told me the story of their unspoken judgments and the words already spoken, in the past when his problems were not so obvious, not so serious.

"He needs to toughen up."

"You need to let go."

"He's too sensitive."

"You overprotect him."

"He's just experimenting."

"You worry too much."

"He just needs to grow up and learn how to deal with his emotions."

"I thought you were going to let him fall on his face and learn from his mistakes."

These and all the other bits of I-want-to-be-helpful thoughts and advice offered with sincerity and tender hearts make me want to shake people by the shoulders and scream, "You can't begin to know what this feels like. Let me change places with you for just one minute, just one fucking minute. You can stand in my shoes, watch your child imploding before your eyes, and feel trapped in this absolute, terrifying hell of helplessness."

Tell me, please—how does a parent watch a child falling apart before her very eyes and not want to cry out to the heavens to make it stop. *MAKE IT STOP!* If only Ben had some other disease. I remember when he was a freshman and sophomore in high school, when we weren't sure yet what was wrong—maybe we should have known, maybe we should have reached out for help sooner, maybe we should have paid more attention, listened more, taken away more, done more—hoping it was anything but addiction. Maybe it's thyroid disease, we thought. Maybe it's simple depression or anxiety and he'll feel better after seeing a counselor or taking antidepressant drugs. Maybe it's the dis-ease of adolescence and it will pass in a few months or possibly years. Maybe it's something that time or a pill will cure, something that we can journey through together as a family, as a team.

A year or two before Ben's troubles began, a probation officer asked me to meet with a seventeen-year-old and his parents. The boy was a meth addict—thin, frail, with dyed blonde hair and black roots. He sat at the end of the table in the small conference room of the Juvenile Justice Center, his hands and feet shackled, his orange jumpsuit baggy and ridiculously bright in that beige-walled room, staring at the table, refusing to lift his head to look at his mother and father.

The room was just big enough for a table and six chairs. He sat at one end, and the mother and father sat across from me. They tried to talk to him, they gave it all they had—tears, threats, pleas, expressions of deep and unconditional love. After fifteen or twenty minutes of calm, composed talking, I felt as if a switch had been thrown. I saw it in the mother's face, her grief metamorphosed within seconds into the fiercest sort of anger, a fiery fury sparked by too many scenes like this, too many futile arguments, too much love met by hateful stares.

"I wish you still had leukemia," she said in a low voice. His head jerked up then, and he looked at her, his mouth dropped open. I could imagine her thoughts, *Oh good, now I have your attention*, and she repeated the words with even more emotion. "I wish you still had leukemia because at least then we were fighting it together."

"What the hell . . . ?" He looked utterly baffled.

"Do you remember?" she continued, because at least now he was looking at her, at least now she had an emotional response, at least now she could see some remnant of the son she used to know. "You were five years old, and I would read you stories. We would cry together and hold on to each other. I was always there with you, and you were always there with me. We went together to all the appointments. We fought it together, and we won. Remember? I was with you the whole time—I never would have left you—and you needed me, you wanted me there. Remember?"

But the moment had passed and he stared back at the table, his mouth a solid line of fury, his eyes narrowed, his whole body screaming the words, *Get me the hell out of here.*

He left the room without looking at them, his shackles clanging, a detention officer next to him with his hand tightly gripped on the boy's elbow. When the door closed behind them, she fell apart.

~

"Why do you put up with him?" My sister Debbie is upset. We're sitting in her kitchen, holding tight to our coffee cups, just the two of us. It's raining—a soft, almost soundless Seattle rain. Tiny translucent raindrops shimmy down windows that look out on the green grass and a dark forest of trees. One glance at the look on her face—lips pursed, eyes filled with concern—and I know she's had it with Ben's behavior, his sullen silences, abusive language, and endless disrespect. I know, too, that she's worried about me, but her concern is filtered through my tormented mind as impatience edged with anger. What I hear in her question is: "What is wrong with you? Why don't you put your foot down? He's destroying your family. You have to do something. What are you waiting for?"

Whether or not those judgments exist, I perceive them because they are the questions I ask myself every moment of every day. I don't have any answer to the question of what is wrong with me. I don't know why or how to put my foot down, and I wonder how putting a foot down can help someone who puts his fists through walls. I know we have to do something, and treatment seems to be the answer, but I can't imagine he'll go willingly. I don't know how to drag him to Montana, kicking and screaming. We're waiting for the right moment. Will it ever come?

I go back to the question of why I put up with him, and I have a simple answer. He's my son. I love him. I can't abandon him. He's sick; he has a disease. I feel the anger boiling up and the almost irrepressible urge to throw her a back-at-you question. "What would you do, Deb? Tell me what you would do if you had a sick-unto-death child who rebuffs every suggestion, who argues with everything we say, who tells me that I'm the problem, who speaks to his father with contempt—his kind, gentle father who waged his own battle with addiction and has been sober now for twenty years? Tell me, please, what would you do?"

Sure, I can shout at Ben, and we can yell at each other until we are hoarse, but I've done that, and I can't do it anymore. I am beaten up, a bloody pulp of a mother who used to be so strong and sure of herself, who knew right from wrong and good from bad, who now walks around in circles of fear and dread, a weak, miserable, terrified shadow of the person she used to be. But I don't have time or energy to think about myself, because my mind is focused on Ben, and my greatest terror of all is that he will die. I know too much about drug addiction. I want to shout at everyone who looks at me with pity or confusion or downright disgust: "This boy is sick with a chronic, progressive, deadly disease. He is not in control of his behavior. Beneath all that horrid awful shitty stuff he is saying and doing is my son, my Ben, my loving, sensitive boy. How do I reach him? Help me with that. Show me how."

I start to cry, and Debbie pats my hand with infinite kindness. "Let's do something," she says softly. "We can go to the bookstore, get a good, long novel, spend the day reading." I nod my head and look longingly at the fireplace. "Can we make a fire while we read?" She smiles and gives me a hug. "Of course we can make a fire. We can build the biggest fire you want." We laugh, then, because it's a gas fireplace. It, too, has its limits.

Pat is outside on the front steps, arguing with Ben.

"All I want is a fucking video game," Ben practically spits the words in Pat's face.

"I think that's a bad idea," Pat says, staying calm. "You've had enough distractions."

"What kind of distractions?" Ben's face is red with frustration and fury.

"Whatever distractions have resulted in you not being able to pass your classes."

"My classes? What the fuck do my classes have to do with this? It's Thanksgiving vacation, and all I want is a fucking video game." He glares at Pat and puts his hand out. "Give me some money."

"I have five bucks. If you want it, you can have it." Five dollars isn't going to buy a video game or a bag of weed. Ben snatches the bill as if Pat had stolen it from him.

"You need to start showing some respect, Ben." Pat's jaw muscles clench in sudden anger. "Christmas is coming up, and if you can't be respectful to me, Mom, and your sisters, you are not welcome in our house." We've been practicing that line, or variations of it, for the past two weeks, but it sounds so harsh and unloving now that he's said it; I want to take it back and tell Ben that he is always welcome at our house, because it's his house, too. I bite my tongue.

"Fuck you! I don't want to go to your fucking house anyway." And with that parting line, he takes off down the street.

Debbie gives Pat a hug as his eyes fill with tears. "We're going to the bookstore. Do you want to go with us?" she asks, patting his back. He nods his head, and I bet I know what he's thinking, because I'm thinking it, too—*Get me the hell out of here. Put me in a different world. Take me away from all of this.*

We drive slowly down the perfectly manicured street with the expensive four-, five-, and six-bedroom houses, each sitting back prettily on half an acre, surrounded by shapely evergreen trees, a perfect little haven of suburbia. *(But what's behind those windows? What dramas are taking place inside?* I always wonder.) Then, we see Ben walking ahead of us, moving fast, head down.

"Should I stop?" Debbie asks.

I look at Pat in the back seat. "I don't care," he shrugs his shoulders. Ben keeps walking as we drive slowly alongside him.

Pat and Debbie roll down their windows. "We're going to the bookstore," Pat says. "Do you want to come with us?"

"Fuck off," Ben says without lifting his head.

A sharp intake of breath as Debbie's shoulders stiffen. She looks at me and then leans out her window. "What did you say, Ben?"

"I told my dad to fuck off." Years later, Ben tells me he still remembers the look on Debbie's face at that moment.

"Just keep driving," I tell her. I look back at him as we pull away. That's our boy walking down the street. But he is not our boy, he is someone else, and we don't know how to save him, how to bring him back, how to hate or love or despise or detest him enough to wrest him free from this thing that has captured him, imprisoned him, taken him away from us. Can we control his mouth, his tongue, his thoughts, his actions? Should we try? From those questions, it's a quick and dirty leap to wondering again where we went wrong. I look at Pat, and the misery on his face matches mine. We are connected by confusion, misery, and tears, when once upon a time we were bonded by joy, laughter, and faith in an ordered world.

That night at the kitchen table, eating leftover turkey and mashed potatoes, I bring out my camera. I feel cheerful for some reason. I adore my family, and here we are together—my sisters, one of my brothers, our spouses, almost all of our children. Sure, Robyn is working in San Diego, and my brother, John, and his family are back in New Jersey. But the rest of us are here, at this long, crowded table, and I want to capture the moment. The camera is a great hiding place, a shield between me and the real world. It collects smiles and arms around shoulders for years to come, and it allows us to look back with the distance of time and say, "See, it really wasn't all that bad." Maybe one day we will say, with the gift of erased memory, "Look how happy we were!"

I click the shutter and look at the image in the LCD panel. Ben is scowling.

"Can you smile, Ben?" Just one smile, I am pleading with him in my mind. Just one smile to erase some of the past two days. Just one stupid little smile. That's all I want. My kids know this about me—I am always taking just one more photo, just one more, trying to capture everyone at their best. It's an impossible goal, but I am always asking them to let me take one more, hoping to get the perfect shot.

I hit the delete button to erase the image of Ben glowering at me. I want a good picture, a happy picture that I can send out to people for our Christmas card, an image that says, "See what a great family we have?" The first picture speaks the truth, and I don't want the truth. I am afraid of the truth, sick to death of the truth.

Ben shakes his head. "Nope," he says. "I'm done."

"Come on honey, just one more." I raise the camera to take another shot.

"Fuck you."

Silence.

I look across the table at Alison, at his cousins Jesse, Jay, Will, Todd, Mac, Emily, Katie. Bits of a second pass, tiny pieces, miniscule moments. We are all holding our breath, waiting. Alison's eyes flood with tears. Debbie told me later that Ben's anger was so over the top, so beyond anything she had ever witnessed, that she wanted to slap him and knock some sense into him.

My sister Billy leans forward from her chair at the other end of the table. "You owe your mother an apology," she says in a calm, low voice.

"Fuck you, Billy," Ben says, pushing back from the table, loudly scraping the chair legs against the wood floor. He stands up, all six-plus feet of him, and slowly raises his middle finger at the table. Then he walks to the front door, slamming it behind him. Hard.

We look at each other, stunned. Then we look down at our plates. In seconds, the conversation starts up again, stilted at first, but gaining in momentum as we pretend what just happened hadn't happened.

Later that night, I knock on Ben's bedroom door. I am angry, and it feels good to be mad. It feels powerful and righteous. I deserve this anger. I own it.

"What the hell is going on?" I say. That's not what I intended to say, but the anger is speaking for me.

"What the hell is going on? What the hell is going on with you?" he says. We speak in loud voices as if the volume can communicate the depth of our mutual despair. I don't mean to, but I slam the bedroom door on my way out.

Debbie hears the whole thing. "You need to talk to him," she says, pulling me into her bedroom and shutting the door. "You need to help him."

"I know."

Debbie has tears in her eyes. "I need to tell you something. This afternoon, before dinner, Ben walked by my office. He was making a beeline for the front door, and he was just sobbing. I jumped up and asked him to come in and talk to me. He looked so beaten, his shoulders slumped. Oh, God, Kath, such sadness in him."

Debbie sighs deeply and reaches for my hand. "He told me his drug use is much worse than anyone thinks—he's using cocaine, hallucinogens, pills. Every day, multiple times a day. He's failing his classes. He's scared. I think he wants help."

Cocaine? Pills? I stare at her. I can't breathe. I didn't know. How did I not know?

"This is so hard," Deb says, putting her arm around me and pulling me close. "I just want you to know that he was sobbing the whole time, his head in his hands. Before he left, he said, 'I don't know how my family will ever forgive me.'"

Forgive. Forgiveness. Oh, Ben, I forgive you. Do you forgive me? Do you forgive yourself? Can I forgive myself so that, in time, I can experience your forgiveness? I remember the passage from *The Spirituality of Imperfection* where Ernie and I write about forgiveness. I can't remember the exact words, but the point is that forgiveness involves a spiritual shift, a turnaround in perspective, where blaming others falls away and we begin to accept responsibility for who we are—imperfect, flawed, broken, torn to pieces. Forgiveness comes, is discovered, when we are able to let go of the feeling of resentment and the vision of ourselves as victims. Only then can we know that we have been forgiven. It is that experience of *being* forgiven that pulls us out of a self-centered focus on our own pain and allows us to forgive others.

Forgiveness is more than a two-way street. It's a circle, a cycle that goes on and on and on, beginning with forgiveness of self and moving outward in ever-expanding circles to the experience of forgiving others. The circle is unbroken when, through experience and the gift of forgiveness, we have embedded within ourselves the understanding that what unites us, one to another, is not our strengths and our successes but our weaknesses and our failures.

Years later, Ben sends me a story within a story within a story that he has written.

> I think Willa Cather said it perfectly—that there are only two or three human stories. The small variations in these stories are as numerous as the number of people who have lived throughout the course of human history, but the archetypes and general threads running through the stories are similar.
>
> I've lived out two of those stories. In the first, the prodigal son, in his subconscious search for enlightenment, neglects what matters most, imbibes a deadly poison disguised as an elixir of life, nearly loses everything, and encounters depths so low that non-existence seems the only solution.
>
> In the second version, the prodigal son, having reached the deepest depths of despair, looks up at the surface and paddles blindly toward it, with the hopes of encountering the faint light glowing miles above him. He changes, using what he has learned along the way, and becomes a true hero in the eyes of those around him, although in his own eyes his mistakes are unforgiveable.

Ah, Ben, I want to call out to him across the years. There is a third story, and you will live that one as well. The prodigal son reaches the surface and begins a new life, knowing he is not a hero at all but merely a human being who, like all other human beings, is flawed and imperfect. And so, he is finally able to forgive himself.

~

I walk down the hallway to Pat, who is sitting on the edge of our bed, his head in his hands. "I'm going to talk to Ben. I'm going to talk about treatment. Do you want to go with me?"

"I'm not sure that would be a good idea," Pat says. "I'm afraid he would feel ganged up on. And I might lose my temper. I'm afraid of what I might say."

"I'm afraid, too," I say, bursting into tears.

Pat puts his arms around me. "Let's practice," he says. We go over the words, repeating them, creating little scripts I can carry around in my brain. *I'm worried about your health. I'm here to listen. I want to help.*

I remember what my friend Debra Jay, the clinical interventionist, once told me: "I often say to families, memorize a few lines and use the broken record technique, repeating the same line again and again. If Ben uses the blame game to get you off track, respond with the words, 'That may be true, but today we're talking about how drugs are hurting you and hurting our family.'"

I also remember the advice another friend—Joyce Sundin, also an intervention specialist—gave me months earlier: "Use simple phrases, such as 'That sounds really painful.' Depending on the situation, you might follow that up with, 'Would you like it to be different?' Don't get caught up in the drama or try to bail him out or offer the wise sage stuff that so many parents try. Remember, the pain comes from natural causes when the person is allowed to experience the fallout from their drug-affected choices. Pain is the motivator or springboard to a different place."

And I remember a scene from the TV series *Boston Legal.* I replayed it several times, writing down the words, memorizing them. Denny is feeling sorry for himself and lashes out at his friend Allen for not being on his side. "You can accuse me of many things," Allen says in a soft, loving voice. "But not being on your side isn't one of them. I'm afraid for you. I don't want to see you hurt."

And I remember that while it is important to speak with compassion and kindness, pleading with Ben on the basis of love is not a good strategy. Right now, he doesn't love himself. He is hurting. He is in the deepest imaginable kind of pain. *Speak to the pain, Kathy. Speak to the pain.*

I walk to Ben's bedroom, knock and open the door without waiting for a response. He's sitting on his bed, his head in his hands. He looks up at me; in his eyes, I see despair.

I sit down next to him and reach for his hand. He lets me take it.

"You need help, Ben," I say, my eyes filling with tears. "You are not yourself. Something is wrong."

He starts to cry. I hold on tight to his hand. He takes a deep breath, ragged with emotion. "Okay," he says. One word.

I struggle with all my might to keep my tone even. "Will you go to treatment?"

"Yes." He's sobbing now, shoulders heaving. "I need help."

I put my arms around him, and we hold on to each other for a long time. *He's here*, I think. *He's still here. I lost him, but right now, in this moment, he is back with me, flesh and blood and bone.*

10

wilderness

December 2005–January 2006

From: Kathy Ketcham
Sent: Tuesday, November 29, 2005 8:41 AM
To: Benjamin Patrick Spencer
Subject: I love you
Dear Benny:
I just want to say how much I love you.
  And how incredibly proud I am of you. How brave I
think you are and how much courage you have.
  I just love you so much.

                                                    Mom

From: Benjamin Patrick Spencer
Sent: Tuesday, November 29, 2005 4:10 PM
To: Kathy Ketcham
Subject: Re: I love you
Mom—
i appreciate the email but i would also appreciate if we
could stop talking about rehab. Im not looking forward
to it, i just want a week where I can still be ben and not
worry about that shit.

On Sunday, December 4, we drive to Wilderness Treatment Center. Ben is in the back seat, staring out the window at the frozen landscape. The windshield wiper fluid freezes up somewhere around Spokane, forcing us to stop every ten miles or so. We are driving blind, looking out at the frozen cracked world with a sense of terrified wonder, as if its stark beauty will swallow us whole.

We keep driving. The snow is falling, the roads are slushy, the sky is gray, and we are all pretending that this is something normal to do on a Sunday—drive ten hours to an inpatient treatment center in the outback of Montana in the middle of winter.

I knit a green scarf. On long drives, I knit scarves, back and forth, back and forth. When the drive is over, I put the scarf in a bag Ben made for me when he was in preschool. Months, even years, go by, and I forget about the scarf until the next trip. I've kept about a dozen half-finished scarves and a few finished ones that I can't bring myself to throw away because of all the hours invested but can't give to anyone, even to Goodwill, because of all the holes and uneven edges.

On this trip to the middle of nowhere, I finish the entire scarf, and I don't drop one stitch. I'm focused, keeping my mind on the needles and the yarn and the back and forth, back and forth, trying not to look out at the gray whiteness, the icy stillness, trying not to think about what has happened and what is about to happen.

Ben asks if we can stop at Pizza Hut in Kalispell. Even though we're late because of the ice and the snow and the frozen windshield wiper fluid, we pull into the parking lot. I watch him eat four or five big slices and find myself thinking that this is a last supper of sorts, the end of our lives as we have known them.

We drive another twenty miles or so, east through Batavia and Kila, until we arrive at the turnoff to Wilderness Treatment Center. As we head down a long, twisting road, Ben asks if he can take his iPod with him. No. His cell phone? No.

"Welcome to Camp Suck Your Dick," he says.

~

On the long ride home, I struggle to keep my mind focused on the copyedited chapters of a book I am writing with William Cope Moyers, son of the famous broadcast journalist Bill Moyers. Titled *Broken: My Story of Addiction and Redemption*, the book tells the story of William's long, disastrous addiction to alcohol and crack cocaine, which came perilously close to destroying everything and everyone he loved. In one scene, just before he entered treatment for the third time, he called his wife and asked her to pick him up at a crack house where he'd run out of money to buy more drugs. When they arrived home, she looked at him, "not with judgment or anger, but with something deeper, some mixture of sorrow, pity, grief, and fear." He begged for her forgiveness.

"I'm a bad man," he kept repeating, not in an effort to get her sympathy but from the depths of his loneliness and helplessness.

"You're a good man, William," she said in a voice that was deeply, desperately tired. "But you have a bad problem, and you will die if you don't do something about it."

Good person, bad disease. William got clean and sober. Ben can, too. William is a good, decent, honest man now that he is released from the influence of drugs. Ben will be, too. *Good person, bad disease.* I put down my pen, close my eyes, and keep repeating those words to myself. There is comfort there; there is hope there.

When we arrive home after midnight, a voicemail is waiting for us. It is Ben Dorrington, Ben's primary counselor at Wilderness. We call him Ben D. I write down every word, replaying the message several times to be sure I don't miss a thing.

"Ben is doing well," Ben D. says. "He's open, talking, polite, appropriate. No red flags. He has lots of resentments, but I see a lot of kids who are more resentful than Ben. He seems to like it here."

The next day, we hear a different story. The honeymoon is over, Ben D. tells us. Ben doesn't feel like he can get sober. He's planning to leave. The staff will do everything they can to convince him to stay, but there are no locks on the doors, no electric fences, no gated entrances.

We have several conference calls with the two Bens. I'm writing notes as fast as the pen can travel across the paper but soon switch to my computer so I can type with my headphones on. I keep all my notes, emails, and letters in ever-thickening folders in a two-drawer oak file cabinet that sits in the corner of my bedroom closet. The paperwork comforts me—no matter what happens, I know I will not forget. I will never forget. These are the records of our unconditional love for our son and our never-ending efforts to help him. These thin papers and thick folders are proof that we tried and that we will not stop trying. Ever. No matter what.

"Everybody here is immature," Ben says in a loud, aggressive tone of voice. "Everybody's a crackhead. I'm bored out of my mind. I can't stay here. These other guys aren't like me; they're all sticking needles in their arms."

My heart is thumping, but I hold fast. I repeat, over and over again, that Ben needs to stay in treatment, and if he leaves, he will be on his own. This is what we've been told to say.

"I hate you," Ben says, his voice a low hiss. "You put me here. This is all your fucking fault."

Hands shaking, I give the phone to Pat, who repeats the message we've practiced over and over again—"You need to stay in treatment; if you decide to leave, you are on your own." Ben D. comes back on the phone a moment later to tell us that Ben stomped out of his office and, on the way out, picked up an office chair and threw it out the door.

"He seems to have his mind made up that he is leaving tomorrow and will hitchhike to Missoula, where his sister is going to school."

I call Alison to warn her. "What do I do if he shows up here?" she says, her voice choked with tears.

"I don't know." A thick blanket of despair creeps over me, cold and dense like the fog that settles over the Walla Walla valley in the winter months. "I just don't know."

Tuesday, December 6

"He says he'll stay out of spite," Ben D. says. I can hear a smile in his voice. "He says he'll spend your $20,000 and then go smoke a bowl in your house. But he apologized for being 'an asshole,' in his words, yesterday."

Ben D. may be my most favorite person in the world right now. I don't know what he looks like, I don't know anything about him, all I know is that I trust him and feel safe with him. I sense the depth of his empathy in the calming tone of his voice, the occasional chuckle that allows me to step back and gain a little perspective, and the way he avoids statements like "I understand what you are feeling and thinking." Even if you've been through a similar situation, how can you know what another person is thinking or feeling? At some level, we are all strangers to each other. We are blindingly unknowable, even to ourselves.

At lunch with a friend I met in a yoga class, she tells me that we all need to follow the Buddhist philosophy and "stay in the pain." I stare at her. "All of life is suffering," she says, with a knowing smile.

I want to punch her in the nose. Here is what I want to say to her: "My experience is not your experience. My suffering is different than yours, although I do not doubt the reality or the depth of the pain you have been through. You do not know—how could you know?—about this all-consuming fear that sends shock waves through me when the phone rings early in the morning or late at night? I am in the pain! I'm in the fire—seared, scorched, burning alive!"

I don't say any of those things. Instead, I go home, curl up with Sophie and Murphy, and let them lick my tears.

Pat writes a long nine-paragraph email to his parents, detailing our decision to send Ben to treatment and asking for their support.

This has been, and continues to be, the most difficult thing we have endured in our 28 years together. Neither of us has spent a great deal of time praying over the years, but if ever there was an issue that is worth a prayer, this is it. The decision had to be made together and with a united sense of purpose. Fortunately, we were able to do that. Ben has gone in and out, as you might expect. One day, he wants treatment in this facility; the next, he wants to be out and going to an outpatient program in Seattle (and thus establishing control over his life, which would allow the addiction to take over once again). One day, he is learning what it means to live life without alcohol and other drugs, and we see and hear the Ben we used to know. The next he despises us for sending him to this place, and despises himself. That is not Ben talking, it is his addiction talking.

Pat's father writes back.

Needless to say we are saddened beyond belief. More will follow but at the moment we are far too emotional and distraught to even be coherent. You both, and Ben, have our prayers. I must stop before I come totally unglued.

All our love,
Mom and Dad

This short email expressing sadness and grief is so uncharacteristic of Pat's father, who keeps his emotions close and tight, that we both start sobbing when we read it. My father died sixteen years ago, when Ben was four; my mother died seven years ago, when Ben was twelve. They died before Ben started using drugs. I miss them so much, and I dream about them often. In my dreams, they are alive, but I am fully aware that our time together is short and soon they will be gone. In my waking hours, I wish they were still here with me, even if just to hold me close one more time.

But I'm also grateful I don't have to write a letter to them.

Wednesday, December 7

Ben has been in treatment for four days when Ben D. calls with good news. "We've had a 180-degree turn," he says. "He's talking about powerlessness. He knows he has no other options. He's relating to all these guys, handing in assignments, starting to gain insight into addiction. It's an abrupt change, but he still doesn't think he can have fun without alcohol and other drugs."

"It's like we're blind on a roller coaster," Pat says. We laugh, and it feels so good, as if we are shaking ourselves loose inside.

But I'm afraid, it seems, of everything. I don't want to answer the phone. When I open the mailbox, my hands shake as I sort through the mail. I'm afraid Ben D. will call and tell us Ben is on a downturn. Or maybe it will be Jody, my sister-in-law, with bad news about my brother, who is dying oh-so-slowly-and-oh-too-soon of pancreatic cancer.

Pat goes hunting with a friend, and I imagine him getting peppered with shotgun pellets as they walk back and forth on opposite sides of the field.

Pat plays poker with his regular once-a-month-or-so group, and I'm afraid to go to sleep before he gets home. We never lock the doors, but now we do.

I can't concentrate. I get up, sit down, walk to the kitchen, look in the fridge, sigh, go back to sit on the couch. I look at the phone, afraid it will ring, willing it to ring. I remember the comments from friends and family: "He needs to learn how to control himself." "He needs to grow up." "Why did you let him join a fraternity?" "He should join the Army." "He won't stop if he doesn't want to stop."

Somehow, somewhere we fucked up.

Saturday, December 10

"He's semi-defiant," Ben D. says. "Not too bad—we expect some of that. He still wants to leave. He's having a hard time with the level of maturity of the other boys. He says he'd work better with more intelligent people."

"That sounds like bullshit," I say, and to my surprise, I start laughing.

Ben D. laughs with me. "Well, there are always a couple of guys who are struggling more. He said he's miserable here, that he can't get sober here, that he's just a pothead and he's in treatment with all these coke and heroin addicts. We talked about how his drug use is pointing to the person he doesn't want to become, and sooner or later he'll have to start confronting this stuff. I said I know he's fearful and that people want to avoid that because they don't want to face themselves. He's making eye contact with me the whole time I'm talking."

Ben D. takes a deep breath and lets it out slowly. *Uh-oh*, I think. "At that point, he stands up and starts calling himself names, using the F-word, accusing me of not caring. He asked me how he could get kicked out of treatment, and then he said, 'Maybe I should just kick your ass.' I calmly asked him why he would want to do that. He called me a few more names, and then he tried to smash his fist through a window. He walked out of my office, picked up the cigarette butt can on the porch and threw it, kicked it a few times on his way back to his cabin, and then kicked open the cabin door. Then he punched himself in the face."

"He hit himself?"

"Three times. He's pretty bruised up. Honestly, I didn't think it would go this far. His inner anger is more than I usually see. He is a young man with so much potential, but he hates himself so much. The anger comes out sideways, and he gets violent."

"But why would he hit himself?" I can hardly find my voice.

"Guys with lots of potential—good athletes, good students—often beat themselves up when they do things they regret or they're ashamed of."

"You think he's so full of shame that he beats himself up?" I'm shaking so violently that I turn up the heat on the thermostat. Ben is in so much pain. Can this much pain be "treated"?

"I do."

"Is there any chance he'll do something that will get him kicked out of treatment?" What I'm thinking is, how long can they put up with this behavior? If his anger is so out of control, if he's throwing things, threatening to hit people, harming himself, how are they going to justify keeping him there? And if he can't stay there, where will he go? What will we do? I picture him walking down the road in the middle of winter—it's minus thirteen degrees in Montana—and wonder if I packed his down jacket.

"It's pretty hard to get kicked out of the program," Ben D. reassures me. "We understand that we'll see a lot of anger, fear, and shame in these kids. Ben is a nice young man; he just doesn't want to confront these personal demons. His anger is escalating rather than de-escalating. I hope and pray he gets through this."

Demons, plural. Not just the monster of addiction but other demons too, unleashed and roaming free, wreaking havoc in his mind. The image horrifies me.

Ben D. offers us advice: "Stick to your guns, stick to what you know is best for Ben. Tell him you cannot support him unless he stays in treatment. Remember this is the chemical dependency side of Ben. We know this isn't really who he is. And it's life or death we're dealing with here. We're fully committed to him. This is a nasty, nasty disease."

Life or death. Fight hard, Benny. Choose life.

Monday, December 12

I open up the picture files on my computer, trying to figure out which digital photos to keep and which to delete. Suddenly I feel over-whelmed and think, *I can't do this.* Then I reason with myself, talking out loud: "Just do two at a time, Kath. Look at two and decide which one of the two you want to keep. Then go on to the next two. One step at a time." I smile, then. Who ever thought this might be true, this one-step-at-a-time stuff?

Ben D. calls around noon. He says Ben did his life story, his peers took notes, and he was honest and open. This afternoon, they will do the "Knees to Knees" exercise, where the other kids sit with Ben, their knees touching, and tell him directly, honestly what they think about how he is doing in treatment.

"He's been avoiding me because he knows he has to face his personal demons," Ben D. says. "He doesn't want to do that."

I don't blame him. At nineteen, could I have faced my "personal demons"? I don't think I was self-aware enough to even recognize that I had personality traits that might be hurtful to myself or others. At

Ben's age, I would have had no idea what the term "personal demons" meant. I would have laughed at the whole concept.

What courage and strength Ben is being asked to pull up from some place deep inside him. Most of us go through life without ever having to look into the mirror of ourselves, removing the outer layers to expose our innards. We stuff our emotions, our fears and our shame, way down inside us, and we close ourselves up tight, resisting all efforts—even our own—to pull them forth into the light of day. It's too painful to admit to our flaws and imperfections; if we are willing to acknowledge them, we also have to be willing to do something about them. We have to be willing to change, which we also resist with all our might, quickly closing ourselves back up again, stuffing those demons back inside before stitching the seams together with unbreakable thread.

I stare out the kitchen window, my hands in the soapy dish water, and realize I am giving myself a safe distance from my feelings—perhaps my own "personal demons"—by using the universal "we." "Get real, Kathy," I say out loud. My demons are all wrapped up in one emotion—fear. I fear losing the people I love. I fear car crashes and airplane crashes. I fear public speaking. I fear big crowds and long lines. I fear not being honest, not being kind. I fear nuclear war.

A memory rises up, maybe because I am in the kitchen, just as I was in 1962 during the Cuban missile crisis. I was thirteen years old, helping my mother clean up the dishes after dinner. I remember the fear building up inside me. "Mom," I said, finally finding the courage to put words to my thoughts. "I'm afraid of nuclear war. I'm afraid I won't be able to grow up and have children."

She turned to look at me, a dishtowel in her hand, eyebrows raised. "Kath," she said, "don't be ridiculous."

I wonder what my mother would say about Ben. If I told her about my fears that he might die, would she say the same words. *Oh Kath, don't be ridiculous.* Or she might say—I can still hear her voice—*You worry too much, Katherine Elizabeth, and where does that get you?*

I smile at the thought. Mom wasn't the most affectionate person in the world—that would have been my father—but she taught us to be tough and scrappy and to take life's bruises and scrapes in stride. But right now, I don't feel so tough. And the fear keeps growing.

Tuesday, December 13

My friend Linda, who cuts and colors my hair, calls tonight. Her five-year-old son, Blake, was born a few months premature. Over the years, she's told me the stories of his birth, her fears, her protectiveness, his pushing back, the speech therapists, the schools, teachers. We talk about thoughts and experiences that are close to our hearts. I tell her things I don't tell many people, even my closest friends. I read the other day that the people who cut, color, straighten, and curl our hair are the repositories of our woes. They do their best to make us look good, while we sit in the chair and reveal what is really happening inside us, beneath the makeup and brave smiles, the "I'm fine" responses and superficial conversations.

What a strange world we live in.

"I know you are about to eat dinner," Linda says. "But I wanted to tell you that I have been thinking about you for the past two days since we talked, and I think you are such a brave woman. You are helping Ben face his problems. You are not enabling him. All the different ways that you could have handled it, but you did it this way, and it is the right way. You have great courage."

I say, "Thank you." I tell her I am writing down what she says because my brain doesn't work anymore. I am brain dead. I have to write everything down. So I write her words on pink sticky notes with a blue marker, and I save the notes for later, knowing I will need them.

I am awed by the kindness of this woman, my friend, who could so easily forget about me because I am just one more face, one more person she sees in the salon. But she thinks about me, and then she picks up the phone to comfort and console me. She calls me brave. She believes I am doing the right thing. She doesn't try to fix me, tell me what to do, or offer advice about how to take care of myself. Gratitude fills my heart.

An epiphany: This is what Ben wants, too—not guidance or instruction, but presence. He wants me to listen. He yearns to be heard.

I think, then, about the receptionist at the dentist's office who was rude and cold toward me, for no reason that I could figure out. I learned later that she was recently divorced, had an autistic child, and had no medical insurance. What was going on for her had absolutely nothing to do with me.

Another epiphany—Ben's fear and anger are about his pain, not my failures. *Hold that thought tight, Kathy*, I tell myself. *Hold it close.*

Wednesday, December 14

I call Ben D. at 7:30 this morning, 8:30 Montana time.

"Ben talked about the death of his friend John yesterday and said, 'I think it's relatively insignificant in the grand scheme of things if I use drugs every once in a while.' We talked a lot about his hopelessness. He doesn't see the program doing much for him. 'I don't know if I want to give pot a break,' he said. 'It gives me more creativity, affects my perception, and I like that.'

"We did Ben's peer evaluation. His peers talked about Ben's anger and how shame-related stuff and low self-esteem feed into substance use. Later he told me he's not ready to surrender. 'The world is such a nasty place,' he said. 'When I'm sober, I feel so pessimistic about the nature of human beings. I'm not happy.'"

Ernie and I wrote about surrender in *The Spirituality of Imperfection*. I look up the section:

> Perhaps the greatest paradox in the story of
> spirituality is the mystical insight that we are able
> to experience release only if we ourselves *let go*.
> This is the paradox of *surrender*. Surrender begins
> with the acceptance that we are not in control of
> the matter at hand—in fact, we are not in absolute
> control of anything.

Friday, December 16

Ben D. calls to tell me that Ben has had one of his best days ever and "a new, open mind-set." He says he's giving up the fight against his disease, he's exhausted, and he needs help.

The results of a psychological test Ben took show that he has considerable anxiety and depression, impulsivity, and some problems with keeping disturbing thoughts out of his mind. His behavior appears to be quite impulsive, which is made worse by substances. The test shows a high likelihood of chemical dependency.

"When I went over the test results with him, Ben said they were 'dead on,' and he couldn't believe a test could tell that much about him," Ben D. says. "He said one reason he thinks he was using chemicals is because they gave him a break, some relief. I asked him when these feelings about needing relief came about. 'When John died,' he said. He keeps bringing up John. He's doing a lot of grief work. And he's doing shame versus guilt stuff. We talked a lot about the shame he feels related to his using and using behaviors and the shame related to ongoing unmanageability and how all these things perpetuate the shame cycle.

"Sooner or later, he'll have to break that cycle," Ben D. says with a sigh. "Whether he can do that on his own remains to be seen. I think there are good signs that he's ready to engage in treatment, but I wouldn't be surprised if he has another one of his episodes again soon. He's had a couple days of clarity and remorse, a few good days, but the pattern seems to be that he will then do something that causes him to feel more shame, and he'll have difficulty dealing with that shame.

"We'll hope for the best and adjust for the worst. He's a good kid. A nice young man."

I take those words to heart—*he's a good kid, a nice young man*—but I adjust for the worst.

Monday, December 19

Three days later. "Ben had his weekly assessment and received the lowest rating—unacceptable and not making any progress," Ben D.

says. "He is belligerent, immature, and at times threatening. Today in group, his peers focused on him for much of the time. He was contradictory, defensive, and angry. He ended up leaving group."

I hear the weariness in Ben D.'s voice. "Two weeks into the program and there has been no substantive change," he says. "Usually we can get kids engaged by now."

"What is it that makes him so resistant to treatment?" I ask. "I wonder if he might be afraid that he will fail, and so he makes that prediction come true?"

"I think you are exactly right," Ben D. chuckles softly. "Recently, Ben said something like, 'If I work hard and fail, where will I be? What's the point?' Then he shifted back to 'I don't have a problem.'"

I remember talking to Robyn after one of her high school soccer games, when she seemed to be holding back, not giving one hundred percent. "Mom," she admitted finally, "if I give it everything I have and it's not good enough, what do I have left to give?"

Thursday, December 22

"Be prepared," Ben D. says. "I talked to Ben about his phone call home on Christmas day, and he told me he's not going to call you."

I take a deep breath and sigh, a ragged, moaning sound.

"I just want you to be prepared," he says. "We had a couple good days, then the level of defiance started to escalate again. I think it's still kind of iffy about what he'll do over the next few days. We often see depression that comes out in anger around Christmas. That might be some of it, with Christmas this weekend. But we have to stop this repetitive pattern of feeling remorse, flying off the handle, then feeling more guilt, shame, and remorse. We'll work on that.

"I do want to tell you about something he said in group today, because I think it's significant: 'It's tough for me to give up the fight, because it's like everyone else has won, it's like my parents have won, and that makes me mad.'

"So now, he gets to be mad at you and not call you."

Christmas Day

I wake up at 5:00 a.m. It's pitch black outside, overcast, and when I step outside for a moment, it feels like rain. I look up the weather in Kalispell, Montana. Light freezing fog and twenty-nine degrees. I turn on the Christmas tree lights, sit on the sofa, and write Ben a letter.

Dear Ben,

We love you more than we can begin to put in words. We miss you more than we can say. You are woven through our lives so that not an hour goes by in which we do not think about you. It comforts us to know that you are in a place where people understand addiction and know what to do to help you get well. But if you refuse to meet them halfway, if you decide to continue to keep using and put your very life in jeopardy, we cannot be part of that decision. Whatever you decide will not change our love for you—we will love you always and forever with a depth and passion that you will not be able to understand until you have children yourself.

You have so much waiting for you in the sober world, Ben—college, a career, children, laughter, the full spectrum of human emotion, energy, motivation, excitement about the world and your place in it, and most important of all, a love of your own self. It's all there. And there's the other side, too, which you have come to know—the sadness, the shame, the fear, the physical injuries, the emotional devastation, the destruction of your relationships, the sickness inside, the anger, the fury, the lashing out, the mean words you speak to people you love, the very disintegration of the self.

What will you choose?

I finish the letter, reading it over and over in the dawning light, and find myself wondering: How many times can you repeat the word *love* without emptying it of meaning?

Just before dinner, Ben calls. He spends most of his time talking to Robyn and Alison. We tell him we love him. He says he loves us.

Tuesday, December 27

"Yesterday was better for Ben," Ben. D says. "He's at a point where he's much more willing to be open-minded and look at himself, look at his issues.

"The biggest thing I'm encouraged by is that before the past couple days, he'd been opposed to looking at the spiritual nature of the Twelve Steps because God killed his best friend. 'Why would I want to believe in something like that?' he said. 'I didn't want to believe that a higher power would allow something like that to happen.'

"Then he said, 'Something has been missing in my life. If you're telling me it's spirituality and the Twelve Steps that will fill the hole that drugs filled for such a long time, then I'm willing to look at it.' He talked about being bullied in elementary and middle school and feeling a general distrust toward people, which in his mind leads to defiance and distrust.

"He's a very insightful young man," Ben D. says. "He's starting to feel better about himself, but there's a long way to go with his self-esteem. And he continues to believe he can solve his own problems."

We talk a bit longer, and I thank him for everything he has done for Ben.

"I don't know where we would be now without you," I say.

Just before we say goodbye, he says, "The miracle hasn't happened yet."

I hear the smile in his voice and interpret it as a promise of sorts. Somehow, somewhere, someday, the miracle will happen.

11

knees to knees

January 1–January 6, 2006

The word *miracle* calls forth a memory from the distant past. When I was in the early stages of writing my first book, back in 1978, I sat in a roomful of patients and their family members at an inpatient treatment center in Kirkland, Washington. My pen was skidding across the paper as I tried to keep up with the man speaking at the lectern, James R. Milam, PhD. His deep, powerful voice resonated through the room. Everyone present, including most of the patients in hospital gowns, sat unmoving, mesmerized by his folksy stories and passionate delivery of the facts about addiction.

After that first visit, I attended half a dozen more lectures on various subjects, ranging from neurochemistry to nutrition. In every talk, no matter the subject, Milam used a reassuring metaphor to explain the metamorphosis that takes place in the process of recovery from addiction. "We have to wait for the physiological change to occur. You can't rush it; it will happen in its own time," Milam explained in his booming voice. "Imagine trying to teach a caterpillar how to fly. The poor thing might listen, take flight lessons, watch butterflies darting around. But no matter how hard it tries, it won't fly. Maybe we get frustrated because we know this little guy has it in him to become a butterfly. So we give him books to read, try to counsel him, scold him, punish him, threaten him, maybe even toss him up in the air and watch him flap his little legs before crashing back to earth."

Everyone laughed; even the sickest patients lifted their heads a little higher. "The miracle takes time," Milam said in a softer tone of voice. "We must be patient. But just as it is natural and normal for caterpillars to become butterflies, so can we expect addicted individuals, given the appropriate care and compassion, to be transformed in the recovery process. The metamorphosis is nothing short of miraculous, as people who are desperately sick are restored to health and a 'normal' state of being."

"So, don't sit around feeling sorry for yourself," Milam admonished, raising his voice again. "Be grateful that you have a disease from which you can make a full recovery."

I remember watching the family members from my seat in the back row—the middle-aged woman sitting alone, dabbing at her eyes with a cloth handkerchief; the businessman with his briefcase, who kept looking at his watch; the grandfatherly man, sitting straight and tall, statue-like, eyes riveted on the lectern; the couple whose heads were bowed, shoulders shaking. I wondered what they were seeing, thinking, feeling. Just twenty-nine years old, I didn't have enough experience with suffering and loss to even begin to imagine what they were going through. I couldn't have known—I never would have dreamed—that one day I would be sitting in such a room, not as an observer but as a participant. That I would be one of them.

~

> We wish to welcome you to the Wilderness Treatment
> Center's Family Week Program.
>   You probably have heard it said that chemical
> dependency is a family disease and that the family and
> concerned persons become affected by the disease. There
> is no doubt that the person who is emotionally involved
> with a chemically dependent person *will* become
> affected, in one way or another, to one degree or another.

I like the way the introduction to the packet of information about Family Week is phrased. No talk about "enabling" or "codependence"—terms that sound so negative and judgmental to my ears. It's just a straightforward acknowledgment that when the demon of addiction enters our homes, the entire family system is turned upside down and inside out. We are "affected," and we need help, no doubt about that. I smile to myself, wondering if the treatment center might consider adding another line or two to this introduction: "We also understand that you will be genuinely terrified, to one degree or another, by the idea of exposing your emotions, thoughts, and behaviors to a group of strangers. Hang in there—you're not alone."

Pat and I look at the five-day schedule. Every morning, 8:45 a.m. check-in is followed by Al-Anon, lectures ("Disease Concept," "Step One," "Family Systems/Roles," "Spirituality," "Continuing Care"), a break for lunch, then videos and groups. The third day's group is replaced by "Knees to Knees." ("That doesn't sound good," Pat grumbles.) "Individual Family Conferences" take place on the fourth day, after the lecture. On the fifth and final day, the "Challenge Course" is followed by lunch and 1:00 p.m. departure.

Robyn flies up from San Diego, and Ali takes a bus from Missoula. We rent a house a few miles from the treatment center, because it's more comfortable than crowding four of us into a motel room in Kalispell, which is twenty-two miles away. We gather our courage Saturday night, New Year's Eve. The girls and I share a bottle of champagne. Pat told me later that it was a rough evening for him. He hadn't had a drink in twenty-two years, but champagne used to be our way of celebrating events, big and small. Just the popping of the plastic cork brought him back to those days and a craving he hadn't experienced in a long, long time. That was the first and only time I've heard him express a desire to drink again.

I knew we were breaking the treatment center's list of "expectations," specifically #3: "Please refrain from the use of mood-altering chemicals while you are participating in family week." I felt guilty for drinking in front of Pat and shame for being the kind of person who knew that wasn't the right thing to do but did it anyway. I can't lie, though—I enjoyed that glass of champagne. Maybe I even needed it that night. Liquid courage.

My stomach twists and my heartstrings tighten as I write these words so many years later, knowing what Ben was going through and thoughtlessly ignoring what Pat must have been experiencing as he watched his wife and two daughters toasting the New Year. Not a proud moment, then or now.

~

"Yeah!" I whisper to Pat when Ben D. introduces himself as our group leader. I'm surprised how young he is—possibly in his late twenties or early thirties. I think he looks a lot like our Ben. Or maybe I'm just hoping that our Ben will look like him in ten years—handsome and broad shouldered with a wide-open smile and a cheerful, confident manner.

"We have a small group," Ben D. says, "because many people wait until after the holidays to send their kids to treatment." The look on his face tells us that waiting isn't always a good idea, but it occurs to me that perhaps the people sitting in this circle are the truly desperate ones. Tim, Susan, and their son Taylor are here for Taylor's older brother, Bryan. Linda is here for Kevin. Steve for Mike. And Pat, Kathy, Robyn, and Alison for Ben.

Bryan, Kevin, Mike, Ben. The boys join us for only an hour or two each day, which is a relief to be honest. We are all excited to see them, but we're nervous, too, because we don't know what to expect—angry outbursts, long tirades, sullen silences or loving embraces, words of gratitude, a sense of newfound self-respect. I hope for the love and gratitude, but given the long conversations with Ben D. about Ben's progress, I expect anger and resentment. I remember what William James wrote about how happiness can be quantified as the ratio between reality and expectations—the higher our expectations, the smaller our satisfaction. Or as Pat put it in group a few days later, quoting a *Calvin and Hobbes* comic, the secret "is to lower your expectations to the point where they're already met." I thought Steve would fall out of his chair laughing.

The first morning, with no boys present, we go around the circle and introduce ourselves. Tim, white haired and blue eyed, is first. "My son Bryan," he begins, as his chin drops to his chest. Susan takes his hand. "My son Bryan," he starts again, "is a heroin addict." He is crying hard now. "I'm sorry," he says, wiping at his tears with the back of his hand. "I'm so sorry."

Ben D. walks over and hands Tim a box of tissues. Tim offers the box to Susan, who is crying quietly next to him. Susan gives the box to Linda, who takes a handful of tissues and gives it to Steve, who is dry eyed and passes it along to Robyn, Alison, Pat, and me. For some weird reason, I think about the scene in *Jaws* when the giant shark leaps onto the back of the boat and one of the characters says, "I think we're going to need a bigger boat." In this small circle, with the tears flowing like rivers, we're going to need a whole boatload of tissues.

Tim is bent over with emotion, his head almost in his lap, his shoulders heaving. Susan continues to pat his hand as she introduces herself.

"We're here because our oldest son, Bryan, is addicted to heroin. He's been here for eight weeks, and in five days, at the end of Family Week, we're taking him home and putting him on a plane to an extended-care facility in Florida. He finished his wilderness trip last week."

I want so much to ask Susan about the trip. The idea of Ben trekking into the mountains in the middle of a Montana winter scares me. In small groups with several counselors, each boy will spend sixteen days and nights (it would have been twenty-one days and nights if they had been in treatment during the summer months) in the million-acre-plus Bob Marshall Wilderness area. I'd never heard of the Bob Marshall Wilderness area, so I looked it up on the Internet. "One of the most completely preserved mountain ecosystems in the world," the description goes. "The kind of wilderness most people can only imagine: rugged peaks, alpine lakes, cascading waterfalls, grassy meadows embellished with shimmering streams, a towering coniferous forest, and big river valleys."

Ben and the other boys will be climbing, traversing, rappelling, or whatever they're supposed to do on those snow-covered mountains, trudging across frozen lakes and streams, camping out in the forests and river valleys or high up on some mountain peak or alpine lake. Three of those days will be a solo adventure, with each boy left alone with a tarp and a shovel to build a snow fort where they can think, reflect, work on the Twelve Steps, write in a journal, and fend for themselves.

I pull my mind back to the circle. Bryan's brother, Taylor, introduces himself. He wears a hoodie sweatshirt pulled over his head. He has disappeared underneath. I watch his hands, turning and twisting in his lap. He says his name, but that's all he has to say.

We continue around the group, telling a little bit about ourselves. We don't say much, but the tissue box keeps making its rounds. When it's my turn, my hands are sweaty, and my throat feels dry. But as soon as I start to talk, I experience a flood of relief. It feels so liberating to be with people who look at me with compassion and understanding, whose eyes fill with tears when I tell my story because my story is their story.

I feel safe in this circle, at home. Then I think how strange that is, to feel at home hundreds of miles from my own home, in a room full of strangers who fate has brought together through suffering. Here, in this room, I am not afraid, and I no longer feel alone. We are fighting together for our children's lives. We are here because we need help ourselves, and we are not afraid to admit it. We are here to help each other by telling and listening to our stories, holding nothing back.

I hold Pat's hand as he talks, squeezing tighter as he reaches for the tissue box. "I miss my son," he says, his voice shaking with emotion. "I want my son back."

~

On the second day, Steve tells a story: "I was seeing a counselor, and every week, it seems, I talked about this huge rock I was trying to push up a hill. I'd get almost to the top of the hill, and then the rock would roll right back on top of me."

He smiles and shifts in his chair. "So, one day, I'm talking again about this Sisyphean task and how powerless I feel as I keep trying to push that thing up the hill. The counselor listens patiently, and when I'm done, she says, 'Why don't you walk away from the rock?' Well, I had no idea what she meant. 'Walk away from the mountain, walk away from the rock,' she says again. I just keep staring at her, trying to figure out what she wants me to do. 'Steve, the rock is your anger and shame. You keep yourself chained to it. You keep trying to push it up the mountain, and it keeps rolling back down and flattening you. You carry that boulder with you everywhere. Why not just walk away from it?'

"Well, damn, I never thought of that," Steve says with a self-effacing grin. "I never thought that I could just walk away from the rock. I thought I was chained to it forever."

He starts to laugh. A moment later, he's laughing so hard, he's having trouble catching his breath. Susan starts laughing, and then Tim, and Taylor, and then we're all laughing, big belly laughs, laughter that brings tears to our eyes. We reach for the tissues and start kicking the boxes across the room, tears running down our cheeks.

~

I don't know exactly when it happened—on the first day when Tim started sobbing, on the second day when Steve told his story, or on the third "Knees to Knees" day—but a switch was thrown, a light came on, and something inside me, inside all of us, gave way. We gave in. We let go. A community was formed in that room, with the snow falling outside in monstrous Montana flakes, with the plastic chairs moving together into a tighter and tighter circle, with the tears and the laughter and the tissue boxes at our feet, ready to be booted across the room or picked up and passed to our nearest neighbor. With the stories being told and the emotions being expressed, with the listening and the talking and the silences, some sort of miracle happened. It wasn't the miracle I expected or originally hoped for, but it was the miracle I needed, the miracle we'd all been waiting for, whether we knew it or not.

I remember Ben D.'s words: The miracle hasn't happened yet. I was waiting for the miracle to embrace Ben, to hold him tight and wake him up to the truth that his addiction was threatening his life. But there is more than one miracle to be discovered in this life, and I found it there, in that room, so far from home, with people I would never have met if it hadn't been for our common story. We became a community, and in that community, we realized how we were all connected—not by being consoled, not by words intended to calm us down, not even by a pat on the hand, a hug, or words of encouragement about our courage, strength, or long-suffering commitment to our children. Rather, we were bound together by our grief and our guilt, by our shame and our soul-sickness, by our fear and our pain. What had been hidden inside for so long was brought to light, our secrets revealed. In the mirror of each other's stories, we discovered ourselves.

For a moment, as I think these thoughts, I step back into the pages of *The Spirituality of Imperfection.* I think about the section Ernie and I wrote on mutuality. It's all coming alive now, the words are jumping off the pages we wrote so many years ago, leaping right into my heart and settling into the folds of my soul. I get it, I finally get it, the number one rule of what Ernie calls "mutuality"—we get by giving, and we give by getting.

> Our need for *mutuality* arises from our very flawedness
> and imperfection; it originates in the fact that by
> ourselves we are never enough. We need others to help
> us; we need others in order to help them. Thus, the
> question "Who am I?" carries within itself another, even
> more important question: "Where do I belong?" We
> find *self*—ourselves—only through the actual practice of
> locating ourselves within the community of our fellow
> human beings.

Of course, of course—this is the spirituality of imperfection come into real life. Once again, I am stepping into the pages of my book. Or is the book stepping into the pages of me? I don't know; it doesn't matter. I realize we are all struggling with spiritual dilemmas, whether or not we call them that, and they arise from the basic awareness, perhaps the most important awareness of all: *Something is wrong with me, and I can't fix it by myself. I need help.* This painful place—this place of grieving, of loss, of fear and helplessness—is being transformed by our willingness to tell our stories and, perhaps more important, to listen to other people's stories, and in the mirror of their pain and despair, discover ourselves.

In that leap of faith that allows us to expose our brokenness—our failures, imperfections, flaws, and limitations—to others (soulmates now, but strangers just hours before), we give them permission to reveal their own brokenness. In the telling of and listening to our stories, we are no longer ashamed. Like the falling snow outside the windows, shame melts into the ground, becoming part of the earth, part of the coming and going of all life.

I look at Susan across the circle, and I realize I am looking at myself. She has bright blue eyes, while my eyes are dark brown. She is five foot seven, and I am barely five foot three. She is from West Virginia, and I am from Washington. She is ten years younger than me. But the differences between us no longer matter, for she is my twin; her story is my story, and when she speaks, I am listening to my own heart expressing its deepest truth.

This is the miracle. We belong together because we are engaged in the same quest as we search for answers to our most anguished questions. In that journey, we reflect back to each other the meaning of our own experience. In telling the truth about myself, I *discover* the truth about myself. I have come to know myself in the honest, unashamed, unedited telling of my story. Like the others in the room, I let go of that vision of myself as someone who is holding it all together, who is in control. I let go, though not without some initial concern that I will be found out, that people will hide from me or laugh at me or feel superior to me. But my self-consciousness quickly fades away, because I am no longer lost. I am found. I am found within this circle of "others," through this community of fellow human beings who are hurting and afraid but fearless when it comes to admitting our need for help and support. This is where we belong, where we "fit." We share our stories, and as we join our stories with others who are on the same journey, we discover a story that is shared.

We are not alone.

~

Ben's hair is cut short, almost to his scalp. He sits across from us with his hands tightly grasped together. He doesn't smile. I look at Susan, whose eyes are filling with tears. She has heard so much about Ben, and now here he is—so close that we can touch him, yet so closed up and closed in on himself that he is beyond our reach.

It's his turn to tell the group his story, revealing the bulk of the iceberg that lies underneath our awareness, beneath even our ability to comprehend. A cold, deep-blue truth.

"Remember that day," he says, looking at me, his tone bordering on belligerence. "The day when you found the pipe?"

"Yes." My voice is almost a whisper.

He looks down at his hands. The knuckles are raw and chapped from the Montana cold. They are red and then they are white as he pushes his hands together and then relaxes them. Red white red white red white.

He starts to cry, the tears become sobs, and the knuckles stay white. "When you left that morning, I went back in the house. I found a bottle of vodka in the basement cupboard and mixed it with orange juice. I got drunk and drove to school.

"I smoked weed every day, before school, after school. Every day.

"Remember when you went on vacation and left me to take care of the house? You told the neighbors to check in on me, but I called them and told them not to worry if I had friends over. Just a small group of good friends, I said, no partying or anything. Well, I had parties every night you were gone.

"I snorted cocaine with freshmen and sophomores. In your house. Kids you know, kids whose parents you know, parents who have no idea what their kids were doing that night.

"I took pills. I smoked crack. I blacked out. One time in high school, I was in the Honda, and I was drunk and blacked out. I was driving down the middle of the road when I came out of the blackout, and a car was coming straight at me.

"I blacked out all the time. I took prescription drugs with alcohol and blacked out. I didn't care what drug I took—I was addicted to getting high.

"I woke up in my own vomit more times than I can count. One time during my senior year in high school, I went to a party and brought a bag of marijuana and six-pack of beer with me. One of Dad's students from Whitman was there. A geology major. He told me how much he liked Dad, and we drank beer together. Later, I was out puking in the yard, and he came outside to see if I was okay. One of Dad's students—and I'm standing there puking."

He shakes his head, as if he is trying to dislodge the memory. He starts to cry, and then, in the next instant, he is angry. "There's so much you don't know. I got the dogs stoned."

I look at Pat. The dogs. Nessie, who died at age fourteen in October of Ben's senior year. And Sophie. Murphy, our new puppy—did he get her stoned, too? I look at Pat and the girls, and they are staring at Ben in disbelief.

Alison can't help herself. "What about Sasha?" she says, her voice shaking. Sasha is her ferret.

"Sasha, too," Ben says. Ali bursts into tears.

~

Ben and I sit on two chairs facing each other, our knees touching. The chairs are placed in the middle of the circle. All eyes are on us as we each take a turn to speak about our regrets, resentments, and affirmations.

I look at the sheet of yellow paper with the heading "Knees to Knees." My hands are shaking. I wish I weren't so nervous. I wish my voice didn't shake. I wish this was all over.

"I have many regrets," I begin, reading from my list. "I regret things I've said to you when I was angry and frustrated. I regret calling you names, saying you were lazy. Once I called you 'useless.' I even called you an 'asshole.'" The tears start and won't stop. I feel so ashamed of myself, so exposed.

I look at the paper in my shaking hands. "I regret being so controlling at times. I regret not being a better listener. I regret not supporting you when you said you wanted to join the swim team."

Deep breath. "Okay. My resentments. I resent your anger. Your attitude. Your harsh words and, at other times, your unwillingness to talk to me—the way you would leave the room and slam doors, punch holes in walls, swear at us."

I read the next item on my list of resentments. *Five fingers, five toes.* I have no idea what I resent about his fingers and toes. Maybe I resent the fact that he was born with everything he needed, all his necessary parts, and yet he turned to drugs. *Oh, Kathy,* I think to myself. *Do you blame him for using drugs? Don't most people who get in trouble with drugs have five fingers and five toes? What's the point?*

I skip ahead to the affirmations. "You have such a good, kind heart. There's a sweetness about you, an openness to life, to new experiences. I love your sense of humor and the way you love to make people laugh. I love your red hair and freckles." Ben has a disgusted look on his face, which throws me off. I shouldn't have mentioned his red hair; he hates his red hair. Why did I write that down? I'm unnerved and quickly read through the rest of my list. "You're so smart, you love to read, and you're a beautiful writer. I love all those things about you."

I don't know how long I spoke. Panic erased most of my memory. I do remember that both of our knees were shaking, and it seemed a struggle to keep them together.

It's Ben's turn to list his resentments, regrets, and affirmations. I listen, but I do not hear him. The words do not register. Panic again, I guess, because even minutes later, I cannot remember one single thing he said.

The only detailed record I have of the "Knees to Knees" exercise is Alison's list. Her classes at the University of Montana start up halfway through Family Week, so she writes him a "Knees to Knees" letter that he received after he returned from his wilderness trip.

Dear Ben,
How ya doin', buddy? You're back from your trip if you are reading this, so how was it? I imagine you in a snow cave (right?) eating berries and singing Kumbaya (sp!!). Ha ha just kidding, but it's a funny image. I'm curious to know how it is going for you—I bet you enjoyed it.

It was so good seeing you, Ben. I was so happy to be able to spend time with you and laugh and joke like we used to do. I'm so proud that you have accepted everything that is going on and decided to change things you want to before it's too late. Life is too short. We all love you so much and want you to be happy. Ben D. asked me to do some regrets, resentments and affirmations, so that's what I'll do now.

Regrets

– I really wish we could have been closer in high school. I know you had your friends, I had mine, and we were doing different things but after what you said in group about feeling angry and the need to bully people, I feel like there is something I could have done. I'm sorry I didn't realize how much pain you were going through. From now on I will be more attentive to your feelings, because you are like that with mine.
– I wish I could have talked to you more about John. It seemed like you had so much anger/emotions built up that you didn't let out because you had no one (or not very many people) to talk to. If you ever need to talk about John, Benny, please know you can talk to me. I didn't realize that his death had such a huge impact on you (as it should of).

Resentments

– I resent that the time we had the most time together, when we both lived at home, when life was easier and we didn't have as many responsibilities, you weren't there. We will never get that time back, Benny, when we can live together as brother and sister. I think of all the things we could have done—watched movies,

done stupid things, played in the snow, music
videos, etc. That time of our life is somewhat gone,
and lost. I know we did have good times, but the
anger, arguments, fights, yelling replaced some of the
happy times we could have shared. And it's not only
you, Benno. I started arguments and fights, etc. The
resentment I feel is on both of our parts. I'm just glad
we have our whole lives to catch up on that.

— Family get-togethers—I know you know all of this
already but it is a big resentment of mine. It not only
includes you changing the moods of our get-togethers
by starting an argument (or more frequently just
being uninvolved because a lot of times it was other
people who started it!!), but that you weren't there
whether physically or emotionally. When you weren't
there it wasn't the same. I wanted to cry all through
Thanksgiving dinner this year because you were sad.
Like I said before, that time is gone now. Who knows
if we will ever get that again? It killed me to see you
so sad and not yourself. That dinner would have
been so much fun if you were there mentally as well
as physically. You make everything 100 times better,
Benny, just remember that.

Affirmations

— YOU ARE SO TALENTED! I have no doubt in my
mind that you are going to be a fantastic writer. Go for
it Benny. . . . I know you can do it.

— You're so damn funny—seriously Ben, Robyn and I
all through Christmas break tried to think of all the
funny things you would do, and I really missed those
things. Even when you weren't trying to be funny
(mashed potatoes on your face, etc.) People love you
for that—you're just fucking hilarious.

– You're compassionate. You love to love and care about others. Your sensitivity is part of this—because you're really open to other people's feelings and don't want to hurt them. That's what was so weird about how you acted the past few years. The compassionate Benny was gone from the surface, but I knew that he was still underneath, and still felt bad for things he said or did, but just underneath. Let him out!! You have no idea how much people love him.

– You're a great brother. You are protective over me and Robyn, which I love because I know I can turn to you if someone needs their ass kicked. Just kidding. But you will always be there for me, care for me and make me laugh. Same goes for you, Benny. Always know that you can count on me.

I love you so much.
Alison

On the last day of the family program, we meet at the treatment center for the "Ropes Course" exercise. The boys join us. We stand outside, where Ben D. and several other counselors blindfold all of us with bandannas and place our hands on a rope. I think Pat and Robyn are behind me and Steve is just in front of me, but we are staggered several feet apart, so I can't be sure where the voices are coming from. We walk slowly over the frozen ground, slipping and stumbling over rocks or tree roots, heading to an unknown destination. We're all nervous as we are led up and down some hilly areas and then through a copse of trees, where I stretch my arm out in front of me to avoid the tree branches. The person in front of me is walking too fast, and I hold back a bit, putting pressure on the rope.

"It's okay," I hear Steve's voice just ahead of me. "You can keep moving forward." Behind me, the rope stretches and tightens, and I find myself echoing Steve's words: "It's okay; you're safe." We walk through an open area, and a few minutes later, one of the counselors gently removes my hand from the rope and guides me to duck under a different rope, placing my hand on yet another rope. Now we are farther away from each other, spread apart, and I feel alone, abandoned, with just a rope in my right hand and no idea where the others are on that rope.

"You are in a maze," I hear Ben D.'s voice off to my left. "You need to find a way out of it on your own. Hold onto the rope, don't let go, and follow it until you can get out of the maze."

I go round and round the rope in a circle, it seems, and then another circle—how many circles are there?—trying to find the exit point. Ten or fifteen minutes go by, and I'm getting more and more annoyed. I change direction on the rope, and a counselor removes my hand for a moment so I can pass by someone going in the opposite direction. I turn back around and then around again. I'm going to beat this thing.

I hear someone say, "I'm out," and now the old competitive fire is really heating up, because he found a way out before I did. I was sure I'd be one of the first people out of the maze.

It's cold; my hands feel frozen. I hear another person say, "I'm out," and then I hear someone laugh softly. I wonder how many of us are still trapped in this maze. What is wrong with me that I'm not smart enough to figure this out? At one point, I try to climb under the rope, but a voice says, "That's not the way," and a hand guides me back into the maze.

I've had it. I stop and just stand there, stubborn, frustrated, pissed off. I realize there's no way out of this damn maze; it's some stupid trick.

"I can't figure this out," I say, fighting back tears of frustration. A counselor who is walking near me—or has he been walking beside me this whole time?—asks, "Do you need help?" Unable to keep the irritation out of my voice, I say, "Yes, I need help."

He takes my hand off the rope, lifts it over my head, and lets me out of the maze. Then he unties my bandanna and says, "You're out."

"How did I get out?" I ask. I really have no idea.

He leans forward to whisper in my ear. "You asked for help."

The "out" group stands quietly, watching the two people who remain in the maze, going round and round and round, getting more and more aggravated. They do not ask for help, nor do they voice their annoyance at being trapped in a maze with no hope of getting out. Like me, they are going to try to figure this out, damn it, and they are not going to ask for help. They stop only when they walk into each other.

"Do you want help?" one of the counselors says.

They both nod their heads. A counselor removes their bandannas. Pat and Ben look at each other, hands still holding onto the rope, eyes blinking in the bright sunlight.

12

help me

January–June 2006

elp me, help me. HelpmeHelpmeHelpme.
Here I am praying nonstop—me, the agnostic, the person who responded to the question posed by a teenager incarcerated in the detention center, "But Kathy, don't you believe in God?" with the words, "I'm not sure yet. My faith is still under construction."

Do I believe in God? I'm getting closer. Not to the God in the clouds or the heavens, not to the God that dispenses special favors to certain people but not to others, not to the God of Thunderous Judgments, Rapturous Returns, or Purgatory and Perdition.

What God, then? The Unknown God, whom I think I see in the wind moving the leaves in the trees or the grasses in the field. The God of Nature—perhaps the same God Henry David Thoreau met in the woods when he perceived that "every little pine-needle expanded and swelled with sympathy and befriended me." The Mysterious God, who might have been there before the Big Bang, thus creating the universe, or who might have appeared afterward in an attempt to generate order out of chaos. The Gentle God, who might have—or might not have—created kindness, forgiveness, mercy, and love.

To the God who might be there but who might not be, who might listen and respond but who almost certainly will be too busy elsewhere, to this nameless mystery, this unfathomable ambiguity, I whisper, "Help me."

And yet, sometimes I wonder if it is God who might need *our* help. The story about God searching for Adam in the garden haunts me. I know the gist of the ancient legend, of course—the serpent, the apple, the bite, the shame, the running and hiding—but I never understood it, really. What's the big deal? The apples were sweet and ripe, Adam and Eve were innocents, and evil existed even in the Garden. Why did they have to run away and hide? Why was God so distraught? There was something about this interaction between God and Adam that got to me, worked its way under my skin, into my bones.

One day, while searching around on the Internet, I Googled "God and Adam." The garden legend popped up, but it was a different version that I hadn't seen before. At the end of the tale is a question.

"Where are you, Adam?" God asks. I hear the anguish in God's voice, and I get shivers from my head to my toes. It happens every time I read those words: "Where are you, Adam?" I think about God looking for his beloved son, but Adam is hiding away in the bushes somewhere, covering his private parts with leaves or twigs or snake skins—who knows. The point is he is hiding, and he does not want to be found. I have to repeat that—*he does not want to be found.* And God, who can see Adam in all his nakedness, who knows exactly where he is hiding—because God, it is said, can see everything—has this sinking heart, because he realizes that his son is hiding from him. His child is lost and does not want to be found.

I see my son standing right in front of me. I see his brown eyes and his dark red hair, the color of brick dust, and his freckles, and his big smile, but I can't find him, because he is hiding from me. He is right there, but he is hiding and does not want to be found.

Where are you, Benny?

At that moment, I want to cry out to the unseen heavens, "Oh, God. I know how you feel."

~

Ben is at Gray Wolf Ranch, a residential extended care facility in Port Townsend, Washington, for four to six months. After his sixteen-day wilderness trip—"he did great," Ben D. told us, "he was a real leader out there"—he spent one more week at Wilderness Treatment Center and then flew directly from Kalispell to Seattle, where a Gray Wolf counselor met his plane and drove him to Port Townsend.

Ben is beyond angry—fury doesn't even begin to capture it—for agreeing with Ben D.'s recommendation for additional treatment. He's also pissed that Wilderness decided to delay giving him his graduation coin—a gold medallion emblazoned with the Serenity Prayer—until he'd spent at least a month at Gray Wolf. They wanted to be sure he got there and stayed there. And every day, according to Kirk, his new counselor, Ben threatened to leave. But he stayed, knowing that we were not going to budge from our position that if he left treatment, he was on his own.

Gray Wolf is expensive; insurance doesn't cover the cost. So, we get a second mortgage on our house and borrow tens of thousands of dollars from relatives. Maybe we're foolish. Maybe we should let him go out into the world, knowing what he knows now about himself and his disease, and either find his way or stumble and fall. He will learn from his failures, and he will keep falling and suffering until he is sick and tired of it all—until he hits bottom. That's the advice we get from friends and experts alike, who believe it does no good to throw so much money into treatment and extended care if Ben isn't ready to quit. I understand the wisdom of that advice, but I also know what happens when people hit bottom. Sometimes they don't bounce back. Sometimes they die.

The money doesn't matter. Going into debt doesn't matter. What matters is that we do everything we can to help Ben find his way. He's lost now, but somewhere in there is the Ben who wants to be found. I know that. I have to believe that.

And so I pray. "Help me!" I am not praying for God to help *me* or to even *help* me; I am praying for God to help me help myself. HelpMeHelpMe. I am praying for strength, for courage. I need help in order to help myself. My prayer is both an acceptance and an acknowledgment: an acceptance of my inability to do this on my own and an acknowledgment that I have to pull my own weight. I can't leave the heavy lifting to God.

"I say my prayers every night," Marc, age fourteen, says in the detention group one day. "I ask God to help me. But I can't blame God when things go wrong. He gives me a path to run down, and if I keep going down the wrong path, He ain't gonna help me." Like Marc, I say my prayers every night. I'm praying for reconciliation, reconnection, forgiveness—not just with or for others, but with and for myself. I need to reconcile and reconnect myself to *what is* rather than *what might be* or *what could have been*. I am struggling to let go and, in William James's brilliant imagery, to give my "convulsive self a rest." I'm not the one in control here. I have made mistakes. I have imperfections—so many of them, I've lost count. And I have wrestled with my lack of control, believing that if I fight hard enough and love deeply enough, I can make miracles happen and bring my son back to me, wounded but whole.

I cannot. I cannot save Ben's life. That is his task, his challenge, his fate.

I add one more short prayer to my daily routine. Waking up I say, "Help me." At night, after turning off the light, I place my hands together, fingers interlaced, and whisper, "Thank you."

~

Ben has been at Gray Wolf for three months when I get the phone call from my sister-in-law.

"I think it's time," Jody says in a voice so soft I have to strain to hear her.

Time, I think. *Time.*

My brother John's cancer has progressed. He does not have much time left.

I fly to New Jersey to spend a week with John, Jody, and their daughter, Casey, age fourteen. Casey is dying, too, of a rare neurological disorder called giant axonal neuropathy. She is unable to walk and spends her days in a wheelchair or propped up next to her father on the couch in their log cabin. Patch, her shih tzu, is always next to Casey and often sits or sleeps on the tray on her wheelchair, keeping her company.

There is something about Casey—some angelic presence pervades her, as if she is here on this earth but also part of another world. When someone is sad, she comforts them with her eyes or a hand raised slowly and with much effort, reaching out to soothe and console.

Never once have I heard her complain. I'll never forget when she was four or five years old, watching her siblings and cousins chasing geese at a park. Pat was with her, holding her hand. She looked up at him and said, "I haven't learned how to run yet. Would you carry me?" He put her on his shoulders, and they ran across the lawn, her pigtails bouncing, her laughter ringing across the open field.

When all her cousins, aunts, uncles, brothers, and sisters are gathered together in the same room, all the loving energy radiates around Casey. It's as if she absorbs that energy and reflects it back, a shining light of love and compassion. I often wonder if she is in pain but somehow doesn't recognize it as pain, or perhaps the progressive nerve death offers this one gift of taking the pain away, purifying her of everything but love and gratitude. It is a mystery to me, and I am in awe of her.

"Be prepared," my nephew Steve says when he picks me up at the Newark airport. Dark circles surround his eyes, and he looks at me with tender concern, choosing his words carefully. "Dad is very thin, very fragile. His liver is failing." He clears his throat, and his voice is husky with emotion. "He's jaundiced, Kath, and his skin is really yellow. Almost orange."

When I see John, maybe I am prepared, because he looks stunningly beautiful to me, as if lit up from inside, a candle glowing in a dark place. I give him a hug.

"Hey, Johnny," I say, willing back the tears.

"Hey, Kath. How are *you*?" His voice is surprisingly strong, and he places the emphasis on *you*. I've spent hours in doctors' offices and hospital rooms with John over the past two years, and whenever a nurse or a doctor appears and asks the inevitable "how are you" question, Johnny always responds with the words, "I'm fine. How are *you*?" They love him, of course. Everyone loves John.

I remember the time, several months earlier, when I walked into his hospital room after the Whipple procedure—what seemed to me a medieval type of torture. In this complex surgery, doctors remove the "head," or wide part, of the pancreas, which butts up against the first stretch of the small intestine, as well as part of the common bile duct, the gallbladder, and the stomach. After all the various and sundry parts are detached, disconnected, amputated, sawed off (I know, I'm being dramatic, but this is my brother's insides we're talking about), surgeons stitch together the remaining intestine, bile duct, and pancreas.

"Can I see your scar?" I asked. I was not morbidly interested; I just wanted to somehow walk this journey with him in every way I could.

"Oh, Kath," he said, looking at my camera. "Really?"

I didn't feel the slightest bit of shame at this invasion of his privacy, because in my mind, I was simply recording his enduring will to live. I wanted photographs that I could show him years later—because I had no doubt he would be one of the twenty percent of pancreatic cancer patients who reach a five-year survival rate after the Whipple. He was strong, my brother—a former national champion swimmer, a self-taught woodworker, father of five children—and both gentle and fierce, quiet and outspoken. I wanted to keep him with me always, Whipple and all, forever.

He lifted his hospital gown and showed me the scar that stretched from one hip to the base of his sternum and looped back around to the other hip. I must have gasped, for he looked down at the scar and then back up at me, a child-like grin on his face. "Maybe it looks like a frown to you, Kath," he said. "But it's a smile to me."

Aw, Johnny. Awe. Johnny.

~

One day, during that last week I spend with him, we are alone in the cabin, and John asks if I would mind giving him a bath. With my help, he strips naked and steps into the round Jacuzzi bathtub. He sits cross-legged with his head bowed. A small moan of pleasure escapes him as the warm water surrounds him.

"It just feels so good," he says smiling, looking up at me. In his face, I see a little boy. I picture my mother bathing him when he was an infant and remember the bath-time song she used to sing to all of us in a high, sing-song voice. "Oh, I wish I was a little cake of soap. How I wish I was a little cake of soap. I'd go slippy and slidey over everybody's hidey! How I wish I was a little cake of soap!"

John asks if I would wash his hair. I put a small amount of baby shampoo in the palms of my hands and massage his head. He doesn't have much hair left, and he is so thin, so terribly frail, his shoulder bones jutting out from his back, his neck muscles stretched forward. His head feels so tiny, so vulnerable. Again he moans an "ahhh" of contentment, even of wonder. I ask him to close his eyes as I fill a measuring cup and pour water over his head; another "ahhh" of pure pleasure escapes him. He is a naked Buddha sitting under a waterfall—yellow skin, white bones, and shining soul, perfectly content, joyfully serene.

The day before I fly back to Walla Walla, I ask if he wants to sit outside in the sunshine. "I'd love that," he says. I pull two chairs into a sunny spot on the driveway, facing a birch tree—or perhaps it is an aspen. It doesn't matter. I cover him with blankets, for there's a slight chill in the air. We sit next to each other, holding hands, looking at the sun lighting up the leaves, which seem to quiver with joy. "Beautiful," he whispers.

He closes his eyes and falls asleep. Matching his breathing, I doze off. When I open my eyes, he is staring at the lit-up leaves, eyes wide in wonder. I squeeze his hand.

"What are you thinking about, Johnny?" I ask in a whisper.

"Oh," he says after a moment. "This dying part."

I want so much to ask him questions. I want to know about this dying part—what it is like, how it feels—to know that life is now to be measured in minutes and hours, not days, weeks, or years. But it is as if a veil has fallen between us. This is holy ground, and I am not to intrude. I have wondered, over the years, if he wanted me to ask questions, to probe with him the meaning of it all—of life, of death, of all that comes between. But I believe now, as I felt then, that words would fail, as words always do when confronted with something so momentous, so indescribable, so terrifying, and, at the same time, so astonishingly beautiful as life just before death.

John dies on May 10, five days after I return home. He is fifty-eight years old.

～

On Friday, June 2, Pat and I drive to Port Townsend for Ben's Gray Wolf "graduation" ceremony. When we arrive, I hand Ben a letter I wrote a few days earlier. He tosses it in his duffel bag, which is packed and ready to go. I have no idea if he ever read it.

Dear Ben:
Life. I think about these last six months and what we have all gone through. Your journey has been the most remarkable. Those first six weeks at Wilderness Treatment Center were not easy for you, not in any sense of the word. They were lonely, miserable, agonizing, terrifying . . . but you stuck it out. You were suffering deeply but you stuck it out. Few people in this world know what strength and courage it took to get through those weeks at WTC—few people will ever have to call on that kind of inner strength. I've heard people say that drug-addicted individuals have no willpower—but I would like to give them an addiction for a few months and see what willpower they have against a disease that takes hold of your body, mind, and spirit and affects most directly the organ that makes decisions, controls impulses, and oversees behavior—the brain. People just do not understand this disease and how powerful it is.

So now you are off, six months clean and sober, starting a new life. You have earned respect from everyone who knows you. You have made us happy and proud, and Robyn and Alison, too. When you love someone as much as we all love you, your life is so inextricably intertwined with theirs that when they suffer, you suffer, and when they are filled with joy or pride, you are, too. I have come to realize that I am happy only when I make other people happy. When I do something that hurts others or when I think only about myself, I feel bad about myself.

As Abraham Lincoln once said, "When I do good, I
feel good. When I do bad, I feel bad. That's my religion."

To me, that sums up the Twelve Steps—when we are
honest, humble, grateful, forgiving, compassionate, and
serve others, we feel good and when we are not, we feel bad.

I want you to feel good, Ben. I want you to BE good
in your heart and in your actions, because that is the
only way you can feel good about yourself.

Be good, my love. For your life affects more people
than you will ever know and what happens to you,
happens to us, too.

I believe in you, I have faith in you, and I love you
with all my heart,

Mom

We arrive at Gray Wolf and meet with Ben in his counselor's office. Ben
likes Kirk. He describes him as "gentle" and a "cool dude." In the four
months that Ben has been at Gray Wolf, Kirk calls us once a week or so
to report on his progress. They are short calls, for the most part. At first
I was disappointed, wanting more information—I had been spoiled
by Ben D.'s long, detailed phone conversations. As strange as it might
seem, there's something psychologically absorbing—some might say
addictive—about living in crisis. Ben's addiction (in my mind, the
demon has metamorphosed into a monstrous spider) spun its web in
myriad directions—physical, mental, emotional, spiritual—wrapping
us in a snarl of confusion from which we could not escape. Our hearts
beat faster; our minds were deluged with terrifying thoughts; our emotions raged out of control; and our spirits were dulled, even deadened.
Over time, this tangled confusion became familiar to us; even as it
kept us separated and pulled apart, it also tied us together, for we had a
common theme to our daily lives, a topic that consumed our thoughts
and our conversations.

As the weeks go by and the daily phone calls turn into brief
weekly reports, often filled with good news about Ben's part-time

job at a golf course and his progress in individual and group therapy, we begin to unspin ourselves. Sleep comes easier. Dreams are less frightening. Conversations turn to other topics—Robyn's life in San Diego and her applications to speech therapy master's programs; Ali's upcoming graduation and plans to move to Ireland for the summer; my book with William Moyers, soon to be released; Pat's preparations for his new geology class based on John McPhee's books, which he titled "Pages of Stone"; and my ongoing efforts to start recovery support services in our community for addicted youth and their family members. We are building up energy for our own lives once again, breathing deeper, reconnecting with friends, expanding our world—and, in the process, finding our spirits lifted and our hopes anchored to reality.

It takes time to readjust to slow, regular heartbeats and a mind that is settling itself back into place, adjusting once again to the common and the ordinary. But as time passes and Ben seems to be adjusting to the routine at Gray Wolf, both Pat and I begin to feel a sense of relief as we have more time to focus on each other and our own lives. The last few months with my brother have also diverted me from obsessing about Ben.

All of which is to say, I'm not at all prepared for what happens next.

Kirk is silent as Ben begins to talk. I expect him to tell us about what he has learned and what he plans to do when he leaves Gray Wolf in just a few hours. I even hope he'll express some gratitude or appreciation for the experiences he has had in treatment and the people who have worked so hard to help him. I should have kept Hobbes's comic advice in mind to lower my expectations to the point where they're already met. But hope dies hard, and we hold on as long as we possibly can—maybe longer than we should.

"I wanted to be part of the family, but you," Ben says, looking directly at me, "made it impossible because you would always glare at me and make me feel uncomfortable. That's why I'd leave the house and go out and use. You hate drugs; you think everyone is like your Juvie kids. There's no way I was ever going to win. That's why everything fell apart.

"It was the way it was handled, always so public. It was everyone else's business that I was struggling—like, 'Let's talk about my son and his revolting behavior, his horrendous addiction.' My aunts and uncles and cousins and our friends were all talking to people, giving details. Why the fuck did they ever need to know about this? Why were they invited to give an opinion about my drug use? About me?"

Ben is sitting on the edge of his chair, red-faced and ready to bolt. "You had a hand in making me who I am. There was always this demonization of drugs. You always had this thing about marijuana being a bad drug for kids, a gateway drug. If someone smokes, you need to do something about it; you need to jump right on it. All that was dumped on me. Why didn't you ask what was going on? Why didn't we have a conversation? Marijuana was my way of dealing with things, with life, with death. But always, always there was this demonization."

I take a deep breath and the tape starts running in my mind, *God, grant me the serenity to accept the things I cannot change, the courage to change the things I can, and the wisdom to know the difference,* over and over and over. I'm trying to create a safe place for myself with the building blocks of serenity, courage, and wisdom. But they are just words, and as hard as I try to make them stand up straight and tall, they crumble before me. Because *nothing has changed.* I am the enemy. Our family is the enemy. Aunts, uncles, cousins are the enemy. We—especially me—are the cause of all his problems. It is all our fault.

Ben leaves the office, and we watch him from Kirk's office window, shooting hoops by himself. Kirk is talking, but my mind doesn't register one word of what he says, because every bit of my energy is invested in trying to hold myself together. I wonder what I look like to this older, experienced counselor. Can he see through whatever mask I'm wearing to the quaking and quivering inside?

I hear the bounce-bounce-bounce of the basketball. I see the trees outside Kirk's window, with the new green leaves lifting and tilting with the wind. I feel Pat's hand reaching for mine and the gentle squeeze of his hand. I am here, I remind myself. I am real. *This* is real.

Let it be.

~

We gather in the community room for the graduation ceremony. Pat and I sit on a couch, flanking Ben. Several dozen boys, all between the ages of fourteen and twenty-five years, line the perimeter of the room. It is a rectangular room, but in my memory, we are sitting in a circle. As I look from one face to the next, I think to myself, "Such beautiful boys."

Ben has chosen six friends and two counselors to speak at the ceremony. One by one, they walk into the center of the room. They lock eyes with Ben, and not once does their gaze waver as they cut straight through the superficialities and platitudes and tell him they're worried about him. They don't think he is ready to leave.

"I wish we had a few more months with you," one of his counselors says. "You're starting to get it; the light is just starting to come on. I only wish we had a few more months."

"I love you, man," Blake says. He's tall, blonde, skinny, maybe sixteen or seventeen years old. He asks Ben if he remembers sharing a tent when they were in the Olympic Mountains on a wilderness excursion. All Blake wanted to do was talk, but Ben didn't want to talk; he just wanted to read his book.

"I never could figure that out about you, Ben," Blake shakes his head, an amused smile on his face. "All you want to do is read books. But like I said, I love you, man. You make me laugh like no one has ever been able to make me laugh."

Daniel, Ben's roommate, sits down on the floor, looking up at Ben on the couch. He says he has too much to say, and he doesn't want to stand the whole time he's talking. Ben laughs and then uses his sleeve to wipe the tears from his eyes.

Daniel talks about his first roommate at Gray Wolf, "the worst roommate in the whole world." He couldn't wait for him to leave and get a new roommate. Finally, the guy packs his bags, and the counselors tell Daniel he's getting a new roommate. His name is Ben.

"So, I figure this Ben kid can't be any worse than the first guy; he's gotta be better, right? But guess what? You were worse. I couldn't believe that I got stuck with you. 'What are they doing to me?' I thought. 'Why do I deserve this?'"

Daniel starts laughing, and Ben laughs with him. "It got better. It got a whole lot better. But man, I wish you weren't leaving, because I don't think you're ready. I'm afraid for you."

I wish I had a tape recording of that hour, when heartfelt honesty triumphed. Pat and I are a mess. Once the tears start, we can't stop them. Ben is crying, too, and we pass the box of tissues from parent to child and child to parent. My heart is breaking—the left chamber pulling away from the right, the valves disintegrating, muscles dissolving, arteries and veins pumping blood into the chest cavity. I swear I can feel the rupture.

A story comes to me at that moment—that's what stories do for me, they appear when I most need them—about a student who asks the rabbi why the Torah tells us to place holy words *upon* our hearts and not *in* our hearts. The rabbi responds: "It is because our hearts are closed, and so God places the words on top of our hearts, until one day our hearts break from the weight of it all and the words fall in."

I look at Ben. Is his heart breaking? I wonder what he is thinking and feeling as his friends tell him how much they care about him and how worried they are about him, because they all say in one way or another, *You're not ready. I wish you would stay. One more month. Just one more month.* I wonder if he wants to stay and get stronger. I wonder if he knows how much these boys love him—they are not afraid to speak that word, *love*—and if he loves them in the same way.

Kris, one of Ben's favorite counselors, is the last person to speak. "The rest of your life depends on who you choose to walk on either side of you," he says, speaking slowly and emphasizing each word. "You have two shoulders, Ben. Two. Not one. Choose wisely, for that choice will determine the pathway you will take in this life."

He hands Ben his medallion with a symbol of Gray Wolf Ranch on the front and the Serenity Prayer on the back. Now it is Ben's turn to speak. His hand closes tight over the heavy coin.

"I love you guys. I love Gray Wolf. I've learned so much here."

He holds up the medallion. "You have no idea how much this means to me," he says, his voice choking up with emotion as his eyes fill once again with tears. "Because those fucking bastards at Wilderness didn't give me my medallion."

We sit in stunned silence. I think Ben was trying to be funny and to somehow lighten the heaviness of the emotions he was experiencing. But no one laughs because it is the saddest statement ever of resentments that continue to fester and burn, altering reality and predicting the future. Whatever hope I have left is gone, crushed. He will use again. I know that. He knows it. Everyone in the room knows it.

As we're leaving, one of the counselors gives Ben a hug. "Remember, Ben, two shoulders. Two."

Then the counselor turns to me. "I wanted to tell you that I've read the book you wrote with Ernie Kurtz more than a dozen times. And on every page, with every story, I think about the line from one of Mary Oliver's poem: 'Tell me, what is it you plan to do with your one wild and precious life?'"

He looks at Ben, then, and I realize his words are meant for him, not me. *Tell me, what is it you plan to do with your one wild and precious life?*

I whisper those words to myself as we drive home in the dark. I think about my future self and wonder what I plan to do now—now that my brother is gone, now that Ben is finished with six months of treatment. In a few days, I will be fifty-seven years old, and in a few more days, Ben will be twenty.

What we do with our lives from this point forward is at once wholly separate and deeply connected.

13

in the shades of sorrow and hope

Summer 2006

Ben is quiet for the first ten miles or so. There are no other cars on the road. Our headlights outline the pine trees on either side of the road in black and white.

I listen to Ben talking on his cell phone.

"Hey man," he says in a voice loud enough for us to hear. "I'm out of prison. Free of my shackles. Let's get together soon."

I look at Pat, imagining his hands tightening on the wheel. In the space between us, there is sadness and fear and even despair. But now, in contrast to the past, the pain is more like a sigh than a howl. An exhalation, a letting go, an acknowledgment, and an acceptance that from now on, our son will choose his own path. We have done what we could. We have done all we could. And now he is free.

We drop Ben in Seattle to reunite with Q. His plan, he says, is to live with her, find a job for the summer, decide whether he wants to return to the University of Washington, and stay clean and sober. He promises to look into schools with sober dorms and recovery programs.

We don't hear from him for a while, nor do we try to contact him. This is his road, and we cannot choose the pathway forward. Only he can do that. He is responsible for his future, for his life. I remember almost word for word what Jim Milam and I wrote in *Under the Influence*:

> The alcoholic must understand that he is not responsible for the things he said or did when he was drinking. The physical addiction controlled his behavior and because he is powerless over the addiction, he cannot be held responsible for it. . . .

No alcoholic willfully became an alcoholic. He didn't know what was wrong with him. Once the alcoholic understands his disease and what it takes to stay sober, however, a moral obligation does enter the picture. *Now he knows*: If he follows the sobriety maintenance program, he will stay sober; if he willfully or carelessly deviates from the program, he will drink again and inflict the illness on himself and others. He has a clear choice now, and he should feel the moral imperative to make the right choice.

One day in mid-June, Ben calls to tell us that his friend Clinton wants Ben to join him and work for the summer at the Oregon coast marina his father owns. "I'll be getting up at 5:00 a.m., fixing boats, painting, pounding nails, helping customers," he says in an excited tone of voice. "The pay is decent, and it will be fun to spend the summer with Clinton. He'll be a really good influence on me, and I think he really wants to help."

We feel good about this plan. In high school, Clinton kept his distance from the drug scene and often expressed concern about Ben's behavior. Working long hours at the marina will also be good for Ben; maybe he will realize how much easier hard work is when he's clean and sober. What we don't know is that a store full of beer and wine is attached to the marina, and Ben can use his paycheck (or charge against future paychecks) to buy whatever he wants. He's just twenty years old—not old enough to buy alcohol, but he works for the marina, and as long as he gets his work done, he's pretty much left alone to do what he wants.

Two weeks into the job, we get a phone call. "I hate my boss," he says, but his voice is not full of bitterness or contempt. It is shaky and sad. "He spends all day yelling at me, telling me I'm worthless. I hate this. I hate life. I can't do this anymore."

"Do what, Ben?" I am holding my breath.

"Recovery. I can't do recovery anymore."

I don't know how to respond to those words, so I try to say something positive, something hopeful. "Sweetie, do you remember the time when you were feeling so discouraged about life, and I said 'This too shall pass'? And you responded, 'This too has meaning.' I thought that was so wise and wonderful."

"I'm tired of your philosophy, Mom," he says and hangs up.

I stare at the receiver for a moment, remembering something else Ben said just a few months ago on a phone call from Gray Wolf. "What if I used just now and then? Would you still love me?"

I walk out to the garden and talk to Pat. There's not much to say that we haven't said before. I go back to my office and email Ernie. He is always honest with me, and I'm struggling with the whole concept of "letting go," which feels too much to me like abandonment. I'm hoping, I write in the email, "to do the right thing." I'm hoping Ernie can help me wrap my mind around the concept of letting go and figure out how to "do" it. I wonder if it's truly possible for a parent to deeply, wholly "let go" of her own child.

Ernie's response does not contain the gentle, reassuring words I am seeking.

"Letting go" does not mean abandoning: letting go means relinquishing control. But did we really have control? Usually not, which is why letting go is so important: it is the surrender of a fantasy, and we are better off living in reality . . . not pretending or striving to possess the chimerical. No?

Those who really "surrendered" and have "gotten it" are usually not that certain of themselves. You speak of your "fear and trembling." It is Ben who must experience the "fear and trembling," and there is absolutely NOTHING you can do to help bring that about. Except, of course, allow him to live with the consequences of his own actions, which, if I can believe you (and I do), is exactly what you and Pat are doing.

You write that Ben called you "in utter despair"—I doubt it. It is too easy to cry for help at the moment of helplessness, yet feel in control again the moment our fingers feel the rope tossed to us.

"Hoping to do the right thing." The better phrase—and, more importantly, "thought"—is to make the effort to "do the next right thing." 'Tis time for bite-sized, baby-steps, one centimeter at a time.

Be brave! According to some statistics, the best realistic estimate is that only 15 percent of alcoholics get into recovery. Tough odds, but if I can do it, surely so can Ben.

With a very real love,
Ernie

I don't know why Ernie had to add that part about fifteen percent. He wants me to "be brave" and face the fact that Ben might never get sober? And then what? Panhandle? Sleep under bridges and park benches (that age-old image of the late-stage drunk)? Get hepatitis? Cirrhosis? Choke on his own vomit? Die of an overdose? Commit suicide?

It happens. I know it happens, right here, right in my own community, because I read the obituaries, and I hear the stories from family members and probation officers. A fifteen-year-old boy commits suicide just hours before he's scheduled to go to treatment. An eighteen-year-old is shot dead by a gang member because she can't pay for the drugs she's been using. A woman in her thirties, a teacher and loving mother of two children, dies of a raging infection from repeated methamphetamine injections. A twenty-five-year-old dies of a heroin overdose in his parents' basement minutes before Thanksgiving dinner, the needle still in his arm.

I know these mothers and fathers. I cry with them. I try to find the right words to say to them. I am silent with them. I know I might be one of them someday. And I know that no words anyone can say, no actions anyone can take, will ease their grief. I even help them write their children's obituaries. One mother, whose nineteen-year-old son hung himself in her basement—he had been sober for almost a year but relapsed just weeks before his suicide—tearfully gave me this advice to offer parents: "Don't give up. That's what I'd want parents to know. Don't give up. You can't ever give up."

How does "don't give up" square with "let go"?

And what about Ernie's advice to be brave? I'd like to know how I steel myself for the possibility that Ben may be one of the eighty-five percent who doesn't recover from drug addiction. How do I prepare for the phone call that will come one night or early morning, from the police or the coroner or whoever calls when people die in car accidents or overdoses or from sleeping outside in the freezing cold? Sorry, Ernie. I know you are trying to help me, I know you love me, but those are not words or images that build up my courage. They make me want to crumple up into a little ball and give up with one last final sigh. Maybe that is what letting go is all about.

A week later, Ben is fired for mouthing off to his boss. He calls us from a pay phone on the highway and asks us to drive to the coast to pick him up. Over the phone line, I can hear the cars whizzing by, and I have to strain to hear him. He says he's been drinking a lot, ten to twenty beers every night, making a fool of himself, getting into fights with his friend, arguing with his boss. "I told him to fuck off, and he told me to pack my bags."

I call Pat at his office. He's been working on his syllabuses for next year's classes and spending his days in the Palouse fields to the north of us, searching in the wind-blown silt for pig fossils buried sometime around 750,000 years ago.

"Shit" is all he says.

We drive to the coast and back in one day, six hours each way. Why do we keep rescuing Ben? I don't have an answer to that question except to say letting go is one tough road to follow. We know what we should do, what we've been told to do. If he's been using, he's not welcome at our house. If he shows up, we'll call the cops. And if he insists on coming home and agrees to our no-drug-use-no-backtalk rules, he can find his own way back to Walla Walla.

We don't do any of that. We pick him up and bring him home.

~

"I guess I really am an addict," he says after we've been on the road for a few hours. "I thought I could go out and drink, just have one or two beers. But I can't. Every time I drink, I get drunk."

I think about a story my friend Jack, in his seventies and twenty-plus years sober, told me over coffee one day. "So," he says in his Irish story-teller voice. "I'm at this AA meeting, and this huge lumberjack of a guy walks up to the front of the room to collect his one-year chip. He stands in front of the microphone—it's a big meeting, a few hundred people—and everybody in the room can tell he is terrified. He clears his throat, tries to say a few words, stops, clears his throat again. The room is dead quiet when, finally, he says, 'If you don't drink, you don't get drunk.' And with those eight words, he walks back to his seat. I turn to the fellow next to me. 'Well, I'll be damned,' I say, 'he just read the entire Big Book to us.'"

Every time I drink, I get drunk.

So when are you going to stop? we want to shout at him, because we have no idea what happens next. We're done. No more treatment, no more "after care" or continuing care or whatever the hell you want to call it. No more money. That's our bottom line. This is our bottom.

I think about all the advice I've offered to parents of youth involved with the Juvenile Justice Center. I even started a weekly parent support group. I'm so full of suggestions for others and yet so unable or unwilling to heed my own advice. Worse, all those suggestions and recommendations seem to me now like mushy, meaningless, direction-less nonsense. More than twenty years ago, in *Living on the Edge*, the book I coauthored with Ginny Lyford Asp, we wrote these words of advice for family members:

> Overcoming the doubts and fears that come from living
> with the disease of addiction takes time, understanding,
> and persistence. But they can be overcome; and they
> must be overcome if you are to escape the pain of the
> past and the fear of the future and begin to live in
> the here and now—the only place in time that makes
> any difference. Living in the here and now also means
> letting go of fear and anticipation about the future.

The word *must* blares out at me. Who was I—who *am* I?—to tell anyone what they "must" do? What a total imposter I was—a thirty-seven-year-old with three children under four years of age, masquerading as an expert, giving advice to other parents before I have even one little bit of experience raising a child with a drug problem. Once again, I think about God, if such a One exists, zapping me with a lightning bolt.

In *Teens Under the Influence*, Dr. Nick Pace and I wrote:

> Rules are rules, and parents need to be clear and
> consistent. Clearly state the rules you expect your
> children to follow, establish the consequences that will
> be imposed if the rules are broken, and list the privileges
> your children will enjoy if they follow the rules.

Have I been "clear and consistent" with Ben? If so, why am I picking up my self-proclaimed drug-addicted son and bringing him back home, when I know—I know, I *know*, I KNOW—that I am breaking my own damn rules? Easy to write a book, huh? Easy to talk about boundaries, eh? Easy to use the word *must*, which is a twin sister to *should*, which is a really shitty word, yeah?

∿

Ben creates a "Contract for Living at Home." At the top of the list, he writes "All subject to compromise or change."

Weeks 1–3

1. Stay at home unless leaving for an AA meeting, counseling, or work (if I get a job at that point)
2. No cell phone
3. No hanging out with any friends unless okayed with you first
4. Willingness (throughout the entire time) to do anything asked (cleaning, yard work, anything)

5. 90 meetings in 90 days
6. Work to pay rent
7. With anything, you may ask me to leave home

Weeks 4–6 (or whenever)

1. Drug tests whenever
2. 8:00 p.m. curfew
3. Finding my own counseling (or helping to)
4. No money unless I buy something with it (with your approval)
5. A certain amount of money placed monthly in bank
6. Regular attendance of AA and other therapy
7. Daily work therapy around the house
8. Breakage of contract means hitting the road
9. Getting a sponsor and doing Twelve Step work

Rules

1. Anything you ask will be done
2. No defiance, anger outbursts, or anything like that
3. No contract breakage
4. No friends over unless first approved by you
5. Pay rent
6. Curfew
7. Drug tests
8. Working a program
9. Fun trips with y'all
10. Ninety meetings/ninety days
11. Restrictions of phone, etc.
12. If contract is broken, I will move out

He doesn't drink or use. For a day. He goes to an AA meeting. Two days. He goes to another meeting. Three days. Two meetings that day. On day four, he spends a few hours on my computer, working on an email to his aunts Billy and Debbie. "This is your nephew Ben

Spencer writing," he begins. "I've got some good news and some bad news, but the bad isn't that bad once you've heard me out." He tells them about the drinking and how it got worse and worse, how he let everyone down—his parents, sisters, relatives, friends, everyone.

So I sat down and started to think. I tried to picture what my ideal life would look like, and when I got the picture in my head, it sure as heck didn't involve any of the things that were happening. I haven't used anything (pot, alcohol, or cigarettes) for more than three days, and I've been going to meetings every day since I've been home.

When I look back at what just happened, I realize that it was supposed to happen that way. If I hadn't screwed up that bad so quick, I would still be drinking and lying about it. And I'm so tired of being the one who screws up. I'm tired of being the one that makes an idiot of their self. I want to be proud of being Ben, and the only way that can ever happen is if I never use anything again. It's kind of cool. I was thinking about how some people can use drugs and alcohol responsibly, and I just thought and kind of laughed to myself that that isn't me, and it never will be.

Sober days stretch into sober weeks. He contacts a counselor and sets up weekly appointments. Every day, he attends the noon AA meeting at the Congregational Church. At first, he complains bitterly about "an old fart" who tells the same old story every day, day after day. "It never changes," Ben says, tossing AA's Big Book on the couch. "He's driving me crazy." But the next day and the next, Ben goes back to the same meeting, and after a while—two weeks? three?—the old man's story begins to make sense. Because it is the same old story, and it is Ben's story, too—the classic story of "the way I used to be, what happened, and the way I am now." It's a story of grief, shame, loss, and despair, altered through time and sobriety to a story of forgiveness, mercy, fellowship, and love.

"I'm getting used to his ramblings," Ben says with a self-deprecating grin. "I kinda like that old fart."

One evening after dinner, we hear a great horned owl hooting in the tree in our backyard. It's a perfect place for an owl to perch—fields on all sides; birds flying here, there, and everywhere to nest for the night; rabbits hiding in the tall grass with their big ears twitching, sensing danger from above, wondering whether to make a run for it across the wide green lawn.

Ben and I decide to see how close we can get to the owl. We walk slowly to the tree, holding our breath. The owl stays put. We walk a little closer. The owl swivels its head to look at us but doesn't move. Slowly we lie down under the tree, looking up at the owl, which stares down at us once or twice and then, unconcerned, gazes out at the fields watching for movement. We don't say a word. The light is dropping down, the night is coming up, the owl is waiting and watching, the sky slowly inks out, the rising moon throws shadows over the lawn and the fields, and suddenly, without a sound, the owl sweeps away, wings stretched, off to dinner.

Walking back to the house, Ben puts his arm around my shoulders. "I never realized how sweet and simple life can be when you're sober," he says in a near whisper.

In midsummer, he gets a job working in the boiler room at Whitman College's physical plant. Pat talked to his friend Dan Park, the plant supervisor, who knows about Ben's struggles and agrees to help him. Dan pairs Ben with Gary D'Agostino, a crusty, straight-talking, hard-living boiler technician. During those long days in the boiler room, learning how to work with his hands, Ben talks to Dag about his drinking and drug use. Dag is a wise old mentor, having some experience with drugs himself.

"I love that man," Ben says at dinner one night. "I want him to be the best man at my wedding."

Toward the end of summer, Ben decides not to go back to the University of Washington. "I don't want to go back to Seattle," he says. "I want to be close to home, have dinner with you guys on the weekends, keep working at the physical plant with Dag. I think I'll apply to Whitman—it would be cool to be able to stop in and shoot the bull with Dad now and then."

In early August, just three weeks before Whitman's fall semester starts, Ben submits his application. Although it's months past the application deadline, a few incoming students have dropped out, and the director of admissions encourages Ben to apply. In the "personal supplement" section of the application, Ben writes about his new-found sobriety—three weeks now—and his desire to give back to the world and his community. His dream, he writes, is to create a recovery community at Whitman, start a weekly AA meeting on campus, and meet with administrators at the college to talk about starting a sober interest house at Whitman.

"I'd be notorious on campus for creating good times without drugs," he writes, "teaching students that you can have more fun than you ever imagined without getting hammered."

In his final paragraphs, he tells the story of the owl.

> I wanted to write about a spiritual experience I had the other day. For the last couple of nights, my parents and I have been sitting around talking, eating dinner, or watching the television when suddenly our dogs start barking. Every night, we look out in the back yard to see this two-and-a-half-foot tall great horned owl sitting in a tree in our back yard. We always go out to watch the owl for ten to fifteen minutes before it gets tired of its perch and flies to another location.
>
> The other night when I was coming back inside, I went up to my mom before we reached the door and told her how happy I am to be sober, because when I was using alcohol and drugs, I wouldn't have appreciated something like an owl in our back yard. I've thought a lot since about those words.
>
> Maybe what affected me most deeply is not so much an appreciation of the owl, or the beauty of

the way the mountains and wheat fields look in the
background at that magical time of night, but more
an awareness of being awake for the first time in my
life. And I can't imagine that awakening continuing,
helping me to achieve the goals I have set for myself, in
any other environment than the one-on-one, friendly,
intellectually stimulating environment that Whitman
College has to offer.

That same week I get an email from Steve from our family group at
Wilderness Treatment Center. His son relapsed. "We are back at Step
One," Steve writes. "I'm sorry for the bad news, but I need some words
of encouragement."

From Linda in Texas, Susan and Tim in West Virginia, and Kathy
and Pat in Walla Walla, loving words arrive in emails long and short.
"Hang in there," we say. "We've been there, too." "He'll make it." "Our
hearts ache for you." "He has the tools." "Relapse happens, and it is
not failure." "He'll find his way." "Remember—take care of yourself.
Take care of YOU."

"Our kids are stumbling," I write to Steve. "A friend in recovery
once compared recovery to learning how to walk again—we expect a
toddler to take a few steps and fall, get up again and fall, and so it goes
until walking becomes easier. But still they fall at times. That doesn't
mean relapse is inevitable, but it happens, and it is not failure."

"Thank you all for writing back and for what you each said," Steve
writes in a long email. At the very end, he adds the most beautiful
words. They take my breath away:

> In the shades of sorrow and hope there is a contour, a
> shape you all gave me to what love is; a shape I could feel.

I think about that sentence for a long time, wondering if hope and
sorrow are shadows of the real thing, the thing with shape and contours,

the thing that is friendship, connection, love. Some realities are *beyond* us—beyond our understanding, beyond explanation, beyond our control—but there is also something solid and substantial *between* us. We cannot control the beyond, but we have some power over the between. It is up to us to create and maintain the between that is friendship and love, and we need to work at it. To keep the connections strong and secure, we do not let go. *Of this, we do not let go.*

We do not let go of forgiveness or compassion. We do not let go of honesty or humility ("I can do some things, but I cannot do everything"). We do not let go of the past or our belief in a future, but we can learn how to live in the present with awareness of what we cannot control, accepting our mistakes as part of being human. For as that grand old philosopher William James put it, "Our errors are surely not such awfully solemn things. In a world where we are so certain to incur them in spite of all our caution, a certain lightness of heart seems healthier than this excessive nervousness on their behalf."

~

When Ben opens his acceptance letter from Whitman, we whoop and holler, laugh and cry. He'll be safe here, I think. He won't get lost. We'll have Sunday dinners together. Dag will keep an eye on him. His professors will make sure he's showing up and doing the work. He's come home.

And so, for the second time, first at the University of Washington and now at Whitman College, Ben begins his freshman year. We move him into the freshman dorm with high hopes. Hopes get ramped up a bit higher when he decides not to pledge a fraternity.

"I think he's going to be okay," Pat says one night. Once again, we dare to dream he's on the right path.

~

Two weeks into the semester, Ben stops by Pat's office to complain about a teacher who gave him a D on a paper.

"Do you know how fucking hard I worked on that paper?" Ben says, red-faced and furious.

"Maybe next time you'll have to work harder," Pat says calmly.

"I hate this fucking place," Ben says on his way out the door.

A college security guard tells us that Ben was drunk and belligerent at a weekend concert. We thank him for telling us, but we don't say anything to Ben. It's his business.

He doesn't show up for Sunday dinner, and we don't call him.

We are not so wise as we are weary. Every Tuesday night, I faithfully attend the parent support group I started and patterned after my much-loved Wilderness group. There are just four of us the first night—Lenna, Marla, Gail, and me—but every week, someone new joins the group. We meet in a cavernous church room and sit on tattered couches that I insist on pushing together into a sort-of circle. The group laughs with me when I start pushing the heavy couches together—they know I'm obsessed with circles.

We tell our stories, and they are among the saddest stories in the world—tales of children who are sick unto death and families torn apart by guilt, grief, confusion, and pain. And yet, in and through the tears, there is healing. Just being with people who have walked the same tortuous pathway, who have stumbled, regained their balance, stumbled again and again, and kept on going gives us strength and courage. In those circles, we do not feel judged and condemned. We do not feel so alone.

Our stories are all different, and yet they are somehow all the same. We see ourselves in the mirror of another person's story. That reflection does not come without the deepest sort of pain, for we connect with each other at the broken places. "There is a crack in everything," as songwriter Leonard Cohen wrote. "That's how the light gets in." The light mixes with the darkness, and we laugh as much as we cry.

One evening, two new mothers come to group. They do not know each other, but they happen to sit next to each other on the same sofa. The first woman tells her story. "My twenty-four-year-old son loves his family. His sister adores him. He was always such a great kid, got straight A's, had big dreams for his life until he started using drugs—marijuana, cocaine, then heroin." She is ripping a wad of tissues to shreds in her lap. "And now—now I don't even know who he is."

The woman next to her leans forward, her eyes wide with wonder. "That's my story," she says, stumbling over her words. "I can't believe it. You just told my story!" The two women hug, holding on to each other as if they have known each other their whole lives.

An everyday experience in a vast, unheated room full of shabby old couches, where strangers gather around to tell their stories—and in the telling and the listening, something unexpected and extraordinary occurs.

A miracle of sorts. And for every miracle, there is a story.

Time before time, when the world was young, a brother and a sister shared a field and a mill. Each night, they divided evenly the grain they had ground together during the day. Now, as it happened, the sister lived alone, while her brother had a wife and a large family. One day, the sister thought to herself: "It isn't fair that we divide the grain evenly. I have only myself to care for, but my brother has children to feed." So each night, she secretly took some of her grain to her brother's granary to see that he was never without.

One day, the brother said to himself, "It isn't really fair that we divide the grain evenly, because I have children to provide for me in my old age, but my sister has no one. What will she do when she is old?" So every night, he secretly took some of *his* grain to his sister's granary. As a result, both of them always found their supply of grain mysteriously replenished each morning.

One night, they met each other halfway between their two houses. When they realized what had been happening, they embraced each other in love. The story is that God witnessed their meeting and proclaimed, "This is a holy place—a place of love—and here it is that my temple shall be built."

And so it was. The holy place, where God is made known, is the place where human beings discover each other in love.

14

order from chaos

March 2007

We're at the beach in a rental house, just Pat and I and Sophie and Murphy, our two springer spaniels. One night after dinner, we walk to the cliff at the end of the beach. The sun is setting, and the sky is pink and purple, with just a touch of blue. The ocean is silver, the white-capped waves relentless. Sophie and Murphy bound ahead of us, chasing the snowy plovers into the frigid water. We whistle them back, afraid they will follow the birds' flight path and get carried off into the deep, darkening sea.

I wonder for a moment: What would I do if a wave took one of them? Would I go after her? Instantly, I know I would, even dressed in my winter coat and fleece pants. I'm a strong swimmer, but I imagine her sinking under the waves and me waiting for her to surface, the ice cold water moving into and through me, draining my energy, threatening to pull me down. Would I be able to save myself and return to shore?

With a grateful heart, I watch them running back toward us, big ears flopping and what looks like a grin on their faces as the wind pushes against them. We laugh as we put their leashes on and start back toward the house. We're almost to the pathway leading up through the rocks when Pat stops suddenly.

"Look at that," he says in a hushed voice. Resting on the beach is a branch, big as a small tree, washed up close to the dunes.

"It's a perfect circle," he says, raising his voice above the crash of the waves. I look and see what I had not seen before. Traced around the branch is a circle. A nearly perfect circle.

"I've never seen anything like it before," Pat says, pointing to the center of the circle, where the heaviest part of the tree branch rests. "There's the pivot point. See, the branch is shaped so it has a bend at the heavy end—that's the pivot point. And here," he points to the tapered end of the branch where it touches the sand, "it's lighter than the pivot point. When the tide came up, the water must have been just deep enough to float the lighter end, and the heavier center stayed grounded. The waves somehow managed to move the tree branch around in a circle until the tide went out again."

He's quiet for a moment, looking at the circle in something approaching wonder. "This is a once-in-a-lifetime thing. It must have happened right when the tide was dropping. The branch had to have been pushed around in a circle precisely when the tide dropped enough to ground both ends because otherwise the waves would have washed the sand smooth again."

I can't take my eyes off the circle carved in the sand by a large piece of wood that happened to be washed ashore at precisely the right time. If Pat hadn't been with me, I would have never seen that circle. I might have stepped around it or straight into it, ruining its near perfection. Most likely I would have considered it an obstacle in my way.

"Chaos produces order," Pat says as he stares out at the sea and then back at the circle.

"What do you mean?" I want—I need—to understand how disorder and disarray can lead to stability and harmony.

"The tide must have been really high to reach this point, so close to the dunes. Imagine it—the waves are coming in all over the place; they're bouncing off the rocks. And this huge piece of driftwood is turning, swiveling, standing its ground but tossed about by the waves. It's chaotic. But out of that chaos, this circle was created."

The dogs are tired and lay down in the sand, curling up next to each other to stay warm.

"Chaos often produces very regular stuff," Pat says. He is usually so quiet, a man of few words, except when he's talking to his students. Then he's animated, full of energy and enthusiasm about the earth and its history. I don't have a long attention span when it comes to science, but I tend to ask lots of questions. In his kindness, knowing the way my mind works, he's careful to keep his explanations short and to the point. But order emerging out of chaos, stability and harmony arising from turbulence and confusion? I'm entranced.

"Tell me how that happens," I say in a near whisper.

"Well, think about the wind blowing across a sandy beach. It produces a whole field of symmetrical ripples. But the way the wind produces a ripple is by chaotic turbulence in its flow. If you look at the air flow in the winds generating a ripple, it's all over the place, spinning, and interfering, but the result is a nearly perfect train of ripples across the surface."

I imagine the wind moving across a lake. I picture the breeze moving through the wheat fields near our home. I see the wind gust on the ocean as it pushes and pulls at the surface to create waves. I think about what Ernie said about the wind as a metaphor for spirituality. We know the wind is there by its effect on things—leaves in the trees, blowing sand, ocean waves. We experience it, feel it, encounter it, but we can't see it except in its influence on the world around us. Like so much that takes place in our world, we cannot control or command it.

"It's such a delicate balance," Pat is saying, "between the tides and the waves and the weight of the log—just enough buoyancy to float one end of the tree branch and push it around in circles, but not enough wave activity to pull it back into the sea and wash away the evidence that it ever existed. You could scour beaches for the rest of your life and never find something like this again."

"So what does all this mean? What does it mean in human terms?" I'm shivering with the cold. The dogs look at us with impatient perplexity as if to say, *What are you talking about? What's so important that we can't go home and lie down in our warm beds?*

Pat stares at the circle. "I think it means we are just where we're supposed to be. If one thing had been changed in our lives, everything else would have gone an entirely different direction. I wouldn't have met you in the tavern playing pool that Friday night. We wouldn't have our children. We would be living an entirely altered existence. Or we might not be alive at all."

We're both thinking the same thing. "Like Ben," Pat says after a moment. "It would be impossible to determine what event was the turning point in his life. Was it the bullying? Losing his best friend at such a pivotal age? Genetics? I don't think we can point to one cause with any certainty. I believe it's just the way things happened. His set of chances ended up with him where he is, at this point in time, and my set of chances ended up with me where I am. It's the way things are."

"So, there's no changing it or wishing it were different," I say, knowing the answer.

"If you change one thing, you change the whole thing."

"Is it all chance, then?"

"That's what I believe. It's all chance."

As chaotic as that seems, I am consoled. *Chance.* Chance events can create order out of chaos. That seems to me a sort of miracle.

We walk over the dunes toward the house. I look back at the circle one more time. It is almost but not quite perfect. When the tide returns, it will be gone. It exists only for this small period of time, and then it will vanish.

We have only this moment.

~

"What about God?" I ask Pat, after we get back to the house, give the dogs a bath, take showers, and snuggle up in blankets on the sofa.

"Well, the chance thing is one of the major arguments creationists have against evolution. The chances of evolving something as sophisticated and complex as, say, a human eye are vanishingly small."

"Ooh," I say. "I like that phrase—*vanishingly small.*"

"Vanishingly small," he repeats with a smile. "How can such a random series of events result in something so perfect as a human eye? It can't, creationists say. Nobody has ever seen a partially evolved eye. Animals don't have half-eyes. So, rather than random chance, it has to be an all-knowing, all-powerful God who created the human eye and who orchestrated all these seemingly random events.

"And that's a valid point of view if you don't believe in the role chance plays in earth history or in the history of an individual's life. Nobody wants their individual existence to be governed by random chance. That's unacceptable to most people. So, we create something or find evidence to support something to make sense of it all. You've heard me say that if it's my day to die, it doesn't matter what I'm doing, I'll die somehow."

"But that sounds predetermined. That doesn't sound like chance."

"The thing of it is, I have nothing to do with it. My chances are unique to me. I don't know what they are or how they will play out in the end. If it's my day, I'm toast."

"You don't really believe that."

"I do."

"But that sounds like you believe in God."

"It does, and it's probably why a lot of scientists end up believing in the existence of God. Ultimately, we can't explain any of this with science. I can talk all I want about what happened a billion years ago on earth, but I can't convince you unless you are willing to be convinced that what I'm saying is true."

"So, is there a place for God in your science?"

"Well, it would be the AA thing." He reaches down to stroke the dogs, who are lying on the floor at our feet. "I view the Higher Power idea in two ways. First, alcohol is more powerful than I am, so I don't challenge or test myself against it anymore. And second, my life is governed by powers greater than my own will or understanding. I make the day-to-day decisions, but the course of my life is determined by events and influences that are not in my control. Things are going to happen regardless of what I do or don't do.

"I can't and won't deny the existence of anyone else's conception of God as a being that plans or oversees our lives, but I'd rather think about the millions of possibilities that exist at each and every turn. Earth is a really old planet, and geological time is deep. There's plenty of time for random chances to become certainties."

Pat is quiet for a few moments. "Scientists are never engaged in trying to find the truth," he says finally. "If they say they are, they are lying to you. What scientists are trying to do is find a reason that something *can't* be true. Does the truth even exist? It's true that the sun comes up every morning. But do you see the same sunrise I see? I can hold a rock in my hand

and say, 'This is a rock.' But do you observe the same shape and substance of the rock I hold in my hand? Truth is subject to an individual's reality."

For some reason, I think about the time Robyn's first-grade teacher showed the class a picture of a snake, a frog, and a lizard and asked, "Which one is different?" Most of the children chose the snake because, unlike the frog and the lizard, it doesn't have any legs. But Robyn, daughter of a scientist, chose the frog. The teacher was flummoxed—why would she choose the frog when the answer was so clearly the snake?

"Because the frog is an amphibian, and the snake and the lizard are reptiles," she explained.

Robyn was right. And the children who chose the snake were also right. There's more than one truth, more than one perspective, more than one way "to be." The "truth"—the one and only right answer—changes, morphs, moves in a never-ending circle, exactly as the tree branch on the beach circled round and round itself, moved by the wind and the tides—an unlikely circle of life forces emanating from the sea, the source. Perhaps this image is an answer to my prayers, an acceptance of the unlikely coexistence of two entities that do not belong together, each acting and reacting to make a whole cloth out of disparate threads.

~

Every morning during that week at the Oregon coast, I get up at 5:00 a.m. The dogs are still sleeping at the foot of the bed. I tiptoe out, make a cup of coffee, and snuggle up on the couch with pillows, blankets, and Martin Buber's slim volume, *I and Thou*—originally published in German in 1923 (*Ich und Du*). Ernie suggested I read Buber for the shame book we are working on. This is my second read. The first time, almost forty years ago in my freshman year in college, I approached the book from a different perspective—as a required text for a college course. Reading it now, I understand Buber in a whole new way.

The sky is dark, and I can hear the waves in the distance. I am content. Actually, this is different from contentment—this sense of peace and serenity—for I am here with a good book, a cup of strong coffee, Pat and the puppies asleep down the hall, the day just barely begun. This is my imperfectly perfect life. I accept and embrace it. I am beyond grateful for it.

I reach for a pen to underline the passages that I am hoping will shed light on the shame experience. I don't get very far, just a page or two, before I begin to suspect that Ernie guided me to this book not for our book but for me and Ben, for the *I and Thou* of the title. The translator, Walter Kaufmann, chose to replace *Thou* with *You*. But as I read, I realize that something—some mystery, some sense of the sacred—is lost in the translation. I find myself replacing *You* with *Thou*. I say "Thou" out loud, whispering to preserve the silence and solitude. The word evokes a sense of the impenetrable mysteries of life. I draw an extra blanket around me.

The book is just over a hundred pages long, but I take hours to read a few pages, underlining sentences and bracketing whole paragraphs, placing stars and checkmarks next to my favorite passages, creating a list of topics with page numbers on the front flyleaf that ends up filling both the front and back of the page.

It seems like random chance when I come across this passage: "I contemplate a tree." My eyes open wide. According to Buber, we can look at this tree as movement; we can assign it to a species; we can divide the whole into parts that exist outside ourselves. But (and I can imagine this bearded man with his gentle brown eyes depicted on the cover of the book holding up a finger of caution), when we divide the tree into parts, it remains an object. Only when "will and grace are joined" and "drawn into a relation" does "the tree cease to be an It." The relation is reciprocal—it gives, it takes, it gives back. "Will" requires pursuit; "grace" requires the willingness to receive.

Wow, I think, *maybe that is life wrapped up in six words*: Pursuit and the willingness to receive.

"A coincidence," it has been said, "is a small miracle in which God chooses to remain anonymous." Just hours ago, walking the beach, we came across a large piece of wood surrounded by a circle in the sand. I saw a tree, an It, but Pat, contemplating the same structure, perceived something of a miracle. He entered into a relationship with the tree, and through his words and his insights, I also began to experience a sense of connection. Perhaps it is fair to say, as Buber wrote, that will and grace were joined in those moments when we were drawn into a relationship with the tree branch, standing before it in awe and wonder, aware of its uniqueness, seeing it not as an object but as a part of our world and ourselves, a seamless joining of the observed and the observer.

The tree branch was once an "It" that became a "Thou." Speaking "Thou" to the branch and its near-perfect circle with my whole being, asking for nothing and holding nothing back, the tree and I became one. "It" became something whole, infused with meaning, and the more I stood in awe of the branch and its circle—the more I came into relationship with them—the more they asked of me.

I am willing to receive.

~

Returning home to Walla Walla, I notice that I am not thinking about Ben in the same way. For all those years, I considered addiction an "It," an object, a thing that separated me from my son. I imagined Ben being taken over by a demon, held captive, imprisoned. So, I felt compelled to do battle with it, trying to reach in and grab the real living thing that was my child, hoping to rescue him from the monstrous force that was consuming him. But in hating the addiction, in trying to crack its ribs and rip out its heart, I was separating myself from my son. For his addiction was and is part of him—not a tumor or an organ to be cut out, but part of who he is, body, mind, and spirit.

I say "Thou" to his addiction, for it is his disease, and he is my son, whom I love with all my heart. I do not wish for a different child. I love him just as he is, for who he is, for all his flaws and limitations. I love him with my imperfect heart in which there are no longer massive spaces for hatred and enmity, for bitter words and shameful secrets.

Ben did not change—I changed. And as my wise friend Joyce reminds me over and over: "We can't change other people, Kathy. We can only change ourselves. And in doing so, we change everything."

15

found

2005–Present

How do you stay clean and sober?"

"I go to meetings," he says.

"I'm wondering if there is something more, some need inside you that compels you to go to those meetings."

He shifts in his chair and shoots me an annoyed look. "What are you asking me? What do you want from me?"

"I want to know how you maintain your recovery."

"I told you—I go to meetings."

"What else?" I am pushing him, but he needs to dig deeper. There's something powerful underneath the surface, a force more formidable than his addiction, giving him the strength and courage to keep moving forward rather than getting stuck or slowly slipping backward.

He jumps up, angrily pushing his chair back, and starts pacing around the room. I know what is going through his mind—*leave me alone!*—but I have to keep pushing. We are getting close. I can hear it in the way he is breathing—shallow, rapid breaths. I can see it in the set of his jaw and the flashing anger in his eyes every time he looks at me.

Suddenly he stops and stares at the side table where he left his cell phone. He picks up the phone with a look of stunned relief on his face, as if he had just found something he'd lost a long time ago.

"You want to know how I stay sober? I email the dead." His hands are shaking as he scrolls through his emails to Paul F., John K., and Mike R. He holds up the phone to show me the messages that bounce back to him with the words "undeliverable," "user unknown," "fatal error."

"I email the dead," he says, tears in his eyes, his voice softened to a near whisper. "And they remind me that when we are gone, we can't hear the cries for help any more than we can reach out to touch and be touched by the people we love. I feel the emptiness, and I am reminded once again that recovery is my life."

He looks at me beseechingly, hoping he has given me what I need. Then he says, simply, "I want to live."

~

That scene created the ending for the book I wrote with William Cope Moyers. William's stunning insight took my breath away. At that moment, I knew we had the perfect conclusion to his memoir. I couldn't know then, two years before Ben's recovery began, that the dead would also accompany my son on his journey.

~

Just before midnight on a clear, cold October night during his sophomore year in college, Ben has what he calls an epiphany. He's been drinking and drugging with his friends, but an overwhelming sense of hopelessness and helplessness (what he later calls a "crisis of faith") moves him to leave the party. Walking home, he looks up at the night sky and suddenly—miraculously, it might seem—he is overcome with a sense of how small and insignificant he is in relation to the vast and immeasurable universe.

"I realized I was powerless and that it was time to accept that fact," he remembers. "That was my surrender."

Ben did not drink or use the next day. Or the next. He hung on through weeks of withdrawal symptoms—tremors so severe, he had trouble holding a pen in his hand; intense, almost overpowering cravings; recurring bouts of anxiety and depression; crushing loneliness. His friends didn't understand the sudden change in his behavior, but for the most part, they left him alone. During those first few months of sobriety, he spent most nights at home. In between classes, he would visit Pat in his office. They would talk, and Ben would often stay for a few hours to study or write in his journal, with his father working nearby. Ben went to AA meetings at the church near campus and spent hours talking to counselors. Lacrosse practices and games filled his afternoon hours, and a new girlfriend occupied his evenings and weekends.

He stayed sober for a month. Three months. Six months. A year. Two years. Despite life's normal frustrations and uncertainties—a night when a drunken friend threw beer on him, a grade on a paper he felt he didn't deserve, a disagreement with his girlfriend—he stayed clean and sober. With time, he became stronger, healthier, happier, more confident. He graduated with a double major and honors in religion, titling his honors thesis, "Show Me How to See Things the Way You Do: Existentialism in Faith, Philosophy, and Film." The purpose of existentialism, he wrote in his thesis, "is not to dissolve all ambiguity and doubt in the world . . . [but] to suggest a way to live with uncertainty and to form meaning in spite of apparent meaninglessness."

"I wasn't sure at first that I could make it through all the ups and downs without something to numb the pain," he told me. "But then I get a glimpse of the beauty in the world and realize the hurt and heartache are worth it. I am never going back. I will never ever make the mistake of trying to numb whatever pain I have in life."

"Chase away the demons," singer and poet Joni Mitchell says, "and they will take the angels with them."

~

As I write these words in 2017, Ben is ten years clean and sober. I think he would agree with me, though this is my interpretation not his, that his recovery is guided by two people who walk with him wherever he goes. John Quaresma stands on one side. Almost exactly ten years after John died, Ben wrote a letter to John's sister, Whitney.

I guess I should start off by saying that I think about
John all the time. After he passed away, I really struggled.
For about 7 years, I got really wrapped up in heavy drug
and alcohol use. I just felt so pissed off at the world. I
loved your brother because he stood up for me and
made me feel loved.

A lot of the work I did in treatment with my
counselor was trying to cope with John's death, but I
just couldn't accept it. And then I relapsed. Again and
again. I just felt so empty without him.

On October 15, 2007, everything changed. I decided
on that night that I was finished feeling sorry for myself.
John never put up with my whining, and I feel that on
that night, he reached out to me in some capacity. Part
of the reason I decided to get sober is because I know
that's what John would have wanted for me.

I can see John's shy smile as he walks with Ben wherever he goes. I imagine him playfully elbowing Ben in the ribs, reminding him that life is short, no matter how you look at it. I watch as he puts his arm around Ben's shoulder and whispers, "Benny and the Jetts," and I picture Ben's smile as he remembers.

Standing by Ben's other shoulder is Gary D'Agostino. Dag, as we called him, was in charge of the boiler room of Whitman College's physical plant where Ben worked for the two summers before his freshman and sophomore years. Something clicked between Ben and Dag as they worked side by side in the physical plant. Dag taught Ben how to do an honest day's work. He showed Ben how to work with his hands, to care about his work, to ask questions and try problem solving if he didn't know how to do something. If Ben slipped up and made a mistake, Dag told him he'd better be honest about it, but he would never hold it against him. Dag demanded that Ben put any and all excuses aside and work his tail off to complete a project that he could take pride in. Bullshitting isn't going to cut it, he said, and if Ben wanted trust, he was going to have to earn it.

"He showed me how to have the courage to stand up for what I believed in. He taught me to be honorable." And then Ben adds, simply, "He saved my life."

Dag died of amyotrophic lateral sclerosis (ALS) on February 22, 2016, almost six years after Ben graduated from Whitman. They stayed in close touch through those years, talking on the phone frequently and even writing a blog together. Ben's great regret is that Dag couldn't be the best man at his wedding. But Dag was there in spirit, walking down the aisle with him.

~

Life sure has its way of taking us where it wants us to go. Once upon a time, I read a story that compares our lives to the underside of an Oriental carpet. I love the image. For most of our moments on earth, our only view of that rug is from the underside. All we can see are the knots and tangles, the broken threads and dull colors, the seemingly aimless, meaningless patterns that appear to begin and end nowhere in particular, with no overarching theme or master thread to pull everything together. But every so often—perhaps only once or twice in a lifetime—we are given the rare opportunity to rise up and look down upon the rug. For just a few, fleeting seconds, we can see the brilliance of the colors, the integrity of the design, the intricacy of the individual threads weaving in and out to create a complex, magnificent whole. And the meaning becomes clear, if just for that briefest of moments.

I wish for a longer look so I can make sense of certain parts of my life. I wonder, for example, what drew me to addiction all those years ago. Why did such a dark subject attract me and then continue to draw me forward, even when I resisted and longed for an easier, more light-hearted path through life? Looking back, with the elevation of age and hindsight, I am curious to see if I can tease out the knots, find the loops and threads that connect to each other so strongly and securely, so I can spin a story that helps me understand the why and wherefore of it all.

A sense of a mystery waiting to be unraveled adds to my fascination. Did my books pave the way for my life? Did the past predict the future? Or could it be that the magnetic force that drove me to write book after book about a subject with which I had no experience was some unearned God-like gift, offering me the strength and courage I needed to face the dark days ahead?

Perhaps it is all chance, as Pat would say. I think he is probably right. But as I imagine the elaborate swirling patterns of my life, I discern a design. The sparkling gold and silver threads of my family and all those I love and have loved shine most brightly. But something draws my eye, some master thread that links all the other strands together. I put my glasses on (why not?) to take a closer look. Thicker and stronger than the other strands, this thread is also more muted, less showy. It does not call attention to itself. Of course, I know what it is. This unifying filament, humble and unbreakable, is spirituality.

As I write these words, I find myself wanting to back away from this line of thought—spirituality has so many distorted, even negative connotations—but Ernie, bless his soul, is encouraging me. I, too, am guided by the dead. He is asking me to offer another image, perhaps a simpler one, to help convey the meaning of spirituality in our lives. *Okay, Ernie,* I answer him, *I'll use one of your stories.*

Many years ago, Ernie gave a presentation on spirituality at the Renewal Center at Hazelden, one of the oldest and most renowned centers for the treatment of alcoholism and other chemical dependencies. Spirituality, Ernie explained to his audience, is pervasive, touching all of our lives, all of our surfaces, all of our depths—physical, mental, and spiritual. Only if we live it, think it, feel it, and practice it in our lives will we come to understand what *it* is.

During his talk, Ernie was momentarily stumped by a question from the audience. "Can you give us an image that might help us visualize what you mean by spirituality?" For several long moments, Ernie stared at the massive stone fireplace, searching his mind for a description that would help bring the concept of spirituality to life. His vision settled on the multi-colored rocks illuminated by the late afternoon sunlight streaming into the room. Perhaps their warmth and beauty would serve as an image of the spiritual.

Then, in one of those strange gestalt switches, his vision refocused and he saw not the individual stones but the bland, gray, pebbly "stuff" that held all those stones together. *That* was "the spiritual," the substance that holds everything together to create a structure of strength and integrity.

"Spirituality is like that mortar in the fireplace," Ernie said, breaking the silence. "Just as the mortar makes the chimney a chimney, allowing it to stand up straight and tall, beautiful in its wholeness, 'the spiritual' is what makes *us* wholly human. It holds our experiences together, shapes them into a whole, gives them meaning, allows them—and us—to be whole. Without the spiritual we are somehow not 'all there.'"

Later, over coffee, one of the workshop participants said he had always imagined spirituality as something unique and spectacular, like angels or saints, something perfect and maybe even beyond human understanding. Running his fingers along the simple, unassuming surface of the mortar, he said, "If my life, my experiences are like a big pile of loose rocks, this plain, old, ordinary stuff is what I want—what I need—to hold everything together."

Stones and mortar—that's the kind of spirituality I need, too. Nothing fancy. No promises of ascending to great heights. Just plain old earthy stuff to remind me that nothing lasts forever. In geologic time, after all, even massive boulders are ground down into dust. But we do have these moments of beauty, of insight, of awe and wonder, and as so many wise men and women counsel, the trick is to stay in the moment, in the here and now. That's not easy for me, with my restless, impulsive nature, but I am learning. I try to remind myself, every day, of writer/poet Jorge Luis Borges's words: "A day does not pass when we are not, for an instant, in paradise."

Right now, what are those instants? I look out the window. A dog is barking. The sky is gray. The roses are not quite ready to bloom—but almost. Wasps are flying in and out of the little tunnels under the roof tiles. I don't like wasps. The dog keeps barking.

What am I searching for? Where are these moments of paradise?

I am breathing. I look at my hands on the computer keyboard, wrinkled and veiny, the skin losing its elasticity. A memory—of my mother and her grandchildren lifting up the skin on the back of her hand and watching it slowly fall back into place. Over and over again, they would play their game and laugh, and she would laugh with them. Did she think about how fast the years were passing, and did her memory take her back to a time when her skin was smooth and beautiful? Did it pain her to watch her grandchildren playing with her wrinkled old skin? I remember her telling me of looking in the mirror, only to be shocked and saying out loud, "Who is that?" I've had the same experience. We look in the same mirror.

The dog stops barking. The wind is moving through the pine trees, the branches lifting up and settling down. I lean closer to the window, craning my neck to look at the crabapple tree, which has lost all of its pink blooms. In the fall, the crabapples fall to the ground and line the walkway by the rose garden, filling the soles of my sneakers with squishy red mush. You would think the birds would eat all the crabapples in the winter, but I think the fruit must be sour. Besides, the birds much prefer the birdseed we put out for them.

A big branch of a tree fell in the yard, and we didn't even hear it, but it filled a third of our large front yard. After two hours of chain sawing, chopping, lifting, and loading, the branch was gone. The grass is yellow where the tree branch fell and lay dead for several days.

A friend emails to say she misses me and asks to meet sometime soon for coffee.

Murphy, almost twelve years old, sleeps quietly downstairs on her blanket on the back of the sofa. I think I will go hug her, wake her up, look into her sleepy bewildered eyes, and tell her how much I love her and how she can never die because I cannot live without her. She will nestle her head in the crook of my shoulder, and I will lean my cheek against her. We will rest like that, breathing in synchrony, thinking our own thoughts. Then she will wonder if we are going outside and, after we go for a little walk, if she will get a treat.

She has bad breath. I don't mind. She lifts her back leg so I can scratch her stomach. Her head is warm against my neck.

It is time for a snuggle and lunch and then the gym, where I will meet Pat, and we will talk about our mornings. My back will ache after the workout, and my knee, too. But it feels so good to move that I don't even register the pain as pain. It just is.

Then back to work and my window that looks out on the world.

So, yes, to these moments of paradise. The day offers them up to me, and I can choose to see them or be blind to them, hold them or let them go, take them for granted or experience gratitude.

A choice. Always, in this life, a choice.

16

coming home

2017

It is mid-November, the wind is strong, and the rain is gathering in thick dark clouds to the west. I look out the window at my rose garden, surprised to see three roses, all on the same bush, perfect, just about to bloom. I put on my coat and pick up my garden shears from the bench on the front porch, just as Pat is walking around from the side yard.

"A little sparrow hawk just hit the window. A kestrel."

"Is it dead?" I ask, fearing the answer.

"It's alive, but I think its wing might be broken."

We walk slowly, hesitantly, to the rose garden. In the far corner of the garden, the kestrel looks at us and flaps one of its wings, moving just a few inches. Then it looks away. Maybe it is gathering its strength, waiting for the moment when it can fly again. But the rain is coming and then the night, and the bird is vulnerable out here in the open, with the owls perched up high in the trees. The bird blinks and stares at the lawn and the sky beyond, not moving.

Maybe—and I know this is a stretch, but still I wonder—maybe the hawk is thinking about "this dying part." Like Johnny, in a different season, wrapped up in a blanket in the chair next to me, gazing at the light filtering through the greening birch leaves, whispering "beautiful."

After a moment, I lean down to the rose bush and slowly, gently cut three roses, leaving long stems. I hold them and take a step toward the bird. I get close—close enough to hold out a rose to its beak.

The kestrel is watching me, but I don't see fear in its eyes. I see connection.

For a few seconds, the bird drinks the fragrance of the rose. Birds, in general, are not known for their sense of smell. They have keen eyesight, but up close, what do they see? What did the little hawk see in the rose? What colors of the rose did it detect—the pink, the yellow, the red? Why did it not move? Why was it not scared? What was it thinking and feeling?

No, no, no, I correct myself. Not an "it." A "thou." I am anthropomorphizing, I know. But when I held out a rose to a wounded bird, it turned to the flower, looked in my eyes, and did not show fear. It was an encounter, as Martin Buber would say.

We keep checking on the little hawk, watching it hop to a bush. Just as the light grows dim and darkness descends, we watch it fly unsteadily to the safety of a copse of pine trees. The next morning, the bird is gone. We look for feathers, searching in the pine needles and underneath the bushes, but there is no sign of an attack or a struggle.

"The bird is alive!" I say, with great relief at the thought of the hawk circling high in the sky once again. "Things didn't look so good, did they? But somehow it lived. What do you think happened?"

"Maybe," Pat says, "the hawk sensed your kindness." *What an extraordinarily loving thing to say,* I think as we walk back to the house. I smile to myself, because I know all too well the other side of kindness that lies within me—the stubborn, quick-tempered, controlling, impulsive, and tactless aspects of my paradoxical personality.

"And maybe," Pat adds, seeing my smile and perhaps reading my thoughts, "the bird didn't hit its head as hard as we thought."

Later that day, I find myself wondering if a bird can sense kindness. If that is possible, if it is true, what does it say for the way we humans interact with each other? When we pass a stranger and smile, what emotions does our expression trigger? When we look into another person's eyes and hold their gaze, what signals are processed through our brains? When we touch each other, laugh together, cry together, what miraculous chain of events occurs within our minds, our hearts, our souls?

Certain words grab me and won't let me go. The word *soul* holds on especially tight. Many people, I know, struggle with the concept of a soul because it's not something we can prove. We can't hold it in our hands, cut it out of our bodies, mend it, stitch it, mold or shape it, weigh or measure it, create or destroy it. The soul is beyond our power and control, beyond even our powers to describe it.

A few days before his great friend Dag died, Ben sent him this email.

I'm sitting here with Cali, my boxer, looking out the window and listening to the crows that congregate around my apartment. Sometimes I feel like I lose sight of the little moments in life, the fact that each second we have on this earth is infinitely meaningful. But even though I sometimes forget, I still know in my heart of hearts that if you pause to reflect about life for even an instant, you can see how precious it all is and how lucky we are to have it.

I think the meaning of life is to be broken, to pick up the pieces, and to start living again, as if for the first time. I'm convinced that there is such a thing as "the soul." It resides in all of us. There's this movie *21 Grams* that I watched when I was new in sobriety and it made a huge impact on my life. There's a quote about the soul that captures exactly what I believe:

How many lives do we live? How many times do we die? They say we all lose 21 grams . . . at the exact moment of our death. Everyone. And how much fits into 21 grams? How much is lost? When do we lose 21 grams? How much goes with them? How much is gained? How much is gained? Twenty-one grams. The weight of a stack of five nickels. The weight of a hummingbird. A chocolate bar. How much did 21 grams weigh?

Your influence on me has weighed a hell of a lot, Dag. *How much is gained?* Everything. All of the good stuff. Everything I have now has been gained from the fact that you never gave up on me.

It feels like I won't be okay after you leave, but I think I'll be okay if I just make sure that I remember everything you taught me. It's a lot to ask, remembering all of those life lessons. But they're filed away in the most important part of me, the part that won't allow me to forget—my soul. And I'll be able to carry those lessons (and the amazing stories you told) with me, wherever I go. I'll have the privilege to impart the wisdom and retell the stories to my loved ones, my kids, and their kids.

The soul—the intangible, untouchable, immeasurable, invisible part of us that won't allow us to forget. I like that. What the soul can't forget is different from what the mind fails to recall. Like Ben, I believe the soul is the repository of our stories, past, present, and future. The soul remembers not dates or names or facts but who we are and where we belong. When we have gone astray, it is the soul that calls us back to ourselves. When we are lost in grief, in sorrow, in loneliness, or in shame, the soul cries out to us in ways that feel like homesickness or, as William James so memorably phrased it, "torn-to-pieces-hood." Responding to the soul's cry, we experience a deep, even desperate, longing for home, for the place where we fit and belong.

I think the meaning of life is to be broken, to pick up the pieces, and to start living again, as if for the first time.

In the detention center, not so very long ago, we were talking about the meaning of life. We rarely talk about the damage that drugs do to the brain, the liver, or any of the body organ systems, because these kids have all heard the facts and statistics many times before. They shrug off those conversations, almost as if to say, "So what? Everyone gets sick, everyone has to die, and if it's my turn, that's just the way it is, and there's nothing I can do about it." Sometimes they add, "And what's the point of it all anyway? What's so great about life?" It's almost as if I am watching them construct a wall to protect themselves.

But when we talk about how their drug use has affected their brothers, sisters, parents, and grandparents, the facade slips away. They hang their heads and stare at the floor. They sigh. Some wipe away tears. For a few moments, they are quiet; then, one by one, they willingly, openly tell their stories about how drugs have changed their relationships with the people they love most in the world. It is a relief to tell these stories, and they are the same story, told in a hundred different ways.

One day in group, fifteen-year-old Laura says she doesn't want to say anything, but she is willing to write down her thoughts. I hand her a piece of paper and pencil, and while the other members of the group talk, she keeps her head down and never once looks up. After group, she hands me what she has written. As I read the words scrawled across the page, I can't stop myself from tearing up. Her words, a stream of desperate consciousness, contain the deepest imaginable pain; they cry out for understanding, for connection.

> I loved my friends. I loved my father. Me and my mom
> were closer than anything. My brother and I loved each
> other. No matter how much we got in each other's hair,
> he loved hanging out with me. I used to know who I
> was and at the beginning of all this shit, I still thought
> I knew who I was. Now I've come to realize that I don't
> know who I am. I know how I feel and I know what
> I want. I know where I need to be, but I don't know
> who I am. I've lost almost everyone in my life. I have
> no family. I have no friends. I've lost everything I had.
> I don't blame this on drugs and I'm tired of everyone
> else blaming it on drugs. I'm tired of making excuses
> for myself. I know what I have done and I knew what I
> was doing while I was doing it. I fucked up. And I can't
> change that. But everyone fucks up. So if you're a real
> fucking person then take me as I am. Accept my fuck-
> ups because they're not any worse than yours.

I am in awe of those words, written by a fifteen-year-old. If we distill her statements down to their essence, isn't this what life is all about? I think Laura would like Ben's thought that "the meaning of life is to be broken, to pick up the pieces, and to start living again, as if for the first time." We all make mistakes. We're human, after all, and if we're going to be real human beings, we need to accept each other, accept ourselves as we are, and find a way to forgiveness.

Acceptance. We can't change the past. Sure, we mess up, maybe we screw up big time, maybe we even lose everything that matters to us. But do we give up on ourselves? Do we give up on each other? Or do we stop making excuses for ourselves, stop judging others, and start realizing that we're all in this together? That's where the soul leads—to the realization that we are all connected. We need each other. We can't make it without each other.

It's the oldest story in the world. Someone stumbles and falls; someone else reaches out to help. In that moment, a spark is created. Between us—in the giving and acceptance of love and commitment—we discover what is beyond us. The South African term *ubuntu* encompasses this sacred way of life. In Archbishop Desmond Tutu's words:

> [*Ubuntu*] speaks of the very essence of being human. . . .
> It is to say, "My humanity is inextricably bound up in
> yours." We belong in a bundle of life.

We are all of a piece, no matter the distance between us, no matter the color of our skin, the country of our origin, or the experiences of our past. We are all connected. *Ubuntu. I/Thou.* We stand in relation, and the longing to find that place where we fit and belong exists before us and will extend after us. We can only find it in each other, in community, in caring for each other, and in the knowledge that others care about us.

What am I seeking? This is Ben's question, but it is mine, too. I used to be filled with an intense, almost fanatical desire to change the world for people struggling with addictions and for their loved ones. When my first book was published, I believed, with all the arrogance of my youth, that perhaps now, finally, we had a call to arms, a manifesto that would alter the way our country approached addiction and its victims. When that revolution failed to happen—when life, in fact, seemed to get even worse for people living with addiction—I kept writing, book after book after book. Then, when I was exhausted by words, I jumped into the trenches to see if and how I might be able to help.

Then the battle came to me, engulfing my family in an agony of helplessness and fear, threatening to take everything good and strong and kind from the son I love more than life itself. In those ditches, in the muck and the mud and the horror of it all, I learned the most important lessons of all about honesty, humility, hope, faith, gratitude, and forgiveness.

And miracles. I've witnessed them, time and time again. I've watched as people given up for dead come back to life. I've seen men and women, young and old, who could not put one foot in front of the other, stand up and start walking, heart heavy but head high. I've witnessed how others, often strangers, step in unbidden to help when we stumble and fall.

Ben is walking in his shoes; it is time for me to walk in my own. For forty years, I stepped into the shoes of my words—shoes that belonged to the world of memory, empathy, chronic pain, alternative medicine, storytelling, and spirituality—but I always circled back to the addiction shoes. They fit me; they fit my life. In some ways—in so many ways—I think the shoes I wore directed my pathway in life.

But now, in this moment in this life of mine, I am ready to walk a different pathway. I don't know where it will take me or what adventures, grief, sorrow, and joy lie ahead of me. Every journey is a pilgrimage. With each day, there is a night; with each dawn, a twilight; and, gift of gifts, on the darkest nights of all, the stars shine through.

Good and evil exist out there in the world, and they reside also inside me. I do the best I can. I lean toward the good. When I make mistakes, I do the next right thing. I do not expect perfection, for then who would guide my next steps? And why would I want to keep moving if I have achieved all there is to accomplish in this life?

I seek out gratitude, for gratitude will not find me if I do not go looking for it. I cultivate forgiveness, for forgiveness is a garden that requires a gardener. When life seems meaningless, I turn my head, fighting my fear, and look into the abyss, where I see beauty and the fragrance of a rose staring back at me. When help is offered, I accept it, and when someone, friend or stranger, needs support, I try to be there to extend a hand. I seek to live by grace, which Dag, that wise old soul, defined as "waking up every morning and making the commitment not to judge anyone."

We are all of a piece. We cannot get through this life alone. To be whole—to be wholly human—we need others to join with us, to tell us their stories, to listen to our stories, to help us, to allow us to help them.

It is all of a piece, this joy and this sorrow, this loss and this gain.

acknowledgments

With gratitude abounding, I thank:

Robyn, Alison, and Ben, my moon, sun, and stars . . . and Pat, who keeps everything in orbit.

Mike, Billy, and Debbie, my brother, sisters, and best friends; and Mom, Dad, and Johnny, who left us all too soon.

Ernie Kurtz, who showed me "a" way but taught me there is no "one" way, and to his wife, Linda, who so lovingly shared Ernie with me all these years.

The staff at the Walla Walla Juvenile Justice Center, especially Mike Bates, Julie Elmenhurst, Norrie Gregoire, Debbie Kelley, and Vance Norsworthy, who gave me a chance and changed my life.

The youth in detention and on probation who are my greatest teachers.

Colleen, who became a friend for life.

Laurie Becker, whose compassion and intelligence shepherded this book through multiple drafts and pulled me from the edge more times than I can count.

Lenna Buissink, Marilyn Dickinson, Debbie Goodeve, Billy Heath, and Robyn, Alison, Pat, and Ben Spencer—my diligent, loving readers who allowed me to speak my own truth, which, of course, may not be their truth.

Nick Dillon, my tattoo guru, and Miriam Todras Spencer, for putting up with me, and the boisterous Ketcham-Spencer clan.

Jane Barragar and Kathleen Hutchison, my Wicked Sisters, who never fail to remind me that book clubs aren't always about books.

Lou Holm, Jeff Jay, Debra Jay, Sharon Kaufman-Osborn, Marie Metheny, William Moyers, Scott Munson, Danny Reese, Marv Seppala, Susan Stough, and Joyce Sundin (among so many others), who led us through the rough and tumble with skill and grace.

Ben Dorrington and the staff at Wilderness Treatment Center and Gray Wolf Ranch, who understand that the process of recovery is unpredictable and unique to each individual and whose patience and steadfastness allowed the miracle to happen.

Susan, Tim, Linda, Steve, and their boys, who brought home the real meaning of community; and Allison, Charles, Connie, Dan, Dana, Gail, Gloria, John, Kim, Lenna, Marla, Sandy, Shelley, Tami, and the entire Trilogy family, including Luis, Megan, and Cari, who have kept the spirit of community alive for all these years.

Gary D'Agostino—we miss you more than we can say—and Liz and Sarah, who so lovingly keep his memory alive.

Bill White, a hero in the addiction and recovery world and a great friend to Ernie—and, to my everlasting gratitude, to me.

Haven Iverson, my editor at Sounds True. Haven is a writer's dream come true, willing to dig into a manuscript and, holding nothing back, offer insightful critiques and detailed suggestions. Her honesty, talent, and sensitivity helped stitch this book into a coherent whole. She's a treasure.

The talented team at Sounds True, who make me thank my lucky stars every day for landing at a publishing house where relationships matter. Thank you especially to Jennifer Brown, director of acquisitions; Sarah Gorecki, managing editor; Tara Joffe, copyeditor; Wendy Gardner, publicist; Chloe Prusiewicz, product marketing manager; and Rachael Murray, Beth Skelley, and Karen Polaski for the book and cover design.

Jane Dystel, my dynamic, indefatigable, never-take-no-for-an-answer literary agent—a true "author's agent"—who has guided my career with a steady hand for many years.

~

After all is said and done, whatever imperfections remain are mine to claim.

recommended reading

This is a very short list of some of my all-time favorite books. If you are like me, having too much information and too many choices can throw you into a tailspin of wondering where to start. Each of these books helps fill out the picture of family helplessness, hopelessness, and resilience, with an emphasis on courage, strength, and wisdom. At the end of this short list, I suggest two invaluable websites that will take you just about anywhere you want to go to learn more about addiction and recovery.

Books

Sheff, David. *Beautiful Boy: A Father's Journey Through His Son's Addiction*. A riveting real-life story written by a father about his methamphetamine-addicted son. Although meth addiction is still a huge problem, the headlines have switched over to the lethal opioid epidemic. Never forget, though, that a drug is a drug is a drug; and, just to make a point, alcohol is the "worst" drug of all in terms of the number of people it kills and maims, either directly or indirectly.

Knapp, Caroline. *Drinking: A Love Story*. Addiction begins in an early stage and progresses, often over a period of many years, into its later stages. For anyone who does not understand the concept of the "high-functioning" alcoholic or addict, this book is invaluable.

McGovern, George. *Terry: My Daughter's Life-and-Death Struggle with Alcoholism*. Former Senator George McGovern wrote this heartbreaking story about his daughter Terry's long and tortuous struggle with alcoholism. His descriptions of what he would do if he had another chance to save her are unforgettably moving.

Lee, Joseph. *Recovering My Kid: Parenting Young Adults in Treatment and Beyond*. Finally, a book for parents written by a doctor who truly understands the family's experience. Dr. Lee writes with the experience of an empathic, highly skilled physician who has worked with hundreds of families struggling to help their addicted loved ones.

Jay, Jeff and Debra. *Love First: A Family's Guide to Intervention*. The most comprehensive guide to intervention, which the authors describe as the most powerful step that a family can take to initiate the recovery process.

Mogel, Wendy. *The Blessing of a Skinned Knee: Using Jewish Teachings to Raise Self-Reliant Children*. If every parent would read this book when their children are still in elementary school and take time to revisit the passages they underlined, they would save themselves—and their children—much anguish and confusion during the tempestuous adolescent years. Forget the rattles, bibs, and onesies and wrap up this precious gem for new parents.

Websites

drugfree.org Filled with down-to-earth advice, helpful tips, colorful graphics, and personalized advice including a telephone helpline, online chat room, and "Ask a parent who's been there" page, this is your first stop for information on everything to do with drugs, addiction, and recovery.

williamwhitepapers.com I can't even begin to list all the valuable resources on Bill White's website but trust me—click on any one of his papers, book reviews, interviews, journal articles, or recovery toolkit tips and you'll begin an astonishing learning adventure with one of the most respected authorities in the addiction and recovery field.

book club reader's guide

1. Katherine opens the first chapter with the words, "Addiction was handed to me, like a gift." What do you make of this statement?

2. Ben grew up in a loving, middle-class family with a mother who specializes in addiction and a father in long-term recovery. And yet, despite their knowledge and experience, they could not prevent the disease from entering their own home. How did Katherine's story influence or alter your thoughts around the subject of addiction?

3. Katherine refers to Ben's addiction as a demon that walked into her house and threatened to destroy her entire family. For Ben, though, addiction is not a demon; it's a spiritual malady. Does Ben's perspective alter his mother's way of thinking about addiction as the story unfolds? How do you characterize addiction after reading this book?

4. In chapter 2, Katherine asks her group at the Juvenile Justice Center what is hurting them. They respond with statements about feeling ashamed and disconnected from their friends and family because of their drug use, even to the point of asking themselves, "What kind of human being am I?" Katherine writes, "We can help these young people understand that they fit in and belong in a world that seems to have turned its back on them." How well do you think she followed this intent when her own son became addicted to drugs?

5. "The Juvie stories are ripping me apart," Katherine writes. "I am too deeply connected to their grief and their longing." Later in the book, Ben confronts her with these words: "You hate drugs; you think everyone is like your Juvie kids . . . That's why everything fell apart." How did Katherine's involvement with the Juvie kids complicate her relationship with her own children?

6. On page 56, Katherine writes, "Ben is not addicted, I keep reminding myself. I would be able to see it, even in its early stages. I know what addiction looks like." How do you think you would react if you were in Katherine's shoes? How would you try to balance a dual role as an addiction expert who counsels others to "let go," and a loving mother whose every instinct is to "hold on"?

7. Hope is an important and continuing theme throughout this book. How did hope help the family stay grounded in all of the chaos?

8. At one point Katherine writes, "Hope dies hard, and we hold on as long as we possibly can—maybe longer than we should." Is it possible that clinging to hope can prevent us from facing reality? Can too much reliance on hope encourage avoidance and inaction when what is needed is active engagement?

9. "There is more than one miracle to be discovered in this life," Katherine writes. What are the different kinds of miracles she discovers in the pages of this book?

10. The theme of "brokenness" appears throughout the book. "The meaning of life is to be broken, to pick up the pieces, and to start living again, as if for the first time," Ben writes in a letter to a friend, while Katherine writes, "We were bound together by our grief and our guilt, by our shame and our

soul-sickness, by our fear and our pain." Do you agree that a deeper connection to ourselves and each other can be found in our "torn-to-pieces-hood"?

11. Do you agree with this advice from Katherine's friend Joyce, an intervention specialist? "We can't change other people, Kathy. We can only change ourselves. And in doing so, we change everything."

12. Katherine claims she is not a religious person and yet throughout the book she talks about God, prays to God, and even has conversations with God. In chapter 12, she tells a story about God, ending with the words, "Oh God. I know how you feel." What do you think about her developing relationship with God, which she defines as "a force in this world that throws color, light, and goodness all around, a hidden power that is greater, stronger, more enduring than the dark energies of ignorance and prejudice"?

13. One of Ben's counselors offers this "two shoulders" advice: "The rest of your life depends on who you choose to walk on either side of you." Do you agree that recovery depends on having the guidance of others who help you take the right path? Or is recovery, at its heart, a solo journey?

14. Throughout the book, Katherine and Ben write letters to each other, sometimes long and emotional, sometimes short and somewhat detached. Have you tried writing letters to your child when you are deep in a conflict or do you have some other communication method that you use? How does your particular method of communication help regulate your emotions and enlarge your perspective on the situation? How does your child react and respond to your efforts to communicate?

15. On page 102, Katherine talks about how shame and guilt overwhelm her after she and Ben argue or fight. "Within minutes—seconds?—I am 'shoulding' all over myself. I 'should' have been patient. I 'should' have given him two minutes or five minutes (why not ten?) to finish what he was doing. I 'should' have removed myself from the situation . . . Should should should." Do you relate to this feeling of immediate regret? As a parent, how do you come to terms with emotions of guilt, shame, and regret? How do you keep yourself from getting hung up on the "what ifs?" and "I should haves?"

16. Were there particular passages that struck a chord with you? Did you find yourself relating to the thoughts or emotions expressed? Did any of the passages call forth memories from your own experiences with your children or other family members?

17. Katherine was compelled to address the way people look at and understand addiction, challenging the stigma and stereotypes that surround it. Do you think she succeeded?

18. How did this book impact your thoughts about addiction, and especially the idea of addiction as a "family disease"? The current state of medical care and treatment for addiction? The need for family support programs in treatment centers and in communities?

19. How did you come away feeling, after reading this book? Inspired? Anxious? Less afraid? Hopeful?

20. Is this a book you will continue thinking about, now that you are done? Do you find it having an impact on the way you go about your days?

about the author

Katherine Ketcham has been writing nonfiction books for nearly forty years. Her first book, *Under the Influence: A Guide to the Myths and Realities of Alcoholism* (coauthored with James Milam, PhD) was published in 1981 and is considered a classic in addiction literature, along with *The Spirituality of Imperfection* (coauthored with Ernest Kurtz). *The Only Life I Could Save* is her seventeenth book. Her books have been published in sixteen foreign languages and have sold almost two million copies.

In 1999, Katherine began volunteering at the Juvenile Justice Center in Walla Walla, Washington, leading educational groups and working individually with adolescents in trouble with alcohol and other drugs. For four years she wrote a bimonthly newspaper column for the *Walla Walla Union Bulletin* titled "Straight Talk About Drugs." She is the founder and former executive director of Trilogy Recovery Community, a grassroots, nonprofit organization in Walla Walla dedicated to developing and expanding community-based recovery support services for chemically dependent youth and their family members.

Katherine lives in Walla Walla with her husband, Patrick Spencer, a geology professor. They have three children: Robyn, a speech pathologist living in Portland, Oregon; Alison, a special education teacher in Seattle, Washington; and Benjamin.

Ben celebrated his tenth year in long-term recovery on October 15, 2017. After graduating from Whitman College in 2010, he worked as a corps member for Teach for America in Nashville and went on to work as the teacher in the Boys Residential Program at Muir Wood Adolescent and Family Services in Petaluma, California. He currently works as senior writer for Fresh Consulting and is finishing his first novel. Ben lives in Walla Walla, Washington, with his wife, Miriam, and their two boxers, Cali and Nessie.

about sounds true

Sounds True is a multimedia publisher whose mission is to inspire and support personal transformation and spiritual awakening. Founded in 1985 and located in Boulder, Colorado, we work with many of the leading spiritual teachers, thinkers, healers, and visionary artists of our time. We strive with every title to preserve the essential "living wisdom" of the author or artist. It is our goal to create products that not only provide information to a reader or listener, but that also embody the quality of a wisdom transmission.

For those seeking genuine transformation, Sounds True is your trusted partner. At SoundsTrue.com you will find a wealth of free resources to support your journey, including exclusive weekly audio interviews, free downloads, interactive learning tools, and other special savings on all our titles.

To learn more, please visit SoundsTrue.com/freegifts or call us toll-free at 800.333.9185.

SOUNDS TRUE
many voices, one journey